A Prison Called School

A Prison Called School

Creating Effective Schools for All Learners

Maure Ann Metzger

ROWMAN & LITTLEFIELD
Lanham • Boulder • New York • London

Published by Rowman & Littlefield
A wholly owned subsidiary of The Rowman & Littlefield Publishing Group, Inc.
4501 Forbes Boulevard, Suite 200, Lanham, Maryland 20706
www.rowman.com

Unit A, Whitacre Mews, 26-34 Stannary Street, London SE11 4AB

British Library Cataloguing in Publication Information Available

Library of Congress Cataloging-in-Publication Data

Library of Congress Cataloging-in-Publication Data Available
ISBN 978-1-4758-1575-7 (cloth : alk. paper) -- ISBN 978-1-4758-1576-4 (pbk. : alk. paper) -- ISBN 978-1-4758-1577-1 (electronic)

∞ ™ The paper used in this publication meets the minimum requirements of American National Standard for Information Sciences Permanence of Paper for Printed Library Materials, ANSI/NISO Z39.48-1992.

Printed in the United States of America

This book is dedicated to the memory of a former student, Josh Julien, who recently passed away at the young age of twenty-nine. He had a heart of gold, a smile that lit up a room, a strong moral compass, and the conviction and courage to stand up for other people and causes. We are better human beings and educators for what Josh shared with us. He was an inspiration to all whose lives he touched, and his legacy will live on in our hearts and our work.

Contents

Acknowledgments   ix

Introduction   xi

Part I   1

  1 Life on the Inside   3
  2 From Idealism to Institutionalism   13
  3 The Prisoners   33
  4 Disempowered to Disengaged   49

Part II   69

  5 New Form, Not Reform   71
  6 Valuing Our Youth, Valuing Our Future   91
  7 The Power of Empowerment   113
  8 Real Learning for Real Life   139
  9 Engaged for Learning   157
  10 Partnerships That Transform   179

Conclusion   187

Resources   191

Bibliography   197

Index   209

Acknowledgments

First and foremost, a huge and heartfelt thank you to former students—Andrew, Ben, Charlie, Feliz, Katie, Lorenzo, Richard, and others—whose experiences and voices were the inspiration for this book. It is my hope that their stories and shared wisdom will enlighten and inspire educators, parents, policymakers, and community members to help change a system that holds too many challenges for too many students.

Working with Andrew, Ben, Charlie, Feliz, Katie, Lorenzo, Richard, and other students in leadership and service learning programming was one of the most enlightening and empowering experiences for me as an educator. The contributions these students made to their communities were extraordinary. By developing and leading a "Walk for Change;" raising awareness, funds, and resources for families and youth who were homeless and who lived with AIDS; raising awareness and funds for human trafficking and natural disasters; building Peace Poles for their schools; educating peers and staff about Tibetan children exiled from their homeland; and addressing many other important needs and issues, these students inspired me and countless other community members with their vision, energy, and efforts.

Thank you to my family members who created and contributed to a foundation that allowed students, who otherwise would not have had the resources, to attend international events such as Peace Jam, where they had the historical opportunity to meet twelve Nobel laureates at a single event. Thank you also to my friends and colleagues who kept waving flags of support along the sidelines for this book, especially my dear friend Susan Strauss, who has been a cherished colleague and mentor in my work, writing, and life. And thank you to Jeff for gifting me a laptop so that I wouldn't have to write in the "old school way" while traveling.

I am ever so grateful to Susanne Canavan, acquisitions editor at Rowman & Littlefield, who saw value in, and had the foresight to publish, a book that highlights the voices and experiences of students who struggle with school. Her efforts to forward this important work hold a special place in my heart. Thank you to Randy Victor who completed the first edit of the book, and whose talents and commitment I greatly appreciated. Thank you to Julia Tagliere, who was instrumental in the *Chicago Manual* style editing of the book, and whose time and efforts were key to meeting my submission time-line.

I extend my appreciation to the educational professionals who took time to review and find value in the purpose and vision of the book, especially considering that their work and/or roots are within the system that requires the change. They are courageous thought leaders in the field, and I am indebted to them. I also appreciate the educators who try to do things differently but run into the thick walls of an oppressive system that makes it difficult to change due to the history, bureaucracy, and standardization of the institution. Stay the course; change is coming!

Introduction

How many more young people will this antiquated institution—school—imprison before we create a system that works *for* and *with* students rather than against them? While many students are able to navigate and succeed in the current system, many others struggle every day to survive. Some make it; others don't. School ought not be a place that is one more hurdle, one more stressor in students' lives. Instead, it should be a place where students thrive, succeed, and prepare for life beyond school. It ought to be a place that students look forward to going every day, not one that feels like a prison where they are fighting every day to survive.

A longtime educational assistant would often say, "I feel there are kids who would be better off today if they had never set foot in a school (especially a mainstream school)." Rather than helping students, sometimes schools end up further intensifying the challenges, disabilities, and barriers that students walk into school with, creating yet more obstacles for students to overcome. Earning a high school diploma becomes an endless battle.

When will education become truly student centered instead of system centered? And where are the voices of our youth in this institution of education? Are they only to be found in classrooms responding to questions from the teacher? Or to answer for a misbehavior in the hall? Why isn't their wisdom and experience part of the inquiry, design, and change process for schools? Young peoples' voices are a significant void in the field that is most responsible for shaping and serving youth in their most formative years. The absence of student voice typifies the oppression that young people experience every day in their schools.

While conducting student interviews for my doctoral research on youth leadership programming, I became acutely aware of how little empowerment students experience in their school careers. For many students with disabilities or other challenges, Leadership class was one of the few (if not the only) experiences where they felt valued and empowered.

In addition, throughout my educational career, I would hear students refer to school as a "prison" when they experienced a loss of personal, social, or cultural freedom. Over time, I came to realize that even in alternative and special education programs, the system still comes first and students second. As educators, we may try to personalize learning environments, but in the end, students still need to work the system that is in place. And when they are not able to, we blame the students rather than take on the monstrosity of the system.

So as a result of my doctoral research findings and many years of witnessing students' struggles, I felt compelled to advance their voices and experiences to highlight the issues and challenges they face in school. My starting point for the book was the interviews I conducted with students—for this book and my doctoral research. I also included stories and voices of students from earlier interviews and my career experiences. As I began reviewing the research and literature, I was surprised to learn that some researchers, organizations, foundations, and even some schools, were advocating and pioneering the learning strategies and environments that interviewed students said they needed. However, these practices and philosophies have yet to reach the larger educational consciousness.

A Prison Called School was also influenced by the diverse roles I held during my twenty-seven years in education—that of educator, psychologist, leader of district professional development, and advocate for youth. All of these roles impacted the perspectives, content, and proposed changes in the book. While all the various roles are important to consider in educational change, the student experience and perspective is the most underrepresented position in school reform.

Hence, this book intends to raise the visibility and voices of young people by highlighting their experiences in our schools where they spend much of their developmental time. The students' voices and stories in this book provide critical lessons for us. These young people were among the fortunate ones who survived, but who did so largely in spite of, not because of, the system. As such, they are messengers of change, willing to share their experiences in the hope that it will lead to a better system for all students.

A Prison Called School is meant to spark inquiry about the effectiveness of current educational beliefs and practices. Are they helping or hurting students, especially those most disenfranchised? Is education more about the students or the system? If it is about the students, do beliefs, cultures, practices, policies, structures, and resources reflect that? Do students feel they are empowered and thriving in school, especially those who are most disengaged? For students to do better and to thrive in school, the system must change, and in deep, substantial ways. Education must center on the whole student and find ways to ensure that all students have an engaging, empowering, and successful experience in the schools they attend.

The philosophical, cultural, and pedagogical changes proposed in this book are derived from the struggles that many students experience in school, but the solutions apply to everyone. The proposed changes can have a positive impact on *all* students, not just those who struggle in school. Likewise, even though the book focuses primarily on high school students and programming, many of the proposed changes (valuation, empowerment, engagement) can be implemented in any grade.

This book is primarily meant for educators, leaders, and policymakers; however, it is important to remember that schools are a microcosm of our society. Social injustices and disparities that exist in our society tend to become amplified in the institutionalized setting of schools. Therefore, communities must also help to support the type of changes that can assist all young people to succeed in school and life. It will take all of us—educators, students, parents, policymakers, and communities—to create the learning cultures, strategies, and environments that work for *all* students.

Part I

Chapter One

Life on the Inside

I'm just another number, teacher is calling me Ramen
and my name is Roberto. Treat them as adults, not kids,
as a human being, not like I'm in jail. School is a place
you should feel welcome, like you want to be there,
a comfortable place and you're proud of it, not,
"this is a prison for seven hours"—seven hours of torture!
—Lorenzo

For some students, school is a welcoming, enriching place. For others it is a place of obstacles, oppression, and failure—a prison to which they are sentenced for twelve or more years. It's not surprising that young people try to escape a system that becomes another barrier in their lives, or that further aggravates their existing hardships; rather, it's a wonder that they stay and push forward.

James could not take another day of emotional torture, another day of being locked in a nightmare that repeated itself each time he stepped inside the walls of the urban high school he attended. He had used up every ounce of coping and survival skills that he could muster to get through the days of school, or "hell," as he had come to know it. When James's mom came home that evening, she found him in his room with a gun to his head. "If you make me go to school one more day, I swear I will pull the trigger; I can't take it anymore! I won't go back!"

Unfortunately, it took that act of desperation for James's mom to realize how painful his school experience had been. James dreaded each school day because of his peers' taunting and teachers who also mistreated him. Fortunately, James's mom was understanding of his anguish and helped him transfer to another school.

Shortly after enrolling at his new school, James began connecting with both staff and peers. He was well liked and respected. Although somewhat quiet at first, James gradually became more comfortable and involved in classes and activities. About midyear, the students were discussing the possibility of holding a major service learning event at the school. James and another student volunteered to organize and lead the event. Teachers were surprised yet pleased that James had the courage and confidence to take on such a strong leadership role.

On the day of the event, James's coleader did not show up for school. The staff asked James if he wanted to proceed with the event on his own. He replied, "Well, I guess I could do it by myself," and proceeded to move ahead with the schedule. James did a remarkable job of leading the event. The teachers were in awe of this young man who had made such a huge leap from the total defeat he experienced in his home school to the place he held front and center in the day's events. As a result of receiving the emotional and academic support he needed to thrive, James developed into a young man who was able to share his talents and leadership and who was able to complete high school.

To think that this gifted young man could have been lost to us in a moment of desperation is inconceivable. It is the worst-case scenario of *leaving a child behind*—when a child ceases to exist as a direct result of his experience with an institution that is supposed to develop, not destroy, him. No young person should have to reach the point of seeing death as a better alternative than returning to school the next day. There are many students who live out their own personal nightmare every day in a place they experience as a prison and where they are relegated to what feels like a life sentence. The fortunate ones survive in spite of the system, not because of the system. Their survival, however, often comes at a cost, a cost to them and society.

Ben's story reveals a traumatizing episode early in his school career that had lasting effects on how he viewed teachers and their attempts to help him. As I asked Ben to recount his early years in school, he was quick to share this story:

> My first memory is a teacher pushing over my desk in first grade. My desk fell to the ground and all my stuff went all over the place—my pens, papers, everything! She was standing by my desk. It scared the crap out of me; I was about to cry. I have never forgotten it!

When I asked Ben what had led up to this, he replied:

> I had wanted to be a teacher at the time, so I was making my own little teacher office at home. I had a whiteboard, file tray, and stapler set up at home already. I just needed some school papers, so my friend and I had both taken some

extra worksheets. Her desk got pushed over too. The teacher did all of this in front of the other kids and then we had to clean up her mess. I was happy getting out of that class!

Although he experienced some difficulties, Ben liked school. He liked it so much that he wanted to recreate the school experience at home. And in return, this was the haunting image he carried forward. It is not surprising that Ben remained suspicious and distrustful of schools and teachers for the remainder of his school career. Many of his interview comments revolved around how school was a constant struggle and a loss of personal freedom:

> It felt like it was always a fight to get through school, even to get my graduation.

Sometimes students' struggles are internal; they experience emotional distress that makes it difficult to thrive in a traditional school setting. Feliz shared her early struggles with school:

> It was very tough! Very tough! I used to get in a lot of trouble and was temperamental. I threw a shoe at my kindergarten teacher and used swear words. First grade I cut my hair off in front of the class. I refused to do anything . . . I was swearing at peers and teachers. Teachers set up meetings and my parents were called in a lot. They told my parents the school wasn't for me and that I needed to see a doctor. They were worried and took me to a doctor. I went for psych evals and got medications.

Feliz went on to say:

> I had bad episodes—behavioral, ADHD, schizophrenia, bipolar. No one knew what was going on, they didn't know why I was like that. I went off all of it in junior high and was fine. I felt pretty fine, more normal.

The emotional distress Feliz experienced was difficult enough to deal with, yet school staff and others made matters worse with their predictions of failure.

> I've been told I won't graduate, I won't get good grades, won't amount to anything. Been told that multiple times by programs, teachers, and others. But I'm not stopping at the brick wall, I'm not giving up. So many things I thought were impossible, now I can do it! I might give up for a second, then I try again and keep at it. I didn't think I'd make it back at mainstream high school, and now I am taking regular classes with a "B" average. I got back up, got my stuff together, and am going to graduate on time.

It is admirable that Feliz had the fortitude to keep pushing forward despite her many challenges and negative messages from the adults around her.

Nevertheless, Feliz ought to have been surrounded by support that lifted her up, not held her back. Not only was Feliz able to transfer back to a large, mainstream high school and maintain a "B" average in her senior year, she went on to enroll in postsecondary education. Feliz's accomplishments extended beyond the classroom and her GPA. She was chosen as the keynote speaker for a state Service Learning event and was one of two student representatives who spoke to Service Learning officials from Washington, D.C. about the many projects she and her peers had accomplished.

These were no small feats for a young woman who had a stormy start to her school career which was further intensified by the prediction of poor outcomes. Feliz's journey was not easy; setbacks happened. However, her self-determination to break through the brick wall of obstacles propelled her through the difficult times. She is truly an example of a young person who survived in spite of the system, not because of it.

Sergio was a tall, sturdy young man sent to us from his home school with a warning to watch out for him. Fighting incidents at his home school resulted in a referral to our alternative school. We kept a watchful eye on Sergio as he came on board, wondering when and where the fighting would erupt. To our surprise, Sergio never engaged in a single fight while he was with us. There was not the slightest indication of emotional or behavioral distress. Quite the contrary. We experienced Sergio as a responsible, kind-hearted, and caring young man who shouldered the responsibility of looking out for his mom and siblings in their single-parent household.

During his stay with us, Sergio shared that the physical education teacher at his previous school had told him he'd never make it, that he wouldn't amount to anything. Thankfully, Sergio did not let that define him. Shortly after graduating from our school, he joined the military and served active duty for a few years overseas.

After leaving the military, Sergio went to work for a prominent technology firm. He happened to stop by the alternative school for a visit one day and told us about his work and position with the company. It was obvious that Sergio was highly valued for what he brought to the organization—so much so, that they were paying for his college tuition and encouraging him to pursue his master's degree. I asked Sergio what his salary was. He quoted a figure that was quite a bit higher than what most teachers make. I suggested that Sergio make a return visit to his previous school and share his success story with the staff there, especially the physical education teacher. He replied that he had actually been thinking about doing that.

Sergio's fighting at his previous school was likely a protective or defensive strategy in response to racial or other harassment. That was not his typical way of interacting with people, but it became his survival mechanism in a predominantly White suburban school. Not only did Sergio have to deal with racial issues, he also had to deal with teachers predicting academic and career failure. As such, this young man battled a system that not only failed to protect him, it created yet another hurdle for him to overcome. Lorenzo had a similar experience:

> I had a teacher in middle school telling me I'd never graduate and would be in jail before I turned eighteen. It gave me the desire to prove him wrong, but it also caused a lot of harm. As a teacher telling young people that they can't or won't make it, just pushes them down. For a lot of kids, they might feel bad and not even bother to try if you're saying that, 'cause if you say it enough, they might want to do that because they don't care anymore.

This prediction of failure was a common theme with many of the students who struggled in their mainstream schools. A young woman who had recently transferred to our alternative school announced on the first day of art class, "I hate art! I don't want to do art and I don't want to be here." Although some students found art to be stressful, Brandi's response was the most aversive reaction I had ever encountered. I reassured her that the type of art and approach used here at the alternative school would be different from her previous experience. Brandi continued to stand in the doorway unconvinced that it would be a positive experience. When I asked her why she had selected the class, Brandi stated that she needed it to meet her home school's graduation requirements.

Knowing that Brandi didn't have a choice, I again attempted to explain that she would be able to work at her own pace and style. With much hesitation, Brandi walked over to a table and sat down, insisting that she wasn't going to do any art. After Brandi had been in class a few days and seemed more comfortable, I asked her what had made art so stressful for her. She replied:

> At my home school, I didn't do very well in art. I was terrible. My art teacher thought I was terrible at art too and said that I shouldn't set foot in another art class ever again . . . I hated it.

I was stunned that this was what Brandi had taken away from her previous experience with art. It's hard enough when students can sense their own struggle with a subject, but when a teacher confirms it and goes on to inform them that they shouldn't even bother to try, it makes for a lose-lose, "why bother" situation. What incentive do students have when their best efforts have been crushed by those who are supposed to be supporting their development?

Brandi's art class at the alternative school consisted of a pottery unit in which students were responsible for completing several projects. One day after school had been dismissed, another teacher and I were admiring the students' final projects that had just come out of the kiln. I said to my colleague, "Look at these three, they're my favorites, they are so unique!" Suddenly a quiet voice from behind us said, "Those are mine." We turned around and there stood Brandi, with a smile on her face. Given that the projects didn't have names on them, I asked, "Are you sure these are yours?" She said, "Yes, those are all mine." I then told Brandi that her work was some of the most creative I had ever seen in my pottery classes. I also encouraged her to not believe everything a teacher says about you, especially if it is something negative.

Although Brandi pushed past her initial despair, she carried a lot of stress and negative self-worth in the meantime. Brandi had internalized the prediction of failure. It takes time, effort, and a great deal of evidence to the contrary to counter that kind of damage. That is time and energy that could be better spent on other needs.

While some educators predict failure for their students, most teachers do not want their students to fail. Educators do, however, get caught up in a system that has limited means and options for serving students that do not fit the ever-narrowing profile of a student that education was originally designed for. With each passing year, schools see more and more diversity, poverty, disabilities, environmental challenges, and the like in their student body. Yet the system falls further and further behind trying to meet the complex needs of students and the ever-changing demands of the times.

Sometimes students' struggles arise from staff, sometimes from their peers, and other times from a system that seems unable to understand and meet their needs. And for many, the challenges come from all directions. Lorenzo's remarks convey the struggle that so many students with disabilities and/or other life challenges experience:

> It's not supposed to be a battle, a war. Teachers are supposed to help us; that's why they went to school and chose this as a career. They're supposed to build us up as people, not shoot us down. They're supposed to turn us from kids into adolescents and then adults. For me, making it through school in general, that was no battle—that was a war!

When a child walks in the school door with challenges and disabilities, the last thing schools should be doing is compounding those struggles. "Do no harm" should be the very least of their efforts. "Build them up and equip them in the best ways possible for life" ought to be the mantra, the standard operating practice. Schools need to assist students in developing every asset that can be of benefit to them—socially, emotionally, and cognitively.

Many of our children walk in the doors of our schools with environmental risk factors, academic deficits, and numerous life challenges. Other students experience social and emotional disabilities that further exacerbate the learning process. For some students, there are even bigger obstacles to overcome.

School is an institution that reflects the larger society, so things that are not well accepted in the larger society become amplified within the school walls. When I interviewed youth who were minority or gay, I became acutely aware of the additional burdens these students face every day in our schools.

Minority students expressed feeling at odds with school—teachers, peers, the system—solely because they were a minority in a predominantly White school. When interviewing students for this book, a racist act was frequently identified as the turning point for when things went wrong in school. Minority students felt the deck was stacked against them because of the color of their skin. For many like Richard, the only way they knew how to survive was to fight, and what felt like, a fight for their life.

> I grew up in a small, racist town, hating school 'cause it didn't seem fair. It sucked! Right from kindergarten on. I was the only Black person and at recess, kids made fun of me and called me the "n" word. I was bullied on a lot! I went to the teachers, but they told me to ignore it. I got in fights . . . other kids started in, but I was always the one who got in trouble. Bus rides were terrible. I always got picked on and had to sit up front. When the driver wrote me up, he used the White kids' names, but wrote "the Black kid" for me. It was always racism.

So began Richard's school career. He found out that he was "different" from everyone else and that being different by way of skin color was not acceptable. Richard likely came to the conclusion that he would need to fight his way through school and life as a means to survive. Charlie came to a similar conclusion around middle school:

> I lived in the deep ghetto, in the shelters full of voucher recipients from the state. Even before that, we lived in inner city and heard gunshots at night—it was a way of life. Getting driven out to the suburban all-White school made me really nervous to go to my new sixth grade class. I was worried that all the suburban White kids would beat me up, jump me, lynch me, be super racist . . . I got in fights, mainly racially motivated.

Despite being a sizeable young man and accomplished athlete, Charlie's fear of racist attitudes and actions permeated his thoughts as he prepared to start his new school. Anticipating harmful racist acts, Charlie braced himself for what was to come. He spent time and energy anticipating the worst and preparing to defend himself—time and energy that likely compromised his ability to learn and thrive in school.

Lorenzo spoke with anger about the racism he experienced being one of a few Hispanic students in a largely White middle-school environment. Feeling the need to defend himself and other Hispanic students, Lorenzo found safety and power by uniting with them and other students who were considered outcasts:

That's when the [racial] harassment started. I started hanging out with my
Mexican homeboys cause of how Whites were treating them. I became the
spokesperson for the Hispanic students. We all said "screw you!" We're not
getting into sports, awards, or things like that, so we're not even going to try.
We would do what we had to, fly under the radar, but not really try. I got sick
of it. Fights started happening and the Hispanic kids united with the loners and
potheads. We had a lot in common—we got in trouble.

Lorenzo went on to say:

I was dealing with the law after that, getting arrested for racial fighting in
school and the community. People were calling me a spic, a wetback, a beaner,
and telling me to go back to my own country. School was a drag, my grades
were bad, and credits were not getting done.

How can students put forth the effort necessary for learning when they
need to be vigilant about their safety and survival? And telling students to
refocus or assuring them they don't need to worry only intensifies their
struggle. When teachers dismiss students' concerns, it implies that staff do
not know or understand students' reality. Those who are in power have
minimized what is very real and very concerning for those who are disempowered, adding yet another obstacle to students' already burdened life.

On Maslow's hierarchy of needs, safety and survival are key basic needs
that must be met before higher-level needs can be addressed. Educators can
pressure students to prioritize school and the learning process, but if their
ethnic or racial identity, essential to their personhood, is being threatened,
learning becomes secondary to protecting one's self. Survival becomes the
pressing need of the day.

It was not a coincidence that a disproportionate number of students who
came into our alternative schools and programs for students with disabilities
were minority youth. Schools are a microcosm of the larger society, and as
such, they tend to play out the same issues present in the general public.
Institutions and systems are built to serve the dominant group and the
masses. The onus is on those who do not "fit" to adapt or change, to align
with the system. And if they are unable to fit, they pay the price, suffering the
consequences that befall those who walk outside the lines of what has been
deemed as "normal."

Our gay, lesbian, bisexual, and transgender (GLBT) youth are another
minority group that is subjected to maltreatment and harassment within our
educational system. Andrew's story is one of trying to find and express his
true identity, a process that was not supported in the mainstream school
setting:

In ninth grade, the beginning of high school, which is supposed to be the "greatest time of your life," I hung out with a group of friends notorious for getting in trouble. I aligned with the "Goth" culture and that led to the entire school not liking me. The close-mindedness of a small town contributed to me being ostracized. Feeling like an outcast led to depression, some cutting, and suicide attempts. In my sophomore year, everything got worse. Things escalated and went to greater levels. My friends had left to go to other schools so I felt more alone. When I switched to an alternative school in my junior year, I still maintained this image for a month and then realized I didn't have to. People reached out to me. I opened up and felt that I didn't have to keep this front up, that I could be me.

Andrew goes on to say:

My mom raised me saying that "you're special, you can do whatever you want," and yet when I was in mainstream high school, the only way I stood out or was recognized was in a way they wanted me to stand out—students with perfect grades, families . . . People who appeared to have a storybook life were recognized. When I was Goth or getting in trouble, I stood out, but not in a way they were hoping for.

As Andrew struggled with his identity, he found out that anything beyond the norm or the ideal was unacceptable, so it was highly unlikely that being open about his sexual identity would be tolerated. Andrew's plight is similar to the many GLBT youth who came through our alternative and special education programs. It's not worth being open about who you are if what follows is tormenting, harassment, and rejection. So instead, young people live in a place of silent, painful turmoil that, at its worst, becomes self-destructive.

Ben came out in ninth grade and feels he suffered consequences because the school was not comfortable with his openness about his sexual identity:

Ninth grade started out good, but then my grades started falling down. I came out of the closet. I was very discriminated against. Kids were spitting on me after I got off the bus. I talked to the cop and they got in trouble. I was sent to another special education school shortly after I "came out." It felt like my [home] school didn't want to deal with it. I didn't want to go to the new school so I left the first meeting and walked home in the rain.

The stories of these students are not atypical. These scenarios play out every day in our nation's schools. It is remarkable that as many young people survive the ordeal. Their survival is a testament to their inner strength and determination to persevere "in spite of." But their survival is rarely without cost. Just because students survive school doesn't mean that they are better off or prepared for life, it means that they were able to meet the requirements deemed necessary to obtain a diploma. Even though students may figure out how to survive the system, some students actually incur more damage, more harm, as a result of their school experience.

As I began sharing the title and focus of this book with people, I was amazed at how many adults said, "That was me, that was my experience with school." They recounted their own traumatic experience as if it had happened yesterday. These are adults in their thirties to fifties who are successful and contributing members of society, yet they continue to carry deep and lasting scars from their school years. No person should have to look death in the eye or carry a lifetime of scars as a result of going to school every day. So why does school go so wrong for many people?

Chapter Two

From Idealism to Institutionalism

The education system failed me miserably!
In a way, they abandoned me, threw me aside.
No child left behind is not happening, because I was left behind.
I say, "Leave the education behind, not the child."
—Richard

Richard's quote is ironic. When education becomes so institutionalized, it can leave behind the very people it was meant to serve. In Richard's case, he felt abandoned and failed by the educational process. He perceived the agenda of education to be more important than his needs as an individual. In trying to educate Richard, we lost him. This is not just one student's perspective. Countless professionals and scholars in the field of education believe that the No Child Left Behind (NCLB) legislation created more harm than help for the very students it was supposed to benefit.[1] Focusing on a specific score took the attention away from the whole child and from some children altogether.[2]

As schools attempt to meet the numerous requirements they are charged with, they push forward even when struggling students are no longer able to keep up. How does education end up leaving so many students behind? The current educational system fails to meet the needs of students for a variety of reasons. Some causes are system generated, while others, like legislation and policymaking, originate beyond the reach of schools.

Many laws and policies are likely designed with good intentions; they are meant to produce ideal learning conditions, outcomes, and supports for students and schools. Yet they can end up missing the mark and even causing harm, as was the case with Richard. It's not only laws and policies that are steeped in idealism; educators enter the field hoping to make a difference in the lives of their students. They fully intend to create engaging and meaning-

13

ful learning opportunities that will help their students to thrive; however, that initial enthusiasm can quickly fade once educators are immersed in the day-to-day demands of the students and the school.

Lynn Groves, a first-year teacher in New York, experienced disillusionment early on in her career as a teacher working with high school youth with disabilities:

> You graduate, you set up your classroom, you think your dream has come true and then the first year, I felt hopelessness—what is this? Just that letdown from that high that you're going to change the world, make a difference. I had to take a step back 'cause I couldn't stay in that hopelessness. I had to figure out how to help them the best I could and at a much slower pace. You start off so positive and passionate, that passion is so strong and then . . . you have to readjust from all those things you were going to forge ahead with.

Coming into her chosen field, Lynn had set her sights high, only to have them come crashing down around her. Her vision and efforts were quickly thwarted. The myriad needs, challenges, and crises of the day undermined all that Lynn had envisioned. So what goes wrong? How does education get so far off track from the noble intentions of those who design and implement education? How do schools become so removed from their core beliefs and goals that they end up missing or even harming the students who most need their help?

INSTITUTIONALISM

Education's failure to effectively serve many students who struggle with school is rooted in the structure and history of education. The education model of today is not much different than it was a hundred years ago. While current societal demands have changed substantially, education has remained largely frozen in time using models and strategies that do not match the learners in our classrooms and schools today. It is an antiquated system that clings to an outdated means of meeting the challenges and needs of our present-day students and world.

John Dewey, an early proponent of educational reform, described traditional education as an institution that is separated from all other social institutions or organizations by its time schedules, examination and promotion process, and rules of order.[3] The intent of education within this institution is to prepare students for a successful future by acquiring prescribed knowledge and skill sets. Content, methodology, and interactions are all stipulated by the institution and have remained largely unchanged throughout the years.

Institutions are not necessarily bad. They can serve society well. However, they can also be detrimental. For example, when serving large groups of people as they often do, institutions impose constraints and standardization, which can ultimately result in *institutionalization*. Institutionalization occurs when the people served are programmed to conform to strict controls that facilitate managing too many people with too little staff.[4] Some of the strategies used to control people and minimize problems include depersonalizing, forcing obedience, and destroying the self. Control is also imposed by taking away people's ability to make decisions, including when they can speak, how they eat, and when they use the toilet.

Institutions are comprised of various systems. Systems originated in the U.S. military in the early nineteenth century.[5] A bureaucracy was created using policies, rules, and a chain of command to control workers, ensure consistent production, and increase efficiency. The American business community quickly adopted these management systems. They were also implemented by education and human services.

Large public schools came about with a dual purpose: to prevent social disorder and to prepare young people to become efficient, productive employees in a manufacturing economy in which factories and assembly lines were the primary occupation.[6] Discipline, conformity, and obedience became the predominant social goals of schooling. As a result, a hierarchical bureaucracy that used rules and regulations as a means to control students and teachers governed schools. Students were divided into grades, taught using standardized lessons, and ruled by a series of bells and periods.

Schools are institutional systems that were created to manage people and processes and to produce specified results. The problem with the current model is that its "beneficiaries" are individuals, each with their own identity, needs, strengths, and challenges. Applying an institutional model to serve them is counterproductive, especially for individuals who are not able to function in the way the system was designed for. There are fundamental differences between programs and processes that are "system centered" and ones that are "person centered." As illustrated in figure 2.1, systems tend to serve the system, not the individuals within them.

In a system-centered organization, labels are the focus.[7] Conversely, in person-centered organizations, individuals, not disabilities, are the focus. A system-based approach emphasizes people's deficits, whereas a person-centered approach strives to help individuals realize their strengths and gifts. Likewise, a system-based approach tends to identify differences and what can be done to "fix" a problem rather than understanding people in the context of their community.

A person-centered approach is not compatible with a system-centered approach because personhood becomes lost or subservient, as explained by Van der Klift and Kunc:[8]

A Comparison of System-Centered and Person-Centered Approaches	
System-Centered	**Person-Centered**
Production and efficiency are the most important outcomes.	Quality of life is the most important outcome.
Subordinates the needs of people to the maintenance of bureaucracy.	Subordinates needs of service system to the needs and interests of people.
People are seen as objects to be processed by the system.	People are critical actors with deep desires who shape their own future.
People's interests are often ignored, sometimes exploited.	Human growth and dignity in the process of change is critical.
Control for decisions is allocated to professionals who know best.	Control for decisions is placed in the hands of the people.
Complex regulations and procedures sustain professional interests.	Quality of support depends on good information and creativity.
Detachment is the preferred stance with people.	Workers develop personal relationships with people.
Workers rely on legal charters, formal authority, and control structures to motivate action.	Workers rely on family, neighborhood, church, and associations to provide social support and stability.
Resources are allocated to increase the holdings of services and the benefits of professionals.	Resources are invested in supports that help people be more effective at meeting needs for themselves.
Offers the promise of perfection at the expense of the diversity of the people and the workers.	Offers the richness of imperfection at the expense of order and control.

Adapted from work by David Korten, as printed in Beth Mount et al.'s *Imperfect Change: Embracing the Tensions of Person-Centered Work*. Manchester, CT: Communitas Communications, 1990. For this publication and other Communitas publications, write: Communitas, Inc., P.O. Box 374, Manchester, CT 06040 (203-645-6976.) For resources related to person-centered work, visit www.BethMount.org. Reprinted with permission.

Figure 2.1.

Systems require compliance. Individuals are expected to go along with whatever behavior is expected of them . . . Self-determination and control over
one's own life often run counter to the goals of the system, which are conformity and uniformity.

Likewise, the onus is on the individual to fit and adapt to the system.

In a system based on an industrial model, individuals are expected to fit into
the services. Programs are developed, and people are slotted into them. Those
in receipt of services seldom have input into their development. Sometimes the
fit is a good one, sometimes not. When it isn't working, the expectation is that
the individual will change, not the system . . . The system simply isn't set up to
accommodate individual preferences.

A FACTORY MODEL

In the past few decades, countless attempts have been made to address and
reform the inadequacies of our educational institutions. More and more demands are placed on schools, yet as broad-scale institutions, they are not able
to respond in a timely and effective manner. The gaps between what students
need, what schools are held accountable for, and what they are actually able
to do continues to widen. Why is it so difficult for schools to effectively
respond to these changing needs and demands?

Education is an institution bound by entrenched traditions that limit its
ability to adapt and meet current demands. The true source of resistance to
change runs deeper than that, however. According to Caine and Caine, education attempts to change, yet it remains largely the same because its underlying mental models of teaching and learning do not change.[9] So before we
try to change the current system, we must first understand what holds it in
place.

Our education system is stuck in a Newtonian view of reality, which
interprets most things as being machinelike.[10] In the Newtonian paradigm,
most everything can be separated into parts and analyzed and fixed. Education applies this perspective by viewing students and issues as isolated parts
that can be fixed or controlled with the right tools such as behaviorism,
rewards, and punishment. When people are divided into isolated parts, it is
easier to view them as objects that we do things to.

At first glance, a mechanistic approach might seem like a good idea.
"Mechanism is extremely compelling because it combines an explanation of
reality with immense power to take charge of that reality . . . for many
people, stability, power, and mechanism represent security and safety."[11]
Being able to identify a cause, effect, and prescribed solution would seem to
make for a well-oiled and well-ordered social machine.

While a mechanistic, assembly-line approach may be an economical model for meeting production goals or serving the masses, it is neither an effective nor an efficient model for serving young people with disabilities and other challenges. Young people with disabilities and other challenges do not thrive among the masses. In fact, being treated as a cog in the wheel of factory-model education is often their demise. Most educators know that this model is ineffective for disadvantaged students. They see the consequences every day in their classrooms.

Jeanne Nehls, a sixth-through-twelfth-grade teacher for twenty-four years in Milwaukee, also taught at a local college. She had a gift for serving students with emotional-behavior disorders (EBD) in her mainstream class-room. However, as time went on and class sizes swelled, Jeanne became frustrated with her inability to serve students with EBD in the manner that was necessary for them to achieve success:

> Class sizes are now so huge it is a challenge to try [to] address the high needs' kids. I build rapport with kids and am good at it. Yet you can't build rapport and relationships with thirty-eight to forty kids, let alone five to seven EBD kids that need the extra attention. Twenty-seven kids that aren't EBD are tough enough. It's like a machine or factory paradigm, and it doesn't work with kids, kids are not machines!

Teaching became the assembly-line mentality that Caine and Caine de-scribed earlier. Jeanne is a model educator who loves teaching her students and others who aspire to teach. She spends her time outside the classroom instructing and mentoring new and upcoming teachers. Instead of stacking the deck against this teacher, the system ought to be supporting her and her students in every way possible.

Students experience the same phenomenon as teachers like Jeanne, only they are at the other end of it, bearing the greatest consequence. Katie, a student with strong academic ability, had a good start to her academic career, but she began struggling in the transition to junior high as a result of in-creased class size and decreased support:

> Once I hit sixth grade, schools and classes were so big, so many kids, so many classes. We were given a schedule . . . here, figure it out. They didn't really help you understand the transition from elementary to junior high. In junior high, it was easier to lose focus 'cause of class size and not getting the extra help you need.

Katie contrasted that experience with the experience she had in the elemen-tary grades:

> It was fun from kindergarten to fifth grade! Teachers broke things down and made it easier for you to understand. In elementary school, it was a different

setting—you were in one classroom all day (except for gym). That made it easier. You were more concentrated on learning.

Another high school student, Lorenzo, did not get the critical help he needed due to the high numbers of students in class and instructional strategies that did not address his needs.

I would try to pay attention, but couldn't focus on what they were trying to teach me. I was a hands-on learner and needed more help . . . with thirty kids I couldn't get the help I needed. You can't give me the instructions and say, "Do it." I would need to read a page three times to comprehend it all.

Charlie also felt the lack of individualized learning support:

The way the system is, the way the teachers are taught; it's "generalized," which is ironic, because every person on this planet is different. How do you generalize when not everyone learns the same?

Charlie went on to address the critical toll it takes on students when schools become overcrowded and depersonalized.

Schools are bursting at the seams; the average class has thirty to forty kids. A kid could walk out of class and not be missed, so how do they get that message [that school is important] and personalization?

Schools are required to serve as many students as possible with limited funding. This seemingly necessitates a factory model to function in an efficient manner. However, a consequence of the factory model is that students who struggle in school become alienated and lost in such a system. They are no longer a person with unique needs, but rather a number among the masses. Students in nonmainstream schools frequently characterize their mainstream school experience as "cattle herding," as Andrew did in his interview:

At regular high school, I was just a number. It felt like a cattle farm, everyone coming and going.

A mechanistic, assembly-line model of education does not bode well for those who do not fit the cookie-cutter approach. The consequences of this approach extend beyond the inability to reach students and offer a personalized learning experience. As the veteran teacher Jeanne noted, students are not machines, and they are not part of a production line. If we treat students and the educational process as such, we lose young people along the way.

On the one hand, the educational system is able to serve and help many students to become "successful" (as defined by the system). While it may not be the best way to educate them, many students are able to work or survive within the traditional model of school. On the other hand, a portion of students does not work well or thrive within the current educational model. Students like Richard, Katie, Charlie, Andrew, and others are challenged by such a system, a system that relies on a defective model of education to meet their needs.

For the system to work, everyone has to work the system. If you don't want to work within the established system or you don't know how to work the system, then you are on the outside. The system may no longer know how to serve you, and sometimes chooses not to serve you. Schools have limited time, options, and resources to work with disadvantaged students. When those aren't enough, schools often give up, place the blame on the student, and turn their attention to the students they know can succeed. It isn't necessarily because staff or schools don't want to help a student, they just don't know what else to do.

As citizens, we must ask some challenging questions: Is it realistic to think that a universal system could possibly meet the learning and social-emotional needs of all young people in this country? Is it ethical or beneficial to impose a factory model of production upon developing children? What is our goal—to educate and graduate our children by investing as few resources as possible, *or* to create and provide all students with meaningful and effective learning experiences along the way to graduation?

OPPRESSION

In the discussion of education as an institution, we must also address a potential consequence of institutions—oppression. Oppression is the systemic mistreatment of a specific group of people by another group of people serving as society's agents. [12] It involves the misuse of power or authority to subdue or suppress others. Often the mistreatment is encouraged or reinforced by the larger society or its culture. As institutions that represent and serve the larger society, schools are at risk for generating and/or reinforcing oppression.

Dewey described the traditional educational system as one that imposes from above and outside. [13] Because this prescribed set of knowledge and codes of conduct are handed down from the past, students are required to maintain an attitude of docility, receptivity, and obedience in order to receive and accept what has been predetermined for them. In other words, young people do not have a say in what they are to learn or how they are to learn it. Not only are they denied voice in their schooling, students must also respond and interact in socially prescribed ways.

Traditional education keeps teachers from considering a key factor in creating learning experiences—the power and purpose of those who are taught. Failure to address this issue results in a lack of mutual adaptation.[14] It is taken for granted that a certain set of conditions suits everyone. Students who can work within this predetermined structure can achieve some level of success. Those unable to work within those constraints have difficulty succeeding. What's worse, when students don't fit the standard model, they are labeled and perceived to be the cause of the problem, creating even more negative consequences for struggling students like Charlie:

> Everyone is different, but yet they (teachers) teach the same. It almost comes down to "it's your fault," like you're dumb or you are the problem, when in fact, they aren't teaching to how you learn. There's automatically a problem if you can't learn like others or "get it," and then after a while, you become the problem.

Not only are the students rendered voiceless and powerless, they are also often blamed for failures of the system to meet their individualized needs. As Charlie experienced, if you can't follow the prescribed course of learning, *you*, rather than the system, are deemed to be at fault. When students cannot fit the system, *they* become the problem.

John Dewey asserts, "It is not enough that certain materials and methods have proven effective with other individuals at other times. There must be a reason for thinking that they will function in generating an experience that has educative quality with particular individuals at a particular time."[15] In other words, we cannot assume that because something works with a group of students it will work for all students. As our present system stands, the responsibility of adaptation is on the student, not the system. We do not question whether the subject matter, instructional strategy, learning environment, or the teacher is at fault; instead, we are quick to blame inadequacies on the student, as was the case with Charlie.

Lorenzo's experience also illustrates the consequences of going against the system:

> You should feel welcome and comfortable as a kid when you're in school. Teachers and schools change that in middle school if they feel you are going to threaten the standards. They treat you like you're robots; you have to do it just how they want. Not everyone runs that way, I sure the hell didn't! They tell you if you can't be like everyone else, there's the door. They don't take time to find out what our needs are.

When students don't fit or work the system, schools often use punishing or controlling tactics with them. Indeed, schools have immense responsibility for carrying out the many academic and legal mandates they are required to fulfill. However, by its very nature and structure, the institutional system creates chaos and then resorts to control and power mechanisms to establish order and maintain the system.

Marana was working on her degree in education and had just begun her student teaching at an elementary school. She was appalled by the restrictive controls imposed on young students:

> On the first day of my internship the school staff had a "dry run" of how the lunchtime routine was supposed to flow. Students were to be instructed to come in one specific cafeteria door and follow an exact path, including the exact floor tile they needed to stand on to reach the lunch line. From there they were instructed to sit at assigned seats at the lunch table. The students were then to be instructed that they were not to get out of their seat for any reason; heaven help them if they should need a ketchup packet. Not an option! At the time I felt the staff was being too "military-like" and imagined the students must feel smothered by having no freedom whatsoever, not even at lunchtime.

Marana went on to say:

> A few hours later I observed the students actually go through the process. What I witnessed was chaos. Even with all of these rules in place the students were out of control! Many kids were pushing, yelling, insulting, and overall disrespecting themselves, the staff, and their classmates. It took football-coach type whistles and threats to take away recess to keep the lunchtime misbehaviors to a minimum.

Movement and noise are restrained throughout schools, classrooms, hallways, and lunchrooms. Yet students are placed in large groups where social interactions and dynamics have the capacity to multiply and intensify. And then when they do, schools respond by imposing ever-increasing threats and sanctions to contain unwanted behaviors. Ironically, schools have created a system that generates and perpetuates the very behaviors they seek to dispel.

John Dewey described this phenomenon in his book *Experience and Education*. The fixed arrangements of rows of desks and military regimes that permit students to move only at fixed signals inhibit intellectual and moral freedom.[16] Passivity and receptivity are the preferred traits in our educational institutions. Schools place a premium on the outward appearance of attention and obedience, creating an artificial uniformity. Consequently, students' true natures are stifled by the enforced quiet and compliance. The pressure of mechanical uniformity and immobility triggers reactions. Disobedient actions become the only escape from the pressures of the institutionalized school.

Institutions work to keep things in order and under control, and schools are no exception. In fact, they may work harder than any other system to do just that. And yet it is not uncommon to see the "out-of-control" students that Marana observed her first day on the job. Dewey suggests that such behaviors and reactions are a direct result of all the institutional controls and oppressive environments imposed on students.[17] In one study, teachers spent over 20 percent of their time on power and control struggles.[18] This is valuable time that could be directed instead to providing students with the academic and social support they desperately need. So why are more and more power and control mechanisms used despite clear evidence that they are ineffective and detract from time and energy that could be better spent with students?

Schools resort to power and control strategies under the premise of discipline or maintaining order. Schools might initially intervene with behavior or performance issues by using lower-level strategies, but when those don't seem to work, things can quickly escalate to a more threatening response. Threats are a common power-and-control response in school systems. Educators threaten to remove privileges, impose sanctions, call parents, hand out detentions, and suspend and expel students. Interventions are certainly warranted in ensuring students' safety and such; however, that is usually the level at which schools start—with threats. And when students don't come into line, educators respond with more serious threats.

Threats create an environment of fear. From grade school on, education is a fearful enterprise for some students.[19] Like threats, instilling fear has become a standard management tool in most of our schools. Classrooms and schools steeped in fear cause children, such as Ben in chapter 1, to eventually hate the idea of school. At worst, teaching becomes about policing and punishing in order to control behaviors or coerce students to do their assignments, and learning becomes a dreaded and frustrating experience.[20]

Along with threats, "hammering" is another tactic schools use to pressure or manipulate students to comply and conform. Students enter school with different abilities, life experiences, and circumstances, yet the traditional model of education presupposes that all students are at the same starting point and are able to learn in the same manner and time frame. When students don't move at the pace and manner that has been prescribed, the hammering process begins. During a professional learning community discussion, one staff member commented that if students fall behind in junior high, they begin to hammer on them to catch up and keep up. Another educator chimed in, "Junior high? I used to teach at the elementary level and we started hammering on them already in second grade!"

For students who struggle, school becomes a deficit-based experience. It can be difficult to diagnose and remediate learning issues. Yet once a student begins to experience difficulties, schools tend to focus only on what students can't do, even faulting them for their deficiencies, as Charlie noted. Educators become frustrated with students' lack of progress or what they interpret to be a lack of effort, so they blame the student and begin hammering them with berating comments, predictions of failure, blame, and threats:

At the rate you're going, you'll never graduate.
With an attitude like that, I don't know how you made it this far.
If you don't like it, there's the door!
You'll never set foot in my class (or school) again!

How do hammering, threats, and predictions of failure help students who already feel the pressure of being behind, not getting it, not fitting in, and failing? They don't. Hammering, threats, and predictions of failure are not an effective way to engage or motivate young people. When you hammer a nail and it starts to bend as you are hammering it, what do you do? If you continue to hammer, the nail bends even more and will not serve its intended purpose.

Educators are often keenly aware that students don't fit into the spaces that have been carved out for them, yet they continue to hammer away at students, expecting that they will "straighten up" or improve with enough hammering. And when that doesn't work, they bring out a bigger hammer in the form of threats. Educators don't necessarily like using hammering or threats; unfortunately, they see it as their only tool for effecting motivation and change. People resort to what they know, helpful or not, when they feel they have no other options.

Brain science supports the assertion that threats and punishments are an ineffective means to achieve positive goals.[21] Behaviors may change temporarily, but emotions and amygdala activity will actually intensify, which in turn triggers an increase in negative emotional outcomes expressed in actions. When negative responses are triggered by the environment, positive outcomes are unlikely.

Those students who aren't easily institutionalized push back, refusing to be controlled by whistles and threats. As a result, these students are labeled as "troubled" or "troublemakers," when in fact they are likely just reacting to the oppressive nature of the system. Could it be that these students are exhibiting healthy, rather than troubled, behavior by fighting to retain their identity and individualism in a system that doesn't encourage or support it? On the one hand, it is irresponsible to defy authority just because it is authority; on the other hand, it is irresponsible to comply with authority just because it is authority.[22]

Although adults want young people to be self-disciplined, they continually order them around.[23] The "obedience" that educators demand requires a myriad of control mechanisms to enforce it. The reality is that young people are less likely to follow a rule they had no part in creating or to embrace learning that is merely a matter of following orders. Coercing students into behaving and learning does not promote intrinsic values and behavior. To foster ownership and self-motivation, students must be granted choices and input; they must be a part of the decision-making process regarding what and how they learn.

Do we need to hold young people accountable? Absolutely. Do we need to keep our schools safe? Of course. But there are better ways of doing it. Young people may require structure and limits; however, there is a key difference between structure and limits and control and coercion.[24] Different students need different levels and types of intervention and support, yet our one-size-fits-all system resorts to using power and control to address academic progress and behavior. When schools use power and control to maintain social order, it's more about preserving the system than it is about serving the students.

Oppression can be insidious, used as a silent weapon that blames, controls, and quiets its victims should they decide to question the system. Oppression comes disguised in seemingly harmless remarks such as: "That's just how it works" or "Never mind, just get it done." It doesn't mean schools and staff can't have expectations, rules, and structure, but people need to have the option to question them, discuss them, and even help change them. Charlie felt the effects of a system that expected him to follow "just because." He pushed back on that.

> So much in school is "generalized." I bucked a lot of the generalized education and challenged teachers, "Why are you teaching me this, why do you think this is important in my life?" I would challenge that. Learning has become so generalized and it needs to be more personalized.

Oppression has significant and long-term effects on our young people in the school setting. When young people not only have to compromise (or give up) their individualization and their ability to assert themselves, they tend to react in one of two ways. They act out, resist, or even rebel against what feels like a loss of personal power and control. Or, they become more passive and compliant. On many levels, a response of resistance may be healthier in that it helps the resister retain a sense of personal power and identity.

Resistance, however, is not an acceptable response in schools. As institutionalized systems, schools ultimately shape and even require students to become passive followers. Students are there to receive instructions and information and respond accordingly. By and large, schools breed passive "followership." Of course, students are encouraged to respond and engage in certain activities, but it is on the terms of the system or those in power.

Educators and parents are often surprised when students graduate and have difficulty transitioning into adulthood. It really should come as no surprise. Students have been conditioned to be passive and reactive, rather than active and in command as learners. School requires students to mainly be in the audience, whereas real life expects them to be on the stage. Pursuing higher education, seeking and maintaining employment, living on one's own, raising a family, and managing finances all require skills and personal initiative that are largely not encouraged or taught in the traditional school setting. As a result, students struggle to move from being students in a desk to independent adults taking charge of their own lives.

A SYSTEM THAT OPPRESSES ALL

Students are not the only ones who are oppressed. Educators are also held prisoner by the system. Much of the pressure and hammering teachers exert on students trickles down from the larger, dysfunctional system. In his interview, Andrew discussed students' need for empowerment. He also realized that teachers were victims of the cascading effects of oppression:

> Empower the teachers because teachers aren't empowered. Even if they want to help, they can't. It makes them feel helpless when they have to teach and get a certain number of students ready.

The external environment makes untold demands of schools, yet provides inadequate resources. Schools have little to no input with externally prescribed directives, but they are obligated to meet these imposed mandates. As a result, the system passes those burdens along to staff. Educators, in turn, press down on the students. A drawing [figure 2.2] by Patty, a junior in high school, provides a powerful depiction of how this process unfolds. Oppression starts with the external environment and becomes internalized by the institution and is passed along until it reaches the individual student. The impact is felt by all.

More recently, teachers feel the demand to teach to high-stakes standardized testing that has been imposed on schools, staff, and students. This can make teachers more controlling; they feel pressured, so they in turn pressure their students. American culture, in general, promotes a relatively controlling orientation in education. [25] Teachers are expected to take control, instruct, and give directions, while students are expected to comply by listening, observing, and obeying. Teachers spend much of their time and effort keeping students under control, administrators try to control what teachers do in the classroom, and larger entities such as school boards retain control as well. Additionally, educators are allowed very little input into the decision-making and policymaking process at the local, state, and national level—a formula for powerlessness.

In addition to cultural and institutional expectations, teachers face countless other obstacles that can leave them feeling disempowered. Educators are confronted with numerous issues that preclude basic learning in the classroom. Students come into classrooms and schools experiencing poverty,

Figure 2.2.

homelessness, substance abuse and addictions, mental health issues, criminal offenses, gang involvement, pregnancy, parenthood, a history of school failure, and physical, emotional, and sexual trauma. Students may also be experiencing discrimination and other challenges as a result of their race, culture, religion, sexual orientation, or disability.

Educators who are faced with these types of issues every day in their classrooms have an overwhelming responsibility. And when the many challenges in a teacher's day or class outweigh the resources available to address the multitude of issues, educators can feel helpless and hopeless. Even the best of teachers can be rendered ineffective when too many demands are placed on them with too little or no support.

This, unfortunately, became the case for Jeanne, the teacher who for years had been so successful with EBD students in her mainstream classroom:

> It's becoming impossible to do my job and the things I know I need to do.
> Teachers really want to help but it's getting harder and harder to do what you
> know is the right way, the best way. Ninety-five percent of teachers are very
> effective and motivated and know what to do, but there are so many demands,
> like standardized testing. I can be more creative when the job is fun; I want to
> be able to do that.

Jeanne goes on to say:

> Every year though, it gets harder and harder to find the energy to do what is
> needed. There are more and more demands to teaching, layers and layers of
> other requirements. That is very, very frustrating. Just let me do my job of
> working with the kids! But with so many demands in and out of the classroom
> it's becoming impossible. The only way I can see to deal with it is to leave
> education or work part time.

Teachers who are effective and highly motivated are slowly, but surely,
depleted by an agenda of too many conflicting demands and too little time,
resources, and support to do what is best for their students. The demanding
academic program educators are responsible for makes it difficult to address
all the needs of every child in their classrooms. Even if they want to do it
differently, teachers often lack what they need to do it "right," as Jeanne
experienced.

POWERLESS TO CHANGE

Caine and Caine ask, "What is it that drains so many teachers and that
renders it so difficult for teachers and students alike to express their creativity, demonstrate their competence, and function at much, much higher levels?"[26] Professionals like Lynn Groves bring hopeful visions of what they
can do as they enter the field of education. Yet once educators are on the
inside, that idealism gives way to a very different reality of what they can
actually do with and for their students. Educators are largely bound by predetermined and non-negotiable procedures with little to no voice or say in the
implementation of policy within their schools.

The oppressive nature of the institutions leaves educators feeling voiceless and powerless about their own field of practice. Even if educators prefer
to do things differently, it takes too much energy to battle the system and
keep focused in the classroom where students need everything educators
have to give. Many educators have tried to bring about change within the
system or on behalf of students. But because education is an institution, it is
wired not to budge. Its survival depends on maintaining the status quo.

When educators continually put forth effort but are unable to effect
change, they can experience a phenomenon known as *learned helplessness*.

Eventually, educators just give up and don't try anymore. They become resigned: "That's just the way it is—it's not going to change." That learned helplessness is then passed along to the students. Everyone becomes a victim in the system as they perpetuate a sense of powerlessness and helplessness.

Lastly, it is probably not a coincidence that many older school buildings actually look like prisons, as Andrew recounted:

> A company that designs prisons designed our school. It really did feel like a prison. Even the teachers wanted to hold class outside when it was nice weather.

The physical structures of schools reflect the philosophy and practices that take place within. If control and containment are critical for a system to function, then we will likely build structures that reflect those priorities. Form follows function. Thick brick walls symbolize the heavy boundaries that are placed around the people inside. They also serve to keep people out that are not part of the system. Long, straight hallways reflect the need to keep everyone in orderly, straight lines. Bells ringing at exact time increments remind us of the military-type routines that keep protocols intact. Strict rules, regulations, and mandates serve as the silent bars on the windows that keep everyone and everything locked into place.

SUMMARY

Schools are well-established institutions in our society. They work to maintain the status quo. By their very nature and structure, institutions are meant to serve the masses, not the individual. Attempts to individualize go against the grain of the current system, which is steeped in standardization and conformity. Those who are served by the institution, those who work on behalf of the institution, and even those who interact with it from the outside are all expected to conform and adjust to the system. As it stands today, the institution of education is incapable of producing the flexible, creative, and timely responses necessary to meet the needs of students and the demands of our current world.

Despite all the variables among students and dynamics within schools, education has developed curriculum and methodologies that are delivered using a mass-scale model. Both the curriculum and methods of delivery are based on the presumption that students will be in school every day, engaged, and ready to work. Likewise, it assumes that students will be able to understand and work with the materials in the way they were intended. While this might work with many students, it is not effective with all students.

And so students and educators struggle every day to do the best they can with what they have, to achieve what is often unachievable. Educators try to meet ever-increasing demands with ever-diminishing resources. Students try to swim upstream in turbulent waters. Hopefully, we won't need to "leave the education behind" as Richard proposed. But we most certainly should not leave any child behind or cause harm in the process of carrying out academic agendas. In a better educational world, one that keeps students at its center, we would be able to meet the needs of all students *and* the standards of a quality academic program.

NOTES

1. Linda Darling-Hammond, "From 'Separate but Equal' to 'No Child Left Behind': The Collision of New Standards and Old Inequities," in *Many Children Left Behind: How the No Child Left Behind Act Is Damaging Our Children and Our Schools*, eds. Deborah Meier and George Wood (Boston: Beacon Press, 2004), 3–32.

2. Dan Laitsch, Theresa Lewallen, and Molly McCloskey, "A Framework for Education in the 21st Century," *Whole Child, Infobrief* 40 (2005).

3. John Dewey, *Experience and Education* (New York: Touchstone, 1997).

4. "Institutionalization," Changing Minds, accessed October 20, 2014,http://changingminds.org/disciplines/sociology/articles/institutionalization.

5. Emma Van der Klift and Norman Kunc, "The Human Service System: Pyramid or Circle?" Broadreach Counseling & Mediation, accessed October 20, 2014,http://www.broadreachtraining.com/advocacy/arsystem.htm.

6. Joan Costello et al., "How History, Ideology, and Structure Shape the Organizations That Shape Youth," in *Trends in Youth Development: Visions, Realities, and Challenges*, eds. Peter L. Benson and Karen Johnson Pittman (Norwell, MA: Kluwer Academic Publishers, 2001), 191–229.

7. Alison Nelson, "Person Centered Services & Outcome Development," presentation at Minnesota Social Services Association on Annual Training Conference and Expo, Minneapolis, Minnesota, March 22, 2011.

8. Van der Klift and Kunc, "The Human Service System."

9. Geoffrey Caine and Renate Caine, *Education on the Edge of Possibility* (Alexandria, VA: Association for Supervision and Curriculum Development, 1997).

10. Ibid.

11. Ibid., 38.

12. Jenny Sazama and Karen S. Young, *Get the Word Out!* (Somerville, MA: Youth On Board, 2001).

13. Dewey, *Experience and Education.*

14. Ibid.

15. Ibid., 46.

16. Ibid.

17. Ibid.

18. Eric Jensen, *Teaching with Poverty in Mind: What Being Poor Does to Kids' Brains and What Schools Can Do About It* (Alexandria, VA: Association for Supervision and Curriculum Development, 2009).

19. Parker J. Palmer, *The Courage to Teach: Exploring the Inner Landscape of a Teacher's Life* (San Francisco: John Wiley & Sons, 2007).

20. James E. Zull, *From Brain to Mind: Using Neuroscience to Guide Change in Education* (Sterling, VA: Stylus Publishing, 2011).

21. Ibid.

22. Edward L. Deci and Richard Flaste, *Why We Do What We Do: Understanding Self-Motivation* (New York: Penguin Books, 1995).

23. Alfie Kohn, "Choices for Children: Why and How to Let Students Decide," *Phi Delta Kappan* 75, no. 1 (1993): 8–21.

24. Ibid.

25. Johnmarshall Reeve, "Self-Determination Theory Applied to Educational Settings," in *Handbook of Self-Determination Research*, eds. Edward L. Deci and Richard M. Ryan (Rochester, NY: University of Rochester Press, 2002), 183–203.

26. Caine and Caine, *Education on the Edge of Possibility*, 32.

Chapter Three

The Prisoners

Let student voices be heard!
I hate how mayors, governors . . . talk about education.
What is education really about?
If it is about us, why aren't we being heard?
We have to abide by everything they say.
Why aren't students' voices and the student body present
at the Board meetings and funding decisions?
Why aren't our voices being heard?
I can see where it wouldn't be the case in elementary school,
but not with older students—we should have a say.
—Lorenzo

No voice, no power. Lorenzo's appeal to "Let student voices be heard!" rings of the oppression discussed in the previous chapter. The voices of our most important stakeholders are missing from the many conversations and decisions that directly impact them. There is a glaring void of student and youth voice in research, literature, policymaking, and the day-to-day issues that surround and impact young people. Not only are the voices of youth sorely missing, but when young people do attempt to share their ideas and experiences, they are quickly silenced by the noise and authority of the adults around them.

So the question needs to be asked, "Why are youth's voices and presence so absent in our schools, society, and in matters that concern them?" The answer lies within a deeper societal issue. It is not just a matter of bringing young people's voices into the conversation, because before we attempt to do so, we first need to *value* their voices, ideas, and contributions. And in order to value their voices, ideas, and contributions, we need to value *them*—young people.

An example of the importance of valuing and empowering young people is highlighted by Maria, a student who had endured a great deal of trauma in her personal life and numerous difficulties in her mainstream high school. Maria transferred to an alternative school after an incident of harassment at her home school. During an interview about the Leadership class she participated in, Maria was asked about the value of the class. She responded:

> Well, the value of Leadership [class] to me is way bigger than any other class at school. I feel like I'm wanted in this class, like you treat me like I'm this awesome kid in this class, and then I go to other classes and I'm not most of the time. I feel like I'm valued in this class, and in my other classes it's all about the teachers and what they have to say.

Maria's comments represent what many youth experience—a lack of valuation and validation by school staff. Their roles as young people and as students render them passive and voiceless in the system. Marie's experience also reflects the hierarchical and oppressive nature of the school system. The teachers do most of the talking and directing, while students are there to engage and respond in a prescribed manner. Their part in the learning process is passive; the focus is largely on what the teachers have to say.

So how did it come to be that education is "all about the teachers" and not so very much about the students it serves? Our educational system, designed by adults, does not provide for student input or student choice.[1] Students are afforded little choice in matters related to their education—what, when, where, and how to learn, who to learn with, and who should teach them.

The hierarchical structure of the educational system places adult educators in the dominant, expert, one-up position while students are groomed to be in the submissive, passive, one-down position, leading to a culture of oppression. These roles and expectations were set up early on in educational institutions and have persisted over time. They came about, in part, as a result of the "cult of efficiency" established in the early twentieth century that bound learners into bolted-down desks and lockstep curricula.[2] Schools attempt to keep students in these prescribed roles by using excessive control, threats of punishment, and coercive tactics.

Ironically, the purpose of education is to empower students through learning—"knowledge is power"—and yet school is one of the most disempowering experiences for many young people. This is highlighted in Feliz's remarks about where education goes wrong:

> There's not so much wrong with the "idea" or purpose of education, but it's the environment—teachers, rules, adult perceptions of youth—where it goes wrong. Their bad perceptions of youth go into their mood and how they treat people.

While interviewing students for my doctoral research and hearing many of them discuss the lack of empowerment in classes and schools, I wondered if school was the only place that youth felt disempowered and devalued. So when my students and I presented at a national youth development and leadership conference, I posed this question to the audience at the onset of the session: "How many of you think we do a pretty good job of *valuing* young people in our society, especially the age group, fifteen to nineteen years old, represented here today?"

Considering that audience members came from all across the nation and represented various fields—youth development, education, juvenile justice, and workforce development—I fully expected a range of responses. Not so. Not a single hand went up. I did not anticipate that over a hundred people would respond in such a way. Surprised by those results, I asked that same question at another conference. The response was the same. Not a single hand went up. After asking the first question, I asked them to consider a second issue: If society does a poor job of valuing youth overall, what happens to the valuation of youth who may have other societal challenges, such as those who are gay, disabled, or in a minority, live in poverty, or have a juvenile record? The unfortunate reality is that their perceived value drops even more.

ADULTISM

John Bell, director of Leadership Development, Youth Build, USA, advised, "To be successful in our work with young people, we must understand . . . that young people are often mistreated and disrespected simply because they are young."[3] This is a consequence of *adultism*—attitudes and behaviors that assume that adults are better than young people and are entitled to act upon young people without their consent. Devaluation and disempowerment of youth is rooted in a cultural phenomenon that affects all of us, because we were all young at one point in our lives.

Adultism is the everyday, systemic, and institutionalized oppression of young people by adults.[4] The oppression associated with adultism is characterized by disrespecting the intelligence, judgment, emotional life, leadership, or physical being of young people.[5] Adultism occurs when adults have both a negative view of young people and the ability to wield control over the lives of youth.[6] Moreover, when adults exert their influence and authority over young people, they do so with little regard for the experiences, feelings, or opinions of youth.

Adultism is manifested through basic assumptions and presumed rights that adults have over children. Adults maintain the right to punish, threaten, hit, remove privileges, and ostracize young people as a means of controlling or disciplining them.[7] In addition, young people's opinions are not valued, and they are not allowed to be decision makers within their communities. As a result of their inferior standing in our society, young people are deprived of voice and power. "If you think about it, you will realize that except for prisoners and a few other institutionalized groups, young people are more controlled than any other group in society."[8]

The concept of adultism is a more recent phenomenon and is not widely accepted, yet young people have long been subjected to the systematic disrespect and mistreatment that parallels the oppression of other *isms* such as racism and sexism.[9] Adultism, racism, sexism, and other *isms* are rampant in our society; however, adultism affects *everyone*. It is an oppression that becomes internalized and passed from generation to generation. Adultism is so ingrained in our society we are not conscious of it. The manner in which young people are treated seems normal and acceptable.

Although the way young people are treated might seem normal, adultism results in harmful consequences for those who are oppressed—young people. One of the most detrimental consequences of an *ism* is that its victims come to see themselves as flawed. When young people are disrespected and mistreated, they are robbed of their fundamental human power, access to their feelings, and confidence in their thinking and ability to act.[10] Not only does oppression erode confidence in one's ability to think and act, it also conditions young people to accept all other oppressions that exist in society.[11]

Adultism is pervasive throughout our society and institutions. In his seminal article on adultism, John Bell outlines the many ways and places that adultism is evident, some of which include the following:[12]

Schools

- Students are subjected to extreme control by way of hall passes, detention, suspension, expulsion, and other penalties to maintain control.
- Teachers can yell at students, but students are disciplined if they yell back.
- Students are forced to accept their grades. This has a profound impact on their lives; however, students do not get to grade teachers. If a student receives an "F" it is assumed that the student has failed, not the teacher.
- Young people do not have any real power over the important decisions that affect their lives in school.
- The rules in schools are imposed on young people and enforced by adult staff.

Verbal Interactions

- In a disagreement with an adult, most young people know that the adult's word will be taken over theirs.
- Most adults talk down to children.
- Adults often talk about a young person in their presence as if s/he weren't there.
- Many young people are ordered to do things or are given rules with no explanation.
- Adults do not really listen to young people and do not take their concerns as seriously as they would adults.
- Young people's ideas are not thought to be worthy of adult respect or to be at the level of adult thinking.
- Young people are expected to listen to adults all the time.

Community

- Adolescents are often followed by security guards in stores.
- Young people are assumed to be up to "no good."
- They are often chased from parks or gathering places by police.
- Media promotes negative images and stereotypes of youth, especially urban and Black youth.

Institutions

- Youth are forced to go to school for twelve years, regardless of whether school is an effective learning environment for them.
- Within the school setting, youth have no voice, no power, and no decision-making capacity to effect change.
- There is an absence of socially responsible, productive roles for youth and no high expectations of young people's contributions to society.

Given their institutional and oppressive nature, schools tend to intensify many of the *isms* that exist in the larger society, including adultism. This is particularly true for students being able to think, speak, and act for themselves. Self-determination is not encouraged, and students are rarely, if ever, asked to express their opinions about matters of consequence regarding their education. As such, schools both disempower and overpower their students. Ben felt the firsthand effects of adultism throughout his school career:

> It feels like a dictatorship; it's their way or the highway! They use the police or county against you. Right now, the teachers are the bosses and they control you. It feels like they are trying to control you, boss you around . . . I needed

my teachers to back off a bit. Pushing me made me not do anything and shut down. I needed leading, not pushing.

Andrew also felt the power imbalance throughout the school; however, it was most pronounced in the main office:

The administration staff were the worst when it came to feeling superior . . . when you went into the main office you would sometimes have to wait twenty minutes for them to talk to us. It made you feel more like a number, like cattle, rather than a person. It made you feel like they were a lot better than you. One dean refused to show emotion, he was always right—his way or the highway. I doubt he knew any of the students.

Similarly, Richard expressed the need for support and advocacy in a system of imbalanced power in which teachers have the right to be disrespectful without consequence, while students are held to another standard.

When everyone in your school is fucking with you, how are you supposed to get through? You really need someone. There was one teacher who, even though kids treated him with respect, he treated them like shit. Teachers should have corrective action if needed.

Oppression in schools is accepted as the natural order of things; it is neither questioned nor challenged. Oppressive practices are prevalent in educational institutions where control, power, and coercive tactics are the primary means of establishing and maintaining order. If adults were treated this way, they likely would not stand for it. But because of the power disparity, and because they can, schools feel free to use oppressive measures with young people.

People tend to attribute a lot of young people's problems to low self-esteem. Paul Kivel, author of books on social justice issues such as racism and violence, argues that the issue isn't one of self-esteem, but rather a loss of power.[13] He maintains that without power to protect themselves, young people are restricted, disrespected, and abused by adults. Adults retain the authority to decide how youth should dress and talk, whom they can befriend, and ultimately, their future through grades, records, discipline, arrests, and such.

Ironically, even though adults hold the power, they blame youth for their failures.[14] They do this by labeling young people as troublemakers, stupid, irresponsible, immature, apathetic, lazy, dishonest, and underachievers. Young people, who end up internalizing the message or attacking others, personalize the message that something is wrong with their body, feelings, attitude, ideas, or skin color. Kivel asserts that issues such as teen violence, gang involvement, chemical abuse, unwanted pregnancy, and suicide are forms of learned helplessness and hopelessness in youth. They have given up on themselves because adults treated them as lesser individuals. Yet in reality, youth haven't failed themselves, adults have failed them.

The oppressive nature of adultism sets youth up to live in and accept a society steeped in exploitation, violence, and hierarchies of race, class, and gender. Not only are youth relatively powerless in an adult-defined world, their opportunities are even more limited if they are people of color, female, gay or lesbian, disabled, or living in poverty.[15] These additional challenges can lead young people to blame themselves for the resulting consequences they experience.

If we only help young people enhance their self-esteem, we are doing them a disservice.[16] Without doing more, we reinforce the notion that they are the problem—that they are to blame. We mislead them into thinking that personal virtue, effort, perseverance, and skill can completely change their lives, which is not necessarily true. Instead, we would increase their chances of survival and success by helping them realize what they are up against.

AN ATTITUDE PROBLEM

Along with adultism, adolescents bear the burden of adults' negative perceptions and stereotypes, which are based solely on their stage of development, as Adrian noted:

> Well, compared to right now, they look down on teenagers like they're reckless teenagers, but once we get out into the community and show them we're doing something, helping you guys, helping ourselves, helping upcoming generations, it will give them the sense that maybe teenagers can do something.

Young people are very aware of the negative stereotypes about their age group, as revealed in Adrian's comments. He hopes that by being involved in positive community action, it will change society's disapproving perceptions of his age group. Teens often feel like they have to prove themselves to gain acceptance in their communities and in society. The underlying assumptions are that their value is limited, or they are in the wrong, and the onus is on them to demonstrate otherwise.

It can be very hard to overcome the negative stereotypes that persist about youth, despite evidence to the contrary. A recent example is driving and texting. Nearly all the marketing campaigns target adolescents, yet a recent survey by AT&T found that adults are more likely to text and drive than adolescents.[17] Survey results revealed that 49 percent of adults admit to texting and driving while 43 percent of teens report texting. While the percentage difference may seem relatively small, there are only ten million teen drivers as compared to 180 million adult drivers. So to whom should those ad campaigns really be directed? Adults are much more likely to endanger others with their texting than teens are. Assumptions like this continue to plague teens and perpetuate false beliefs about a group of people based strictly on their age.

Troubled youth are no longer seen as the exception but as the dysfunctional rule, when in fact, today's teens are healthier, better educated, and more responsible than teens of the past.[18] Over time, nearly every generation of young people has been regarded as deviant and out of control. These misperceptions can be attributed to *ephebiphobia*—a fear and loathing of adolescence. Our current pathological perspective on adolescence tends to emphasize the negative; adolescence is seen as an incurable social disease.

Research efforts also contribute to an exaggerated prevalence of adolescent maladjustment as they tend to focus primarily on a storm, stress, or deficit paradigm for adolescence. Likewise, studies that investigate general beliefs and perceptions about adolescents are discouraging, as they tend to portray teens in a negative and undeserving manner.[19] Until Shepherd Zeldin's 2002 study, "Sense of Community and Positive Adult Beliefs Toward Adolescents and Youth Policy in Urban Neighborhoods and Small Cities," no research had explored adults' beliefs of adolescents as prosocial contributors to their communities.[20]

Adults believe that teens today are different from teens in the past. Only 16 percent of Americans say that young people share most of their moral and ethical values.[21] In a Gallup poll people were asked what word(s) applied to young people in their teens and twenties today, and the most common responses were *selfish* (81 percent) and *materialistic* (79 percent). On the other hand, words such as *patriotic* (65 percent) and *idealistic* (49 percent) were used to describe youth of past generations.

The results of other research studies are consistent with previous findings. When adults and college students were asked what phrase first comes to mind about teens, more than two-thirds of adults used negative terms such as *rude*, *irresponsible*, and *wild*.[22] In addition, adults were more likely to describe teens in more negative terms than they described children and less likely to ascribe positive characteristics to teens than to children.

Mass media plays a strong role in how young people are perceived. Depictions of youth and youth-related issues by TV networks create and perpetuate negative images and stereotypes of adolescents:[23]

- Only one out of every twelve local newscast stories and one in twenty-five network news stories focuses on young people.
- Nearly 60 percent of all media coverage about young people focuses on negative outcomes such as crime victimization, accidents, and violent juvenile crime.

- Rather than challenge negative media stereotypes about teens, most adults assume that their own adolescent experience was an exception to the norm.

There is a significant disconnect between how adults view adolescents and what teens actually think and do. In contrast to how adults perceive them, teens rank being honest, working hard, and giving time to help others as some of their most important values.[24] Moreover, young people are at least as healthy as or healthier than their parent's generation; SAT scores have remained constant since 1970; and the number of high school students who volunteer has remained constant since 1975.

Another research study revealed a disturbing finding: adults were unable to change their negative beliefs about young people, even when provided hard evidence to the contrary.[25] When groups of adults were given a "true news story" about recent trends among teenagers, the adults consistently overlooked the positive data that dominated the story. Instead, they focused on the few negative items. When asked to reexamine the story and explain why they thought it was negative given all the positive factors, the adults responded that they thought the numbers were incorrect. After they were reassured that the numbers were indeed correct, the adults still found ways to reinterpret the information to reach an unfavorable conclusion about the teens.

The fact that adults hold and convey primarily negative views and images of adolescents is alarming enough. It is even more disconcerting that when presented with hard data refuting those perceptions, adults reject the positive evidence rather than change their biases about teens.

Society views young people, both collectively and individually, in negative and stereotypical ways. Richard experienced this on a personal level, and like Adrian, he felt the need to debunk the stereotypes and prove his worthiness through positive community involvement:

> People that know me think I am a hoodlum—that feels like ignorance to me. All I really want to do is make people happy and do something right . . . Almost everything we did in Leadership and the community was good for me—people we met, connections we made, being able to help others. If youth get involved in these things, it might help people to really see the inside of the person and not just judge us, only seeing the funk, the negative, 'cause even though we are different on the outside, we are all the same on the inside.

As a result of teens' lesser status, adults can be quick to judge, label, and write young people off, as revealed in Richard's remarks and in the stories of students in chapter 1. This judge, jury, and sentence approach is yet another form of adultism. Young people are in a one-down position and must continually prove their worth as individuals and as a group in society. This is a double standard. Would adults judge and label their peers as quickly and frequently as they do youth? Likely not. Perhaps it is adults, not youth, who have an "attitude" problem.

In sharing his experience, Richard asks people to not make assumptions or jump to hasty conclusions. He encourages them to take time to really know and understand young people and what they have to offer, and to view them as worthy individuals. Young people should not have to endure all of this to earn acceptance in our society. They should be able to trust that they are valued members of our communities, as there are consequences when youth aren't accepted and perceived in a positive light.

Adultism, negative perceptions, and stereotypes cause harmful consequences for youth and for our society. Young people are aware of societal stereotypes and can internalize these skewed beliefs. Perceived exposure to stereotyping has been associated with reduced feelings of self-worth and negative self-attributions for both females and ethnic minority adolescents. [26] Likewise, adults' negative beliefs of youth, along with internalized negative self-perceptions, likely contribute to adolescents' lack of confidence in their ability to have a positive impact on their communities.

In addition, negative and limited perceptions of youth and their capacity tend to marginalize youth and severely limit the roles they are granted in society. [27] The primary roles that an adolescent can occupy in society are mostly limited to student, athlete, or consumer. As a result, young people miss out on the opportunity to attain a sense of full membership in society and in their communities.

Negative views and stereotypes of youth exist not only in general society, they also prevail throughout our school systems, as schools reflect the beliefs and values held by the larger society. Along with a commonly held pessimism about adolescents in general, students with disabilities face additional negative and limiting perceptions: "too many school boards, administrators, principals, and teachers continue to devalue the unrealized potential of students with disabilities." [28]

A prime example of this "devaluation of unrealized potential of students" occurred at a state conference for alternative programming. The students in my Leadership class were setting up for a workshop we were facilitating on youth leadership. Several educators who had arrived early for the workshop struck up a conversation as we continued with our preparations. They wanted to know where the students were from, so I explained they were from alternative high schools and programs for students with disabilities.

After hearing my explanation, they responded, "There's no way our students would be able to do something like this. We don't have any kids that could do what your students are doing." While they likely meant it as a compliment for our students, their comments devalued the potential of their own students. They were predicting failure for them even before their students were provided an opportunity to demonstrate competence.

Unfortunately, this experience is repeated by many educators who see only the challenges and disabilities of their students. Often these staff members are frustrated by the many challenges they face in their daily work. They find it hard to imagine that with the appropriate supports and opportunities, these same students can achieve productive outcomes.

This was likely the case in a highly publicized incident of a high school English teacher who was found to be blogging damaging and profane comments about her students.[29] Ms. Munroe was upset with her students and chose to vent through personal blog entries. She was suspended by her school district for using profanity and referring to her students as "noisy, crazy, sloppy, lazy loafers, and lazy whiners," among other derogatory labels. She also proposed "colorful comments" that could be put onto report cards about students.

Ms. Munroe's duty to her students is to be their helper and advocate, not their critic. Ms. Munroe's words perpetuate the negative and harmful perceptions that already exist about young people, which in turn, reinforce the devaluation of youth. Educators often see and work with the by-products of a "bad fit" situation (with school) rather than a "bad kid" issue. However, people working in education often come to view the young person as the problem, rather than viewing the young person as an individual with challenges, as Charlie experienced firsthand in school.

Not only do adults perpetuate negative stereotypes of young people, they also do not trust them. Educational institutions and practices in the United States, historically and presently, reflect a basic lack of trust in students and serve to keep students under control and in their place—as passive recipients of what others deem as education.[30] Adults' distrust of young people, and their resolve to be in control, dehumanizes students and reduces them to products. Distrust keeps students from being seen as knowers, people who have legitimate knowledge and authority for policymaking and practice shaping.

Research studies confirm that adults do not view youth as effective decision makers.[31] Many adults believe that young people cannot or do not care to participate in decision making, and in fact, they may actually hinder the process. So instead of helping young people become acclimated to decision making and action in their communities, adults isolate them. Adolescents in the United States, more than in other countries, operate on the fringes of adult life. Preventing adolescents from participating in decision making contributes to and sustains stereotypes, resentment, and suspicion.

THE RIGHT TO BE OPPRESSED

In addition to being victimized by adultism and negative stereotypes, young people have very few rights as people and citizens. This is especially evident in schools. When it comes to education, we tend to see education as something adults do "to" children. Not only are young people not included in the planning and implementation of education, they also have very few rights as recipients of that education. Young people are prohibited from having a voice in crucial matters that impact them as students, as Lorenzo pointed out in his opening quote.

In an oppressive system, it is the individuals running the system who hold the power, not the people it is meant to serve. As such, people are granted very few, if any, rights that would provide them active voice and participation. In fact, it is quite the opposite. Oppressive systems devise and enforce a lot of rules and regulations while minimizing autonomy and liberties.

Students in our district were working on a service learning project about "student rights." They obtained a sampling of student high school handbooks from around the state, including rural, urban, and suburban schools. In examining the handbooks, they found that 22 percent of the handbooks contained no student rights and 39 percent had only one or two. Together, nearly two-thirds of the school handbooks sampled afforded students few, if any, rights. One of the handbooks that listed no rights for students had more than fifty rules and regulations by which students were required to abide. Of the schools whose handbooks offered only one student right, one handbook contained thirty pages of rules and regulations to be observed by students.

Another school providing only one student right described it as follows: "All students have the right to learn." Any and all privileges, safeguards, and opportunities for representation were diluted into this one lackluster statement. Considering that all students are mandated to attend school and learn, it wasn't much of a "right." Among the other school handbooks that students reviewed, 17 percent listed four to six student rights and 22 percent had ten or more.

Out of curiosity, one of the students working on the Student Rights project obtained the *Client's Rights* document from a juvenile detention center he had spent time at. The juvenile center handbook listed more rights, and more humane rights than most of the school handbooks. Furthermore, many of the rights, itemized in the juvenile center handbook related to personhood, dignity, and other attributes that assured individualized and respectful treatment. It was a glaring contrast to the school rights that mostly focused on legal and safety rights (e.g., access to records, data privacy, nondiscrimination).

The limited number and type of rights granted students in educational institutions is indicative of their status as an oppressed population. Schools and policymakers are reluctant to grant young people rights and privileges, but they are willing to impose an inordinate amount of rules, regulations, and consequences on our youth.

Not only are young people denied rights and voice, they also lack representation in policymaking that directly affects them. In a recent attempt to address bullying and harassment issues occurring in schools, policymakers in one Midwest state set up a task force and invited citizens to apply to serve on the task force. Although students applied to be on the task force, they were not accepted. Students were rendered voiceless on an issue that greatly affected them.

Once again, we have an issue that directly impacts students, and yet not a single youth voice was invited or allowed to be at the table to represent their interests and voice. Typical of what happens in our schools and society every day, adults assume that they know best and discount the importance and value of young people's involvement. We will never be able to fully and effectively address issues that impact youth until we have their full participation in the decision-making and planning processes.

Despite the lack of national and local rights and representation for youth, the Convention on the Rights of the Child compiled the first legally binding instrument that incorporates the full range of human rights—civil, cultural, economic, political, social, and humanitarian—for children worldwide.[32] Developed in 1989, these rights were established on behalf of children to ensure special care and protection, and to promote the awareness that children have human rights too. The four core principles of the Convention include:

1. Nondiscrimination
2. Adherence to the best interests of the child
3. The right to life, survival, and development
4. The right to participate, including respect for the views of the child

The last principle, respect for the views of the child, implies the right to participate in the dialogue, to express opinions and be heard, to access information, and to freely associate with others. Engaging these rights as they mature helps children to realize all of their rights and prepare them for an active role in society. One must ask, "Are we implementing the spirit and intention of these internationally recognized rights within our public schools and communities in the United States?" As Lorenzo alleges in the opening quote, likely not.

Participation rights for young people are sorely lacking in our schools and communities. Young people are excluded from most of the decision making that affects them. Not only is participation a fundamental right that young people should be granted, it also fosters empowerment and the full development of young people so they can learn and practice their roles as active, energized, and responsible citizens in their communities. [33]

SPEAK TRUTH TO POWER

How do we, as a society, presently address devaluation and oppression of youth? We don't. We ask youth to become involved with social change and world betterment, yet they have no role or voice to improve their own environmental conditions. In our schools and in our communities, young people are asked to step up their game and help address the oppression of others while remaining a prisoner of their own oppression. Not only does oppression of young people go unrecognized, but young people's voices, experiences, and wisdom are also absent from the places that should be benefiting them (e.g., schools, research, policymaking).

Before any real and lasting change can occur in our school systems, educators first need to examine how they view and value youth, especially older youth. Until perceptions change, reform in our schools will be limited and unsustainable because only the symptoms, not the underlying causes, are being addressed. Educators (and society) need to value the population they are serving in order to serve them well. Schools need to have a philosophy, guiding principles, and systemic practices that recognize young people as individuals of worth whose voices and involvement are welcomed, not only as active participants, but also as key informants and decision makers in the processes that most affect them. This valuation needs to extend to those youth who are most marginalized by our society and educational systems.

Another consideration is that devaluation is not limited to the youth alone; it extends to those who work with youth, including educators, members of community youth organizations, those who work in the juvenile systems, and the like. The consequences of extended devaluation can take many forms such as a lack of social support, negative perceptions, omission of relevant voices, oppression, and low priority when it comes to formal decision making and resources.

SUMMARY

By the very nature of their developmental stage, young people are disregarded and disrespected. It is a universal reality that all young people must deal with regardless of gender, ethnic background, and socioeconomic status. Consequences associated with the devaluation of young people are detrimental and long lasting. The effects are carried forward from generation to generation at the expense of our youth, and ultimately, our society.

Young people come up against adultism and persistent, negative stereo-types every day, especially in our schools. Youth internalize the oppression that is rampant in our society and institutions. And yet they hold out hope that by doing extraordinary things for the community, they will be able to change people's perceptions of them and be valued by their communities.

We need to speak truth to power. Young people are not second-class citizens, nor are they less valuable members of our communities and schools. They should not have to prove their place and value in society. Rather, it is for society to recognize and nurture young people for who they are and the value they bring to our lives and communities, our present and our future.

What goes unrecognized fails to be challenged, and in turn, continues to be accepted and reinforced as the acceptable status quo. It is time to awaken to the realities of what our youth deal with every day—devaluation and oppression in our schools and communities. It is for the adults in our society, with the involvement of youth, to recognize and forward this much-needed change. Our children and our future depend on it.

NOTES

1. Richard Cohen, "Adultism," *The School Mediator* 3 (2004), accessed October 28, 2014,http://www.schoolmediation.com/newsletters/2004/01_04.html.

2. Alison Cook-Sather, "Authorizing Students' Perspectives: Toward Trust, Dialogue, and Change in Education," *Educational Researcher* 31, no. 4 (2002): 3–14.

3. John Bell, *Understanding Adultism: A Major Obstacle to Developing Positive Youth-Adult Relationships*, YouthBuild USA (1995), accessed October 28, 2014, https://www.scoe.net/actioncivics/pdf/UnderstandingAdultism.pdf.

4. Paul Kivel, "Adultism," Getting Together for Social Justice (2009), accessed October 28, 2014,http://www.paulkivel.com/component/jdownloads/finish/1/81/0?Itemid=31.

5. Richard Cohen, "Adultism," *The School Mediator* 3 (2004), accessed October 28, 2014,http://www.schoolmediation.com/newsletters/2004/01_04.html.

6. Jorge Velázquez Jr., and Maria Garin-Jones, "Adultism and Cultural Competence," *Children's Voice* 12 (Child Welfare League of America, 2003): 20–21.

7. Bell, *Understanding Adultism*.

8. Ibid., 1.

9. Ibid.

10. Ibid.

11. "Challenging Adultism," The Free Child Project, accessed October 30, 2014,http://www.freechild.org/adultism.htm.

12. Bell, *Understanding Adultism*.

13. Paul Kivel, *Adultism* (2006), accessed October 28, 2014, http://paulkivel.com/component/jdownloads/finish/1/5/0?itemid=31.

14. Ibid.

15. Ibid.

16. Ibid.

17. Larry Copeland, "Texting in Traffic: Adults Worse Than Teens," *USA Today*, March 28, 2013, accessed October 28, 2014,http://www.usatoday.com/story/news/nation/2013/03/28/adults-worse-than-teens-about-texting-behind-wheel/2026331/.

18. Kirk A. Astroth, "Beyond Ephebiphobia: Problem Adults or Problem Youth?" *Phi Delta Kappan* 75, no. 5 (1994): 411–13.

19. Franklin D. Gilliam Jr., and Susan Nall Bales, "Strategic Frame Analysis: Reframing America's Youth," Society for Research in Child Development, *Social Policy Report* 15, no. 3 (2001).

20. Shepherd Zeldin, "Sense of Community and Positive Adult Beliefs Toward Adolescents and Youth Policy in Urban Neighborhoods and Small Cities," *Journal of Youth and Adolescence* 31, no. 5 (2002): 331–42.

21. Meg Bostrom, *Teenhood: Understanding Attitudes toward Those Transitioning from Childhood to Adulthood*, FrameWorks Institute (2000), accessed October 21, 2014,http://www.frameworksinstitute.org/assets/files/PDF/youth_understanding_attitudes.pdf.

22. Zeldin, "Sense of Community and Positive Adult Beliefs Toward Adolescents and Youth Policy."

23. Gilliam Jr. and Nall Bales, "Strategic Frame Analysis: Reframing America's Youth."

24. James Youniss and Allison J. Ruth, "Interim Report: Positive Indicators of Youth Development," unpublished manuscript, The Catholic University of America, Washington, D.C., 2000.

25. Meg Bostrom, *Teenhood*.

26. Shepherd Zeldin and Dimitri Topitzes, "Neighborhood Experiences, Community Connection, and Positive Beliefs about Adolescents among Urban Adults and Youth," *Journal of Community Psychology* 30, no. 6 (2002): 647–69.

27. Linda Camino and Shepherd Zeldin, "From Periphery to Center: Pathways for Youth Civic Engagement in the Day-to-Day Life of Communities," *Applied Developmental Science* 6, no. 4 (2002): 213–20.

28. Drew Allbritten et al., "Will Students with Disabilities Be Scapegoats for School Failures?" *Educational Horizons* 82, no. 2 (2004).

29. Matt Rourke, "PA Teacher Strikes Nerve with 'Lazy Whiners' Blog," *USA TODAY*, February 16, 2011, accessed October 21, 2014,http://usatoday30.usatoday.com/news/education/2011-02-16-teacher-blog-suspended_N.htm.

30. Cook-Sather, "Authorizing Students' Perspectives: Toward Trust, Dialogue, and Change in Education."

31. Shepherd Zeldin et al., *Youth in Decision-Making: A Study on the Impacts of Youth on Adults and Organizations*, University of Wisconsin-Madison Department of Human Development and Family Studies, University of Wisconsin Extension (2000), accessed February 26, 2015, http://www.theinnovationcenter.org/files/youth_in_decision_making_brochure.pdf.

32. "What Is the Convention on the Rights of the Child?" UNICEF, accessed February 24, 2015,http://www.unicef.org/rightsite/433_468.htm.

33. "Adolescence: An Age of Opportunity," Executive Summary in *The State of the World's Children 2011*. New York: United Nations Children's Fund, 2011.

Chapter Four

Disempowered to Disengaged

I am smart, but when you have someone talking to you
like the "Clear Eyes/Red Eyes" commercial, so monotone and robotic,
it's hard for you to understand and comprehend what's going on in class.
It's like watching paint dry.
—Katie

In addition to the oppressive nature of school, early and ongoing educational challenges cause many students to become disconnected with classes and school. Katie's quote expresses how many students feel about school when they are not engaged or interested. They cry out, act out, or check out because they are at odds with a system that seemingly works against them, not *with* or *for* them. Not only does every day feel like a battle, but for many students with disabilities and/or other challenges, classes also seem tedious and uninspiring. Students often complain that they have done the same work in previous schools or programs and are not motivated to repeat the same material. Further, much of the work feels beneath their ability level.

The importance of engaged learning is supported by ample research, yet classes are not very engaging for students. Students become more disengaged from school as they move from elementary to middle school, and by high school as many as 40 to 60 percent of students are chronically disengaged from school.[1] Classroom disengagement translates into school disengagement, as nearly 7 percent of students drop out of high school each year[2] and 20 percent do not graduate with their class.[3] Dropout rates are even higher for minority youth, reaching 8 percent for Blacks, 12 percent for Hispanic students,[4] and 13 to 15 percent for Native American and Native Alaskan students.[5]

In addition to dropping out, many students do not graduate in the allotted four-year time frame. Minority students, students from low-income households, and students with disabilities are less apt to graduate in four years. Graduation rates for African American and Hispanic students are at 69 percent and 73 percent, respectively, as compared to 86 percent of White students,[6] and the graduation rate for Native American /Alaska Native students is 67 percent.[7] Graduation rates for minorities differ significantly between states, with Minnesota showing the highest racial disparities.

Low-income student graduation rates vary as well, ranging from 25 percent in Maine to 63 percent in California, with the national average at 45 percent.[8] In some states (Minnesota, Wyoming, Alaska) with lower-than-average numbers of low-income students, they still have lower-than-average overall graduation rates (59 to 65 percent) for low-income students. Students with disabilities also experience low graduation rates, nearly twenty points lower than the average graduation rate for all students.

Dropouts identified "uninteresting classes" as the top reason they left school.[9] Other reasons cited by students were apathy, boredom, and a perceived lack of relevance. Many students said that they found the world outside of school more interesting and engaging than school. Typical classroom instruction fails to engage students cognitively, emotionally, or behaviorally.[10] Subject matter tends to be disconnected and unrelated to students' lives outside of school. Students are passively listening to lectures or doing repetitive tasks that are often either too easy or too difficult. Moreover, getting the right answer takes priority over understanding.

Other nonacademic factors contribute to disengagement and eventually dropping out. Teacher-student interactions, disciplinary procedures, and school size and climate can impact whether students remain engaged and in school.[11] When students perceive that teachers are not caring or invested in their learning, it can drive them away. Likewise, when students sense that discipline and conformity—controlling the students—takes precedence over education and a caring and supportive environment, students can end up feeling stressed and unsupported. And if students don't feel that they are valued or that their opinions are respected, they become alienated from their schools.

Disengagement is a slow process that begins in earlier grades. School engagement declines steadily from fifth grade through twelfth grade.[12] Disengagement is widespread and not limited to students who struggle with school, as 45 percent of students report disengagement with school. In one study, fifth-graders spent 93 percent of their time sitting and working alone.[13] Students who are bored or working in isolation are not actively engaged in the learning process.

Students are disconnected and demoralized as a result of being required to do work that holds little interest or value to them. And if it is work they have already attempted and didn't succeed at the first, second, or third time, why bother going through the motions one more time? When students detach from the learning process, educators often conclude that they are unmotivated. Teachers assume that students aren't willing to invest the effort to learn, but that assumption is usually incorrect. The real cause of students' struggles likely has more to do with earlier environmental challenges and unmet learning needs that led to school failure.

THE "SUCCEEDERS"

When I met Charlie in his junior year, it was obvious that he was a bright young man who demonstrated high verbal and analytical abilities. His early life experiences included homelessness, limited income, and numerous moves. Charlie struggled with his classes and his schoolwork and was eventually referred to another high school. Although he was aware of his challenges with school, Charlie didn't understand why he couldn't "do school" like his peers:

> Now when I look back, I feel like a fool, 'cause it seemed like everyone knew and did what it took to get the work done, be successful, and go to college. It felt like teachers focused on the "succeeders" and not on me, 'cause they already thought I would fail, I wouldn't make it. They put their attention on the students that knew how to succeed. It felt like everyone else knew something I didn't and I didn't know what that was . . . my friend could get it like they taught it, so he was successful.

Charlie recognized that many of his peers, including his friend who excelled in school, seemed to be able to do school with ease. It was as if they had inside information on how to succeed at school. Unlike his friend, Charlie didn't hold the key that could unlock the gates to learning. He was further discouraged by teachers who seemingly gave up on him and turned their attention to those students who got it.

Andrew had a similar experience. He was frustrated by teachers who used methods that were ineffective for him. And like Charlie, Andrew also felt that teachers' attention was directed more toward those students who were able to learn from traditional methods.

> The way things were taught, I didn't really get it. Some teachers I excelled with and others I didn't. It was their method or style I couldn't pick up on, so I didn't do as well in those classes. It was difficult to get attention from teachers when I needed it. I did stay after school for a few classes 'cause I wanted to get my grades up, but even though it was just me and the teacher, they still taught me in the same way and used the same examples and I still didn't get it. I didn't get it when they taught that way in the class and I didn't get it one on one.

Andrew went on to say:

> I could tell by how teachers taught. They didn't take the time to understand
> how you learned. If you weren't in that group, "high clique," or one of the
> people that got how they taught, you had more struggles.

Andrew and Charlie's experiences are unfortunately all too common in
the classroom. Out of necessity, teachers are under pressure to teach to what
Susan Neuman calls the "bubble" kids—the ones who have the requisite
knowledge and readiness to learn.[14] Given the large number of students in
their classes, teachers face the dilemma of pacing the instruction for the
majority of students who are ready to move on, or pacing it to the few who
are struggling. More often than not, even the most effective teachers compromise for the group and teach to the middle. Consequently, students who
haven't obtained the prerequisite concepts are left behind as the teacher and
other students move forward. Even if some students are lucky enough to get
additional help, only about one in three will likely benefit and achieve success.

Students need the objectives and strategies for doing things in school to
be explicit and not left to chance to figure out on their own.[15] If things are not
explicitly modeled or explained, students can have difficulty understanding
expectations related to doing work and the use of strategies to solve problems
or learn content knowledge. When expectations and strategies are not made
clear or tangible, students end up underperforming and not knowing why, as
may have been the case with Charlie and Andrew.

LEARNED HELPLESSNESS

There are multiple and varied reasons why students become disconnected
and disengaged with classes and school. One well-researched cause is a
phenomenon known as *learned helplessness*, in which students learn to "not
learn."[16] At least five million children between the ages of five and sixteen
struggle with learned helplessness in our schools. Learned helplessness occurs when there is an overload of achievement failure. When children experience continuous frustration and failure in school, they come to the conclusion
that all tasks are too difficult and not worth the effort. They believe that
outcomes are out of their control and that their actions will not result in
success. Learned helplessness is an adaptive response to life circumstances
and can take hold as early as first grade and result in students dropping out of
school.[17]

Learned helplessness leads to deficits in three areas—motivation, emotions, and cognition. Deficiencies in these areas destroy the student's natural
desire to learn.[18] Educators usually perceive lack of motivation as a behav-

ioral or moral decision on the part of the student, when in fact, it is actually a motivation deficit created by a continuous pattern of failure that stymies the student's willingness to try. As a form of self-preservation, students stop putting themselves in the position of potential failure.

When educators encounter motivational issues, they tend to apply more pressure on the student.[19] However, hammering on students, as discussed in chapter 2, has the opposite effect. Misconstruing underachievement as a motivation issue and applying undue pressure does not help to motivate students; instead, it increases negative feelings, depression, and self-concepts of failure. It is critical that educators understand that underachievement is not a motivation issue. Nor is it a moral decision on the student's part. Rather, much of what educators perceive as motivation issues is actually a conditioned response, a learned behavior.

Along with the motivational deficits, emotional deficits occur and can lead to depression and low self-esteem.[20] Struggles with school tend to intensify students' negative feelings regarding self-worth and helplessness. This can leave students at risk for depression. Children who are depressed exhibit more achievement-related problems and social skill deficits.

Cognitive deficits are another consequence of learned helplessness.[21] Faulty thinking, a breakdown in logical perceptions, occurs when students experience learned helplessness. Thinking becomes blocked, and consequently, students use avoidance and other maladaptive strategies as a means to cope with failure. And the longer students practice ineffective responses, the more challenging it becomes to break out of those patterns.

A number of factors contribute to learned helplessness in the school setting. In addition to continuous academic failure, grouping students with various disabilities with a teacher who has generic training, excessive use of external reinforcement, lack of early identification of disabilities, and reinforcement of achievement rather than effort can lead to or reinforce learned helplessness in students.[22]

It is not just the occurrence of failure, but rather students' perceptions about failures, that determine how they approach future incidents.[23] This is known as *attribution theory*. What students attribute to their failure determines subsequent success or failure. By third grade, children already have an optimistic or pessimistic style of seeing the world. This is manifested in school by either mastery or a learned-helplessness orientation. Mastery-oriented students attribute their achievements to personal abilities and efforts. Students who experience learned helplessness attribute success to uncontrollable factors, while they attribute failure to their personal lack of ability. This pattern of attribution negatively affects students' future efforts.

SELF-EFFICACY AND SELF-ESTEEM

Similar to learned helplessness, self-efficacy also impacts how people perform. Self-efficacy is a belief in one's own capacity to succeed at tasks; it is a judgment about whether "I can" or "I can't" perform a particular activity.[24] Self-efficacy is the perception that one has the necessary skills to achieve one's goals.[25] How people feel, think, behave, and motivate themselves, and the choices people make in life, are all impacted by self-efficacy beliefs.[26]

People with strong self-efficacy view difficult tasks as challenges to be mastered.[27] They increase and sustain their efforts when confronted with failure. If they encounter failure, it is attributed to insufficient effort, knowledge, or skills. On the contrary, people who have weaker self-efficacy avoid challenging tasks, as those are viewed as personal threats. They tend to have lower aspirations and lesser commitment to goals. People with low self-efficacy minimize their efforts and admit defeat more readily. Failure is interpreted as a lack of ability on their part. Students with low self-efficacy do not expect to do well, and often do not achieve at their ability level.[28] They don't believe they have the skills, so they don't even attempt the task.

Just as self-efficacy is strengthened through successful mastery experiences, it is undermined by experiences of failure, especially if failure occurs before a sense of efficacy is firmly established.[29] Early childhood and school experiences are critical to the development of self-efficacy. Repeated mastery or failure will directly impact the degree to which people feel in control of themselves and their environment.

How students interpret their past successes and failures influences what activities or goals they select, how much effort they put forth, and how persistent they are when facing difficulties.[30] If students have been successful with a certain skill in the past, they will likely believe that they will succeed with it in the future. If students haven't been successful, they will likely believe they will fail at future attempts. The connection between self-efficacy and achievement increases over the years. By the time students are in college, their self-efficacy beliefs are more strongly related to their achievement than any other measure of their ability.

Although self-efficacy is formed early on, certain learning and school experiences can promote a positive sense of self-efficacy. Positive self-efficacy can be fostered through activities and assessments that encourage problem solving, provide opportunities to improve performance through practice and feedback, and involve collaboration versus competition.[31] Focusing on task goals rather than ability goals also helps increase positive self-efficacy.

Another factor that can affect learning and school performance is self-esteem—feeling good about yourself. Self-esteem is based on how one feels about one's overall worth or value and is different than self-efficacy.[32] However, like self-efficacy, there is a connection between self-esteem and school performance.[33] Correlations exist between self-esteem and school factors such as participation, completion, self-direction, and various types of achievement.

Self-efficacy and self-esteem are linked in other ways as well. Students who believe they have limited capacity to achieve decrease their feelings of self-worth as a means of protecting their egos.[34] By not trying, they don't have expectations, and consequently, don't incur as much pain when they fail. Students go from failure avoidance to failure acceptance. It's a natural instinct to minimize pain—better to not put forth effort and fail than to work hard and fail.

Environment is a powerful influence on self-perceptions.[35] It is the interaction between the individual and the environment where self-esteem has the potential to develop or diminish. The environment (e.g., home, school), rather than the child, is responsible for creating the conditions that will cultivate self-esteem. Many aspects of the school (e.g., climate, learning strategies, curriculum, teachers) create conditions that either enhance self-esteem or impair self-esteem. Unfortunately, for many disenfranchised students, it is the latter.

MOTIVATION

Disengaged or underperforming students are frequently perceived as lacking motivation. Yet as noted in the earlier discussion on learned helplessness, students do not consciously choose to be unmotivated. In fact, quite the opposite is true. They are usually highly motivated to finish school and do well. Even students who have dropped out of school recognize the importance of high school graduation to success in life.[36] Students want their family and friends to be proud of them. Students like Lorenzo want to achieve the goals and mile markers (i.e., high school diploma) that have been designated as benchmarks for success in life:

> I felt the pressure to perform like my sisters—their awards were displayed at home and family events, so I felt that pressure. I wanted to see my mom smile, be proud of me, wanted to get the recognition and awards like they [sisters] did . . .

This is not the voice of an unmotivated student, someone who is not interested in excelling. Although some of his motivation is extrinsic, Lorenzo is compelled to perform in school. And yet listen to what happens when that initial drive is overwhelmed by work and assignments that are beyond his reach:

> . . . but I couldn't hang at that level. Everything seemed so hard . . . too much,
> so I gave up, stopped caring about school in seventh grade. I was failing tests
> and didn't do homework.

Lorenzo's initial motivation was overpowered by a buildup of stress, and he seems to have experienced the learned helplessness discussed earlier. At first glance, it might appear that a lack of motivation caused Lorenzo's decreased performance. In fact, it is not uncommon for students who experience a drop in performance to be labeled "lazy" or "unmotivated." However, this was clearly not the case with Lorenzo. He was highly motivated to achieve in school; however, his struggles with school became overwhelming. Underperformance, as with learned helplessness, is not an outcome students choose. Students do not make a conscious, moral decision to underachieve.

Richard was also highly motivated to be in school and learn, even though he experienced challenges at school and in his home.

> I love to learn! I always liked my school, classes—it was my getaway from my
> dad. No one knew that my mom and I were getting beat every night by my dad.

Daunte was another student who was motivated to finish school but who experienced a great deal of stress in the school setting. Similar to Lorenzo, Daunte was eager to obtain his diploma; however, the stress-inducing environment of school eventually impacted his progress in classes and school in general.

One day at the start of a new school year, Daunte mentioned that he had passed all the necessary exams and obtained his GED over the summer. I asked him why he had returned to school. Daunte responded that he felt the GED was a lesser standard, that he still needed an actual high school diploma. I reassured Daunte that the GED was a rigorous assessment, that it was difficult to pass, and that it was recognized by many employers and colleges. Also, given his current success as a shift manager at his work, I felt that Daunte would continue to experience success in the workforce with his GED.

Nonetheless, Daunte insisted that he was going to see school through until he obtained his diploma. Watching Daunte the next few months was heart wrenching. The fact that he was willing to put himself through a very stressful environment in order to reach society's benchmark speaks to the strong motivation that many young people have to graduate from high school even when the odds are against them. Most students enter school with motivation and the end goal of graduation; however, their day-to-day drive and commitment become eroded over time as a result of ongoing struggles and the school's inability to meet their needs.

Research supports the notion that most students have high aspirations when it comes to school and graduating. The 2009 *High School Survey of*

Student Engagement revealed that 91 percent of students expect to attain at least a high school diploma, and 87 percent expect to obtain some type of postsecondary degree.[37] Only 1.5 percent of students expected to leave high school without graduating.

Motivation, however, does not just materialize on its own. In order for anyone to be intrinsically or self-motivated, certain criteria are necessary. Edward Deci and Richard Ryan have conducted years of research in the field of motivation. Their Self-Determination Theory (SDT) holds significant relevance to education. SDT asserts that three basic psychological needs must be fulfilled in order for people to persist and thrive: competence, autonomy, and relatedness.[38] Students need to experience all of these to be self-determined. This topic will be addressed more in depth in chapter 9.

STRESS

> In first to fourth grade I was not at the academic level as other students (reading and writing), so I was getting frustrated. I didn't speak fluent English the first few grades. Things picked up by third grade, no more barriers. I went to an all-Hispanic school K–first grade. Moving from Kansas to Minnesota was a big change. It took me longer to adjust than my sisters; I wanted to go back.

As Lorenzo recounts his early school experience, it is obvious that a major barrier was his limited proficiency with the English language. He encountered difficulty with academics, most likely due to the initial language barrier. During that same time, Lorenzo's family moved to a different state. Any one of these can present a challenge to school performance, and then to have cumulative stressors only intensifies the struggle.

> As a kid, I had to kill myself to get good grades—not sleeping at night due to workload and stress. Fourth grade I got straight A's all four quarters, not even an A-. I was so exhausted, I couldn't do that level anymore.

Lorenzo's struggles increased:

> In eighth grade, I got into fights, got out-of-school suspension twelve times in three months. My mom searched for smaller schools. They accepted me at a private school—wrong move. It was really hard and there was only one other Hispanic student in with the upper-class white kids. The academic work was really hard. If I killed myself in fourth grade, I committed suicide twelve times that year. I got very little sleep (three to four hours) trying to do the homework and was still failing my classes.

And eventually, the stress became too much:

It was too much, not worth it. Then because of my GPA, I lost sports, so that was the end for me. Coach saw my performance went down in sports 'cause of all the homework. I went to school, but basically I hated it! Other kids would tease you when you came out of the Special Ed resource room . . . call you "retarded." I got in a fight, grabbed my backpack, loaded up all my stuff—books, pencils—and left there for good.

Stress compounded and increased exponentially for Lorenzo. He struggled to handle a homework load and academic work that was beyond his reach, he changed schools, experienced racism and harassment, and was dropped from sports. A high level of emotional distress is evident through Lorenzo's use of words like "it killed me" or the metaphor of "committing suicide" regarding his unrewarded efforts. In addition to experiencing emotional distress, Lorenzo's high self-expectations were going unmet. The antecedents for learned helplessness are in place as Lorenzo experiences stress overload and the domino effect of failure.

Stress is cumulative. The more exposure children have to stress, the more reactive they are to stressors.[39] Every stressor builds on and exacerbates other stressors and slowly changes the student. Each risk factor in a student's life increases impulsivity and decreases capacity for delayed gratification. While young people who grow up in poverty and stressful environments may have exaggerated responses to stress, those most likely to survive in that environment are those who have an exaggerated stress response.

Extensive research has been dedicated to the effects of stress on the brain, learning, and other social functioning. There is an epidemic of brain damage being caused by harmful experiences in a child's life.[40] Factors that lead to stress such as poverty, violence, sexual abuse, neglect, family breakup, and drugs continue to rise in our society. Over sixteen million children live in poverty in the United States.[41] The number of children living in poverty has increased from 16 percent in 2000 to 23 percent in 2012, an increase of nearly 50 percent in twelve years.

Violence is also on the increase. A study in an impoverished neighborhood in Chicago found that 74 percent of students had witnessed a murder, shooting, stabbing, or robbery and nearly half of them had been a victim themselves of a rape, shooting, stabbing, robbery, or other violent act.[42] Teachers may not be aware that a student like Richard suffers abuse when he goes home at night. Though traumatized by past or recurring stressors, students often suffer in silence within the walls of the school. Teachers are more apt to see the consequences of students' attempts to cope with the stress and trauma.

Unsafe psychological conditions can also stress students and impact the level of safety they feel within the school environment, as Andrew experienced:

There was a definite sense of "norm" when it came to race, orientation, cloth-ing, things like that. A family of Asians had moved in and left within a year to go to a different school due to all the harassment. There were about ten minor-ity youth in this small rural high school. One of my friends was Black and she strongly identified with her ethnic background. None of that was apparent or seemed to matter in middle school, but it did in high school. "Coming out" wasn't even an option. I didn't want to draw more attention to myself. I just wanted to get in and get out. I kept it very hidden, especially because I was in a lower clique group.

Myriad other stressors may impact a student's engagement and ability to learn. Racism and other *isms* can dramatically impact a student's school experience, as illustrated in students' stories in chapter 1. Students might experience stress as a result of being removed from their current program or school or not having their disabilities identified. Countless environmental factors such as divorce, loss of family income, death, illness, moving, legal issues, and the like can influence whether students are engaged in school. Students' own substance abuse and mental health issues, or those of family members and friends, can substantially impede the learning process.

Another source of stress in school is a phenomenon known as *stereotype threat*—the vulnerability one feels about confirming a negative stereotype about their group as a result of their performance.[43] The perceived potential to confirm a negative stereotype has been shown to impair intellectual perfor-mance. Even simply indicating one's race on a form can trigger a stereotype in a person's mind, which in turn can lower performance or test scores. This can impact a minority student's performance on tests and in the classroom. Furthermore, when a stereotype is evoked, minority students can be reluctant to ask questions or seek extra help out of fear that doing so will demonstrate a lack of intelligence or reinforce a negative stereotype.[44]

Efficient learning does not take place when the learner is experiencing fear or stress.[45] Stress can have significant effects on both physiological and cognitive functioning. The main emotional system within the brain is the limbic system, which is composed of the amygdala and the hippocampus. If the amygdala is activated, it interrupts action and thought and triggers bodily responses critical for survival. The emotional brain also has strong connec-tions with the frontal cortex, a key area for reasoning and problem solving. When a student is stressed or fearful, the frontal cortex becomes impaired, causing a negative impact on learning.

Major threats to physical or psychological well-being cause a cascade of neurochemical changes in the brain.[46] The brain directs the body to produce adrenaline and cortisol, which puts the body in a high alert state. If the stress persists, it can increase the complexity of neurons in the amygdala, the brain's emotion center, making the brain's neurons considerably more sensi-tive to memory modulation.[47] When both the hippocampus and the amygdala are involved, children may experience increased emotional memory (of traumatic events) and decreased declarative memory (responsible for storing basic knowledge and learning).

Threats activate defense mechanisms and behaviors that are conducive to survival but are counterproductive to learning.[48] In addition to physical reactions and chemical imbalances, threats and threatening environments can trigger impulsive and aggressive behaviors. Students who have had early and constant exposure to threats and stress can experience a heightened alertness and sensitivity to their surroundings as they anticipate and fend off potential threats as a means of survival.

Chronic or acute stress becomes hardwired into children's developing brains and has overwhelming effects.[49] Stressed neurons generate a weaker signal, handle less blood flow, process less oxygen, and extend fewer connections to nearby cells. The areas of the brain critical for cognition, learning, and working memory are the prefrontal cortex and the hippocampus. They are also the areas of the brain most impacted by the stress hormone cortisol. Some of the effects chronic or acute stress has on learning include the following:[50]

- Absenteeism
- Impaired attention and concentration
- Reduction in cognition, creativity, and memory
- Diminished social skills and social judgment
- Reduced motivation, determination, and effort
- Increased likelihood of depression
- Reduction in growth of new brain cells

Stressed brains do not learn in the same manner as nonstressed brains.[51] People's ability to do math and process language is compromised. Chronic stress impairs people's ability to generalize or adapt old information to new situations. Executive function, which is needed to excel in school, is impeded. Chronic stress also triggers emotional and physical reactions. Anxiety, post-traumatic stress disorder, increased detachment, and helplessness are the most common adaptive behaviors resulting from chronic stress.[52] Aggressive and acting-out behaviors are other potential responses to stress. Chronic stress also weakens the immune system, resulting in more frequent illness.[53]

Teachers see the effects of stress every day in their classroom. They see the toll it takes on students and the learning process and feel frustrated by the inadequacies of the system. Lynn, the teacher from chapter 2, explains:

> There's Maslow's Hierarchy—those needs need to be met first. You're not going to do well at school if you're scared at home or worried 'cause you don't

have health coverage or you're hungry. Learning is secondary. How can you learn Algebra if you have migraines from not eating in twenty-four hours? I think that's where we see the behavior—when these needs are ignored and not met. The brokenness of the system becomes apparent—the system that is supposed to be in place to help these kids. And it's not that teachers don't care, there's not a system in place to be able to do what we need to do.

While Lynn has an understanding of how stress and unmet basic needs inhibit learning, other educators can be quick to blame or demean a student for misbehavior or inadequate performance. More often than not, students are responding in the only way they know how in that moment and circumstance. Such was the case with Daunte, who mustered up every bit of coping ability he had on a daily basis to obtain his diploma. Richard reinforces that in his remark about how students are doing what they can to persevere in spite how defeated they feel:

Students want to drop out 'cause they have no faith in the educational system, but they need that diploma. It takes a strong person to go through this and keep going to school.

Young people usually cope with life and learning in the way they know how and given the skills and resources they have. People are hardwired with six emotions: joy, anger, surprise, disgust, sadness, and fear. [54] Every other emotional response must be taught; it is not intuitive. If students lack patience, empathy, cooperation, gratitude, and forgiveness, then educators must teach these skills and attributes rather than label or judge students for not practicing them.

In addition, stress, threats, and learned helplessness must be minimized or eliminated from the environment in order for students to achieve optimal learning. [55] While educators have minimal control over the stressors students experience outside of school, they can work to minimize the level of threats and stress that occur in the school environment and provide the necessary supports to help students cope with threats and stress while they are at school.

POVERTY

One thing I hated, we had no computer at home. When we did a paper for school, I had to type it at school. I offered to handwrite, double space, but I failed, 'cause it was not typed. How can you fail someone that doesn't have the money for a computer? You can only spend so much time at a library [to type]. I was ready to give up.
—Katie

Poverty has devastating consequences on a child's development, their capacity to learn, and their success in life.[56] Over the past two decades, differences between rich and poor children have doubled in America, resulting in the greatest economic disparity since 1979. Nationally, 23 percent of all children live in poverty.[57] More concerning is that 40 percent of African American children live in poverty, which is nearly three times the rate of White children. Other minority children experience high rates of poverty as well, including 37 percent of Native American and 34 percent of Hispanic children.

Nature and nurture both influence a child's development and success, but growing up in poverty trumps children's genetic capacities.[58] DNA is thought to be responsible for about 30 to 50 percent of our behaviors; the other 50 to 70 percent is determined by environment. So even if it is brief, poverty can have unforgiving effects. And the more persistent and earlier in life poverty occurs, the more adverse effects it has on a child's life.

Poor children in America are far worse off on almost every aspect of well-being than peers with greater financial resources. They score about 60 percent lower in cognitive performance when they start school and remain at that level throughout high school.[59] Middle-income students will have heard or seen forty-five million words, compared to a child in poverty who will have heard or seen only fifteen million. School readiness scores indicate a six-month gap between low- and middle-income children. Twice as many children in poverty will have short attention spans, and five times as many will be in poor health. These differences are associated with future problems in adolescence and adulthood.

According to the Child Trends organization, of the 3.9 million kindergartners entering school, 2.2 million lag behind in at least one area, and 610,000 lag behind in at least two areas.[60] Starting behind, poor children will face a continuous battle to catch up, especially if they struggle with the critical foundational skills of reading and comprehension.

While students in poverty may be just as motivated to learn as their higher-income peers, they lack the skills and prerequisites.[61] These deficits can set them on a path of low academic achievement and negative personal, emotional, and social outcomes. By the time they reach adolescence, students may already be incapacitated by the consequences of poverty. Their struggles and pattern of nonachievement can eventually cause low-income students to drop out of school. Some 38 percent of all children have spent a year or more in poverty, yet they account for 70 percent of all children who do not graduate.[62]

Poverty also affects brain function. Socioeconomic status (SES) is highly associated with a variety of cognitive factors, including IQ, achievement tests, retention rates, and literacy.[63] There is a gap between low- and higher-income children on nearly every measure of cognitive development. Correlations between SES and cognitive ability and performance are significant and last throughout an individual's development, from infancy to adulthood.

School functioning requires an "academic operating system" in the brain.[64] In order to be successful in school, students need to have an operating system that includes these essentials:

- The ability and motivation to defer gratification and make a sustained effort to meet long-term goals
- Auditory, visual, and tactile processing skills
- Attentional skills that enable the students to engage, focus, and disengage as needed
- Short-term and working memory capacity
- Sequencing skills (knowing the order of a process)
- A champion's mind-set and confidence

Together, these building blocks comprise the academic operating system that allows students to focus, work hard, think critically, and process and sequence content.[65] If students have these fundamentals, it can override the adverse effects of poverty. The components of the academic operating system enable students to focus on, capture, process, evaluate, prioritize, manipulate, and apply or present information in a meaningful way. Although all students need an academic operating system, significant differences exist between the operating systems of low and high SES individuals. These differences occur in critical neurocognitive areas such as language, memory, working memory, and cognitive control.

A developing brain needs coherent, novel, and challenging input or it will scale back its growth.[66] Low SES children tend to receive less cognitive stimulation than middle-income children. They are less likely to be read to, coached in learning skills, or helped with homework. Children in poverty have less access to computers and the Internet, culturally enriching activities, and healthy after-school activities. They have fewer toys and learning materials. Instead of actively engaging their brains, they are likely to spend more time watching television, a relatively passive activity. Limited resources put children at a huge disadvantage.

Adding to the effects that children experience from impoverished environments is the tendency for children in poverty to be underserved in the schools they attend. Significant inequality exists in funding, staff, and resources for schools that serve children in poverty.[67] The wealthiest public schools in the United States spend at least ten times more than the poorest schools, ranging from $30,000 per pupil at the wealthiest schools to only $3,000 at the poorest. Schools that serve large numbers of low-income students and students of color have larger class sizes and fewer teachers and counselors. They also have fewer and lower-quality academic courses, books, computers, libraries, materials, supplies, extracurricular activities, and special services. These disparities contribute to a wider achievement gap in the United States than in any other industrialized country in the world, most of which fund schools centrally and equally.

Furthermore, students who are least likely to have learning supports at home are also least likely to have teachers who understand how children learn and develop, who know how to teach them to read and problem solve, and who know what to do if they are having difficulty.[68] Low SES students are more likely to be taught by inexperienced teachers or educators who are teaching outside their area of expertise, especially in the areas of math and reading, two of the most critical subject areas.[69]

Students also bear the ill effects of teacher turnover in schools with high-poverty populations. More than 30 percent of beginner teachers leave the field within five years, with low-income schools experiencing an even higher rate of turnover.[70] Teachers are less likely to stay in schools where salaries are lower and working conditions are poor. They are twice as likely to leave if they lacked mentoring and adequate preparation for teaching.

In addition to cognitive and learning difficulties, children in poverty face social and emotional challenges. Chronic socioeconomic deprivation can create environments that undermine the development of self and the capacity for self-determination and self-efficacy.[71] Low SES children develop more stress-based attachments with parents, teachers, and adult caregivers. They are also less likely to receive positive reinforcement from teachers. Many factors often associated with low-income households interfere with the healthy attachments that help cultivate self-esteem, a sense of mastery, and optimistic attitudes in children.

Instead of redirecting children in poverty toward a pathway of success, schools tend to recreate or reinforce the social inequities that already exist in the larger society.[72] Given the severe effects of poverty on school and life outcomes, children who experience poverty need the support of every group or institution in their environment, including schools. Education must provide a much-needed advantage, not disadvantage, in their life.

SUMMARY

Disengagement, repeated failure, compounded stress, poverty, and other factors make for a difficult journey through school. As Richard so fittingly noted, surviving twelve grueling years of school requires a lot of tenacity. Educators must be cognizant of the many challenges young people confront in their lives on a daily basis, both inside and outside of school. There is usually not one simple reason for students' disengagement or underachievement. More likely, it is due to a complex web of factors such as an inability to be taught in a way they can learn, learned helplessness, lack of self-efficacy, stress, poverty, and societal and environmental stressors.

When educators perceive students who struggle in school as problems, rather than as individuals with problems that affect their achievement, they exacerbate students' struggles. If students could have learned by traditional methods, they likely would have. Students' seeming lack of effort is likely a learned, protective response, rather than a conscious decision to underperform. So blaming students for their disability or inability to learn only compounds and intensifies their challenges, adding more obstacles and frustration that they must overcome.

For students who have the necessary prerequisites and know the formula for succeeding in school (the "succeeders"), traditional school may prove effective. They know what it takes and they can do it. For other students who are not able to do traditional school, different learning environments, strategies, and supports are required. Until schools can become more effective for *all* students, it is important that educators do not blame students for the inadequacies of the current system and do not add to the challenges students already face in their lives and schools.

NOTES

1. Adena M. Klem and James P. Connell, "Relationships Matter: Linking Teacher Support to Student Engagement and Achievement," *Journal of School Health* 74, no. 7 (2004): 262–74, accessed December 24, 2014,http://ceep.indiana.edu/hssse/Klem.pdf.

2. "High School Dropout Rates," Child Trends Data Bank, Appendix 1, accessed December 9, 2014,http://www.childtrends.org/wp-content/uploads/2012/10/01_appendix1.pdf.

3. Marie C. Stetser and Robert Stillwell, *Public High School Four-Year On-Time Graduation Rates and Event Dropout Rates: School Years 2010–11 and 2011–12: First Look*, National Center for Education Statistics, U.S. Department of Education (2014), accessed December 6, 2014,http://nces.ed.gov/pubs2014/2014391.pdf.

4. "High School Dropout Rates."

5. "Statistics on Native Students," National Indian Education Association, accessed December 6, 2014,http://www.niea.org/Research/Statistics.aspx -Grad.

6. Robert Balfanz et al., *Building a Grad Nation: Progress and Challenge in Ending the High School Dropout Epidemic*, Civic Enterprises (2014), accessed December 17, 2014,http://gradnation.org/sites/default/files/17548_BGN_Report_FinalFULL_5.2.14.pdf.

7. Stetser and Stillwell, *Public High School Four-Year On-Time Graduation Rates and Event Dropout Rates: School Years 2010–11 and 2011–12*.

8. Balfanz et al., *Building a Grad Nation*.

9. John M. Bridgeland, John J. Dilulio Jr., and Stuart C. Wulsin, *Engaged for Success: Service Learning as a Tool for High School Dropout Prevention*, Civic Enterprises in association with Peter D. Hart Research Associates (2008), accessed January 16, 2015,http://civicenterprises.net/MediaLibrary/docs/engaged_for_success.pdf.

10. National Research Council and the Institute of Medicine, *Engaging Schools: Fostering High School Students' Motivation to Learn* (Washington, DC: The National Academies Press, 2004).

11. Kimberly Knesting, "Students at Risk for School Dropout: Supporting Their Persistence," *Preventing School Failure* 52, no. 4 (2008): 3–10, accessed December 19, 2014,http://cpedinitiative.org/files/Students at Risk for School Dropout.pdf.

12. "Gallup Student Poll, Montgomery County Public Schools, MD," Gallup, Inc. (2012), accessed December 24, 2014,http://www.montgomeryschoolsmd.org/uploadedFiles/info/gallup/GallupStudentResults.pdf.

13. Eric Jensen, *Teaching with Poverty in Mind: What Being Poor Does to Kids' Brains and What Schools Can Do About It* (Alexandria, VA: Association for Supervision and Curriculum Development, 2009).

14. Susan B. Neuman, *Changing the Odds for Children at Risk: Seven Essential Principles of Educational Programs That Break the Cycle of Poverty* (Westport, CT: Praeger, 2009).

15. Linda K. Schlosser, "Teacher Distance and Student Disengagement: School Lives on the Margin," *Journal of Teacher Education* 43, no. 2 (1998): 128–40.

16. Robert Gordon and Myrna Gordon, *The Turned-Off Child: Learned Helplessness and School Failure* (Salt Lake City, UT: Millennial Mind Publishing, 2006).

17. Jensen, *Teaching with Poverty in Mind.*

18. Gordon and Gordon, *The Turned-Off Child.*

19. Ibid.

20. Ibid.

21. Ibid.

22. Nicki G. Arnold, "Learned Helplessness and Attribution for Success and Failure in LD Students," LDOnline (1996), accessed December 6, 2014, http://www.ldonline.org/article/6154/.

23. Gordon and Gordon, *The Turned-Off Child.*

24. Del Siegle, "An Introduction to Self-Efficacy," accessed December 6, 2014,http://www.gifted.uconn.edu/siegle/selfefficacy/section1.html.

25. Karen Reivich, "Self-Efficacy: Helping Children Believe They Can Succeed," *Communique Handout* 39, no. 3 (2010): 1–4, accessed December 6, 2014,http://www.nasponline.org/publications/cq/39/3/pdf/V39N3_FT_Self-Efficacy.pdf.

26. Albert Bandura, "Self-Efficacy," in *Encyclopedia of Human Behavior* 4, ed. V. S. Ramachaudran (New York: Academic Press, 1994), 71–81, accessed December 6, 2014,http://www.uky.edu/~eushe2/Bandura/BanEncy.html.

27. Ibid.

28. Siegle, "An Introduction to Self-Efficacy."

29. Bandura, "Self-Efficacy."

30. Ibid.

31. Atelia Melaville, Amy C. Berg, and Martin J. Blank, *Community-Based Learning: Engaging Students for Success and Citizenship*, Coalition for Community Schools (2006), accessed December 6, 2014, http://www.communityschools.org/assets/1/AssetManager/CBLFinal.pdf.

32. Reivich, "Self-Efficacy: Helping Children Believe They Can Succeed."

33. James A. Beane, "Sorting Out the Self-Esteem Controversy," *Educational Leadership* 49, no. 1 (1991): 25–30, accessed December 6, 2014,http://www.ascd.org/ASCD/pdf/journals/ed_lead/el_199109_beane.pdf.

34. Gordon and Gordon, *The Turned-Off Child*; Nicki G. Arnold, "Learned Helplessness and Attribution for Success and Failure in LD Students."

35. Beane, "Sorting Out the Self-Esteem Controversy."

36. Bridgeland, Dilulio, and Wulsin, *Engaged for Success.*

37. Ethan Yazzie-Mintz, *Charting the Path from Engagement to Achievement: A Report on the 2009 High School Survey of Student Engagement*, Center for Evaluation & Education Policy, Indiana University (2010), accessed December 21, 2014,http://ceep.indiana.edu/hssse/images/HSSSE_2010_Report.pdf.

38. Edward L. Deci and Richard M. Ryan, eds., *Handbook of Self-Determination Research* (Rochester, NY: The University of Rochester Press, 2002).

39. Jensen, *Teaching with Poverty in Mind.*

40. Ronald Kotulak, "The Effect of Violence and Stress in Kids' Brains," in *The Jossey-Bass Reader on the Brain and Learning* (San Francisco: John Wiley & Sons, 2008), 216–25.

41. *2014 Kids Count Data Book: State Trends in Child Well-Being*, The Annie E. Casey Foundation, accessed December 6, 2014,http://www.aecf.org/m/resourcedoc/aecf-2014kidscountdatabook-2014.pdf.

42. Kotulak, "The Effect of Violence and Stress in Kids' Brains."

43. Claude M. Steele and Joshua Aronson, "Stereotype Threat and the Intellectual Test Performance of African Americans," *Journal of Personality and Social Psychology* 69, no. 5 (1995): 797–811, accessed December 6, 2014,http://mrnas.pbworks.com/f/claude+steele+stereotype+threat+1995.pdf.

44. Bryan Goodwin, *Simply Better: Doing What Matters Most to Change the Odds for Student Success* (Alexandria, VA: Association for Supervision and Curriculum Development, 2011).

45. Usha Goswami, "Neuroscience and Education," in *The Jossey-Bass Reader on the Brain and Learning* (San Francisco: John Wiley & Sons, 2008), 33–50.

46. Neuman, *Changing the Odds for Children at Risk.*

47. Jensen, *Teaching with Poverty in Mind.*

48. Eric Jensen, *Teaching with the Brain in Mind* (Alexandria, VA: Association for Supervision and Curriculum Development, 1998).

49. Jensen, *Teaching with Poverty in Mind.*

50. Ibid.

51. John Medina, *Brain Rules: 12 Principles for Surviving and Thriving at Work, Home, and School* (Seattle, WA: Pear Press, 2008).

52. Jensen, *Teaching with Poverty in Mind.*

53. Medina, *Brain Rules.*

54. Jensen, *Teaching with Poverty in Mind.*

55. Jensen, *Teaching with the Brain in Mind.*

56. Neuman, *Changing the Odds for Children at Risk.*

57. *2014 Kids Count Data Book: State Trends in Child Well-Being.*

58. Jensen, *Teaching with Poverty in Mind.*

59. Neuman, *Changing the Odds for Children at Risk.*

60. Ibid.

61. Ibid.

62. Donald J. Hernandez, *Double Jeopardy: How Third-Grade Reading Skills and Poverty Influence High School Graduation*, The Annie E. Casey Foundation (2012), accessed December 6, 2014,http://www.aecf.org/m/resourcedoc/AECF-DoubleJeopardy-2012-Full.pdf.

63. Jensen, *Teaching with Poverty in Mind.*

64. Ibid.

65. Ibid.

66. Ibid.

67. Linda Darling-Hammond, "From 'Separate but Equal' to 'No Child Left Behind': The Collision of New Standards and Old Inequalities," in *Many Children Left Behind: How the No Child Left Behind Act Is Damaging Our Children and Our Schools*, eds. Deborah Meier and George Wood (Boston: Beacon Press, 2004), 3–32.

68. Ibid.

69. Jensen, *Teaching with Poverty in Mind.*

70. Darling-Hammond, "From 'Separate but Equal' to 'No Child Left Behind.'"

71. Jensen, *Teaching with Poverty in Mind.*

72. Neuman, *Changing the Odds for Children at Risk.*

Part II

Chapter Five

New Form, Not Reform

Start over! Do it a new way. Stop and think
before you mess up all education and all students.
You've been doing it this way for so many years
and still so many kids are failing.
—Ben

So much reform, yet so little transformation. As Ben points out, educators keep trying to solve problems by using many of the same strategies and thinking that have been used for decades, yet their efforts don't produce the desired results. It's like doing the same thing over and over but expecting different results. And in the process, more students are harmed; more disengage, fail, and drop out. "For too long we have maintained a status quo in education that has at best prepared children for our past and at worst marginalized those families least able to access a better life for their children."[1]

Albert Einstein once said, "No problem can be solved by the same kind of thinking that created it." This is true for education. Problems in education have arisen because we are using an outdated model that no longer fits the needs of our twenty-first-century students, society, and economy. If we continue using the same obsolete paradigm to solve problems, we end up with just another variation of what we already have—reform. What is needed instead is "transformation."

Transforming education requires innovation—new ways of thinking, doing, and relating. Unfortunately, the United States has one of the lowest levels of educational innovation compared to other OECD (Organisation for Economic Co-Operation and Development) countries.[2] Countries such as Denmark and Korea earned ratings of 37 and 32 points respectively on an innovation measurement, while the United States had one of the lowest rates at 17 points. Instead of innovative pedagogy like relating lessons to real-life, higher-order skills, data and text interpretation, and personalization of teaching, U.S. innovations consisted mostly of student assessment and testing changes.[3]

ASKING THE RIGHT QUESTIONS

Those involved in educational reform continue to ask the same questions but expect different answers. Before we recreate more variations of the current model of education, we must stop and ask different questions: compelling and transformative questions that can lead us to new forms and different places. But first, we must give considerable thought to the questions we ask, because they will serve as the guiding compass for educational change. The questions we ask will take us down distinctly different roads, each with their own unique outcomes.

Asking, "How can the United States have higher, or the highest, achievement scores in the world?" leads us to very different paradigms and practices than if we ask, "How we can support all young people, including those who struggle in school, to optimize their development and preparedness for success in school and beyond?" The first question focuses on test scores and numerical outcomes that serve the system and not so much the students. The second question redirects education to determine what young people need for success in school and life and how schools can facilitate that process. The first question narrows the vision and keeps the system at the center, while the second question broadens the vision and keeps young people at the center.

Placing young people at the center of learning and education begins with them—not the system and not the adults. If the questions focus on students, then the solutions will also center on the students. Other compelling, student-centered questions can help propel us to new territory:

- What do young people need to optimize their development and success in school, adulthood, citizenry, careers, and life?
- How can students be supported in these pursuits by educators and schools?
- How do young people learn best?
- Are educators, educational strategies, and learning environments addressing students' needs and how they learn best?
- How can the community support students in their learning?
- What do students have to say about their school experience?

Other key questions can help reveal and challenge the beliefs, values, assumptions, and expectations currently held about young people and how we work with them in our schools:

- Do we value young people in this country?
- If so, to what degree and in what ways? Do our decisions, plans, and budgets reflect how we value young people?
- What do we believe to be true about young people? Are they seen as a problem or a resource? Upon what do we base our beliefs and assumptions?
- How do we elicit and validate young people's ideas, experiences, wisdom, and contributions?
- What is the role of young people in our schools? Are they active or passive participants? Are they one-up, one-down, or equal partners? How are young people engaged and empowered in school?
- How would young people respond to these questions?

We also need to consider who gets to ask the questions that drive educational innovation, and who gets to answer the questions. Will it be educators, students, parents, policymakers, community members, researchers, or all of the above?

Asking questions will help us reexamine and redefine the purpose of education—what young people need to develop and succeed in school and to effectively navigate future education, careers, citizenship, and life. Students interviewed for this book were asked what they thought the current purpose of education was and what they thought it ought to be. Charlie responded:

> The purpose of school [now] is to teach kids to be generally knowledgeable of the main subjects, like math and English and history. There should be a lot more time on preparing you for "life" rather than school. Things like caring for one another, the value of life, making this a better world, making sure that kids know they have that power.

Similarly, Feliz felt that school should focus on a child's overall development and preparation for life:

> To get someone ready from kindergarten to college. For social development and educational development. To be prepared for life—the steps to being an adult. Help you for your future, jobs, life. School is a good thing for social development and maturity. School's a basic life need; you need education, food, and water for life.

Other students shared their perspectives:

> It should be a place to learn, to work with people, communicate, to care . . . a place to have help getting your life set up to succeed at a job and life. —Ben

> What it should be is to help you set your goals, reach goals, and set more goals for your future, maybe even as president of the United States. —Katie

Teachers will have time for you . . . see you as an individual vs. [a] trouble-
maker. Education should be something people want. See what the world is . . .
you start on that path. It's supposed to get us ready for what we want to do in
life. —Lorenzo

A proper education is not being taught. It shouldn't just be about books. Teach
people to be human again. Teachers and schools didn't take the right steps to
address racism. —Richard

Students felt that school should be a place that supports the full development of children. They wanted school to help them set and achieve goals,
navigate transitions, and prepare for life beyond school. Students also felt
that it was important for schools to foster compassion, empowerment, and
opportunities to contribute to world betterment. In addition, Lorenzo felt that
education should be something that people are drawn to pursue.

Although the United States tends to focus on preparing students for college as a primary goal of education, other countries embrace a broader sense
of purpose for education. For example, in Finland, the purpose of teaching
and learning is to pursue happiness of learning and cultivate development of
the whole child.[4] This aligns with what students deemed important in their
reflections about the purpose of education.

As the primary normative institution for youth in the United States,
school affects adolescents' lives more than any other institutions.[5] Schools
hold immense potential for supporting young people to become productive,
healthy adults; however, inherent conflicts exist between what young people
need and what schools are able to provide. So we must continue to ask
questions, especially as they pertain to what students need for their development and success in school and life.

NEW LEARNERS, SKILLS, AND COMPETENCIES FOR NEW TIMES

This country is different from how it was one hundred, or even twenty, years
ago. We are part of an ever-evolving world. Likewise, what and how students
need to learn has changed. Imparting a large amount of basic information
may no longer be as necessary as it once was. Besides, memorizing or learning the vast amount of information available in any given field is impractical
and impossible. In our age of technology, knowledge and learning are a mere
click and seconds away. Anyone can access the 5,500 videos on the Khan
Academy website that cover nearly every topic and allow learners to obtain
knowledge and practice skills at their own pace.[6]

So rather than just requiring facts memorization and knowledge dissemination, schools need to help students build other necessary, world-based skills and competencies and provide opportunities to practice those skills in meaningful, real-life situations.[7] The International Youth Foundation promotes "education for life," as opposed to education for academic achievement.[8] Education for life encompasses a broader range of educational outcomes, including the competencies that young people need to succeed in life now and as adults.

Ben valued what he gained from the "learning for life" he experienced in his Leadership class, much of which took place out in the community:

> Leadership helped me be a better person—I grew up, I had more responsibility, things to worry about, meetings to go to, businesses to go to, projects to finish, timelines to meet. It shows you how real life works, how businesses operate, how to make connections, how to get into a company.

Not only is it a new age for learning and working, it is also a new generation of learners. What students want and need is different from previous generations. In a study of individuals aged eleven to thirty-one, eight common themes distinguished them from the previous generation.[9] They want and expect the following:

- Freedom in everything they do, including freedom of choice and expression
- Customization and personalization, the ability to change things to suit their needs
- Scrutiny and transparency—stakeholder access to pertinent information
- Corporate integrity and openness when deciding what to buy and where to work
- Entertainment and play that is integrated into their work, learning, and social life
- Collaboration and relationships to be a vital part of all they do
- Speed in communications, getting information, and getting responses
- Innovation in products, entertainment, learning, and work

This new and different generational profile creates new demands on our educational institutions.[10] The one-size-fits-all factory model of education and the lecture-memorization, drill-test model of instruction no longer work for today's students. Rather, they need learning to be interactive, collaborative, and innovative in order to be actively engaged in school.

Educational departments across the world are shifting to align with the needs of the twenty-first century.[11] It is less about eliminating all the traditional ways of teaching than about finding a balance—one that includes blending traditional practices with newer methods and philosophies that are becoming more effective in meeting the demands of present and future times. The continuum and shifting in practices is represented in the figure below.

Embracing new ways to educate, however, is not easy. Transforming education to meet the demands of a new age and a new generation is complex and challenging. Tradition and other obstacles impede innovations in teaching and learning. Schools still cling to the Industrial Age approach of delivering mass education as efficiently as possible.[12] Decades of teaching practices that rely on transmitting knowledge through direct instruction are difficult to overcome. Further, educators are used to teaching and measuring knowledge, not skills.

21st Century Learning Balance

Teacher-directed	Learner-centered
Direct instruction	Interactive exchange
Knowledge	Skills
Content	Process
Basic skills	Applied skills
Facts and principles	Questions and problems
Theory	Practice
Curriculum	Projects
Time-slotted	On-demand
One-size-fits-all	Personalized
Competitive	Collaborative
Classroom	Global community
Text-based	Web-based
Summative tests	Formative evaluations
Learning for school	Learning for life

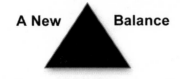

A New   Balance

Figure 5.1.

The rigidity of standardization in the current system also makes it difficult to apply the real learning that students need.[13] Things are done in prescribed ways at prescribed times. Students are expected to master a core curriculum of facts and skills, specified by the state, in the same amount of time. The institutional and bureaucratic nature of education poses yet another barrier. Bureaucracies serve to ensure conformity of practice and resist change. This makes it difficult for innovative programs or processes to succeed. Change becomes so diluted that new programming turns out to be very much like the old.

STUDENTS: THE CENTER OF LEARNING

As it stands today, learning is *system centered*. Traditional curriculum has limited capacity to adapt to differences among students and changes in the environment.[14] For the most part, students must express or demonstrate what they have learned in exactly the same way. So it is up to students to adapt to the system and overcome its barriers, inefficiencies, and rigidity.

New learners and new times call for student-centered, rather than system-centered, education. In a survey of K–12 public school teachers, 76 percent agreed that schools should adjust to the needs, interests, and learning styles of individual students rather than expecting students to meet the norms of the school.[15] According to the Nellie Mae Foundation, student-centered learning is the most promising approach to achieving equity and excellence for all students, especially those who are underserved.[16] It allows young people to be treated as unique individuals, rather than as a singular, homogeneous group.[17]

Student-centered learning is an approach that focuses on the real needs of students.[18] Four essential features define a student-centered approach: the student's experience and identity is a key starting point for education; individualized pacing is allowed and advancement is based on demonstration of proficiency; the role of the educator is expanded and reshaped (more of a facilitator and coach versus instructor); and learning experiences can happen anytime, anywhere.

In a study of six exemplar schools that effectively use student-centered practices, researchers identified eight core elements that define teaching practice in student-centered learning.[19] These elements do not exist in isolation; they operate in a dynamic relationship with one another. They include the following:

- Strong relationships with students
- Personalization and choice in curricular and instructional tasks
- Appropriate challenge levels for each learner

- Support of students' social and emotional growth and identity development
- Anytime, anywhere, and real-world learning
- Technology that is integral to teaching and learning
- Clear, timely assessment and support
- Practices that foster autonomy and lifelong learning

Along with student-centered education, a *whole child* approach to working with students is essential. The Association for Supervision and Curriculum Development (ASCD) launched the Whole Child Initiative in 2007 as a means to move the narrow focus on academic achievement in education to a broader vision that promotes the long-term development and success of young people.[20] ASCD is committed to a whole-child approach to learning, teaching, and community engagement that puts students first and aligns resources to their needs.

Among other qualities, a "whole child" is one who is intellectually active; physically, verbally, socially, and academically competent; empathetic; creative and curious; autonomous; a critical thinker; confident; and cared for and valued.[21] Five main tenets comprise the whole-child approach.[22] These tenets assert that each student:

- Enters school healthy and learns about and practices a healthy lifestyle
- Learns in an environment that is physically and emotionally safe for students and adults
- Is actively engaged in learning and is connected to the school and broader community
- Has access to personalized learning and is supported by qualified, caring adults
- Is challenged academically and prepared for success in college or further study and for employment and participation in a global environment

A whole-child approach to school means that young people's needs are met at the very basic levels of health, safety, and belonging.[23] Meeting these essential needs takes precedence over academic achievement, because when these needs aren't met, students likely will not be as motivated, engaged, or academically successful. When their basic needs are satisfied, students are more apt to engage in school, act in accordance with school goals and values, develop social skills and understanding, contribute to the school and community, and achieve academically.

Brain research also provides support for a more balanced approach to educating young people. Studies indicate that since children develop along multiple, interconnected domains, focusing on only cognitive development can hinder development of other domains.[24] In other words, if one developmental domain is ignored, other domains may suffer.

A student-centered and whole-child approach to learning and education is critical for students' personal, social, and cultural development, which in turn impacts how they feel and respond in the school environment. Students should not have to check their identities, cultures, languages, and values at the school door, as these attributes comprise a student's authentic self and the personal, social, and cultural collateral students need for developing their identities and the motivation needed to succeed in school.[25]

Being able to meet students' basic needs and support their full development, including their cultural identity, requires a much more personable, individualized, holistic, and culturally aware approach than our current educational system allows. However, by adopting student-centered and whole-child approaches, schools can provide the kind of learning and environments that young people need.

Learning should not only center on students as whole human beings, it should also involve students in matters relevant to their school experience. Progress in educational policy and practice cannot be done without engaging education's most important stakeholders—young people.[26] Their involvement is critical for shaping beliefs about the purpose and nature of effective strategies for transforming education. "Students must be empowered to change schools if education is going to change."[27]

Involving students in educational improvement is the right and ethical thing to do, considering how much they are impacted by the process and outcomes. Including students in the school improvement process is also a component of quality pedagogy.[28] Students provide the unique perspective of how educators' practices are experienced from the student's view, which is essential for the educational improvement process.

The reality, though, is that youth are rarely involved in educational reform.[29] Efforts to include young people in the process have mostly been sporadic, limited to small groups of students, and led by outside organizations. "There is something fundamentally amiss about building and rebuilding an entire system without consulting at any point those it is ostensibly designed to serve."[30] Furthermore, students' overall role in the learning process needs to become more active and empowered. Research demonstrates that students learn best when they take on active roles, have opportunities for meaningful choice, and become contributors and change makers instead of just consumers of knowledge.[31]

EDUCATIONAL REFORM ON A GLOBAL LEVEL

American education differs from education in other high-performing global communities, including Finland and Japan. Japanese-style learning requires more thinking, while American-based learning involves mostly memorization and guesswork.[32] Japanese teachers refuse to be authorities in the classroom; they facilitate student discussion toward a collective agreement on what makes sense to the students (and avoid one single, correct answer). Both learning and teaching are collaborative.

Another way the United States differs from other countries is in its curricular focus. Academic-only agendas are dominant in countries like the United States and Canada, yet nonacademic youth outcomes, such as connectedness, civic involvement, mental health, and social skills, impact whether students will succeed academically.[33] The International Commission for Education in the Twenty-First Century conceptualized education as being based on four pillars: learning to know, learning to do, learning to live together, and learning to be.[34]

Learning to know refers to broad general education and lifelong learning.[35] *Learning to do* involves the competence to participate in the workforce and to work in teams. *Learning to live together* refers to an understanding of others and our growing interdependence. *Learning to be* is about developing one's full potential and exercising autonomy. The U.S. educational system tends to focus on the first pillar, learning to know, at the expense of the others.

The United States also differs from high-performing countries such as Singapore and Finland in teacher training, practice, and evaluation. In America, there are more than 1,500 different teacher preparation programs with differing levels of quality.[36] Conversely, there is only one academically rigorous teacher education program in Singapore and Finland. Quality of teaching is controlled at the front end, rather than at the service end. Teacher education is standardized, while actual teaching and learning are not.

In Finland and Singapore, teachers are trained in high-quality preparation programs, typically at the master's level, while receiving a salary.[37] Teachers are well paid, supported by mentors, and have fifteen or more hours a week to learn and work together on shared planning, action research, lesson study, and peer observations. Collaboration is another important aspect of teacher practice in Finland. Finnish teachers collaborate with other teachers to jointly plan and develop curriculum.[38] Schools are also encouraged to work together by sharing materials, practices, and innovative approaches, all of which help to build lateral capacity.

Unlike teachers in the United States, teachers in Finland can exercise their professional knowledge and judgment openly and widely in their schools; they have autonomy and power.[39] They are the ones who control the curriculum, assessment, school improvement, and community involvement. And in Singapore, teachers are not evaluated on students' test scores, but rather on how well they develop the whole child and contribute to each other's efforts and the well-being of the whole school.[40]

Not only does what we teach, how we teach, and how we train teachers contrast with other high-performing countries, but how the United States handles educational reform also differs. Pasi Sahlberg, Finnish educator, scholar, author, and visiting Professor of Practice at Harvard University, identified certain patterns of education reform in countries that are trying to improve public education (e.g., America, England, Australia) and refers to it as GERM, or the Global Educational Reform Movement.[41]

Key elements of GERM-based reform include competition, standardization, test-based accountability, human capital, and school choice.[42] These approaches have not yielded the intended results and stand in stark contrast to the way that Finland, a top-performing country in education, addresses educational reform. The "Finnish Way" of educational reform emphasizes collaboration, personalization, trust-based responsibility, human and social capital, and equity.

Also, rather than tightening controls over schools, enforcing stronger accountability for student performance, firing bad teachers, and closing troubled schools, as the United States tends to do, Finland embraces a different approach to educational improvement.[43] Finland focuses on improving the teaching force, minimizing testing, placing responsibility before accountability, and keeping school- and district-level leadership with educational professionals.

In its pursuit of educational reform, the United States has done nearly the opposite of high-performing countries such as Finland. It has imposed more standardized curriculum and testing, reduced innovation in teaching, relied on outside sources for solutions, and adopted a system of high-stakes accountability that uses rewards and punishments.[44] This, in turn, has led to more inequitable conditions in local schools.

Finland, however, was not always a top-performing country in education. It experienced a sizable achievement gap in the 1970s that was tied to socioeconomic status.[45] Finland began shifting from a highly centralized system emphasizing testing to a more localized system supporting equitable funding and extensive preparation for teachers. It expanded the capacity of local teachers and schools to meet the needs of all students. Finnish education reform was based on equal opportunities for all, equitable distribution of resources, intensive early interventions (prevention), and trust building among educators.

Finland also moved from a more traditional model of presentation-recitation instruction, age grouping, fixed teaching schedules, and classroom-based seatwork to one that provides more flexible, open, and interaction-rich learning environments where an active role for students is primary.[46] In the revised model, Finnish students have more flexibility to complete their studies as a result of personalized learning plans that are not tied to age groups or classes.

These new forms of teaching and learning did not all originate in Finland, however. Many high-performing school systems that have successfully reformed education, such as Finland, Singapore, and Canada, acquired many of their educational practices from America's innovations.[47] Finland credits much of its success to pedagogy practices that were researched and designed in the United States, including cooperative learning, problem-based teaching, and portfolio assessment.[48]

Pasi Sahlberg stated: "This [United States] is the only education system in the world that is self-sufficient in terms of ideas, knowledge, research and innovation, and financial resources. All others, more or less, depend on knowledge and ideas generated in the United States."[49] Ironically though, the United States has not applied many of its own innovations.

Finland's educational success is also a result of high-quality and equitable student learning. High-performing countries such as Finland, Canada, and Korea generate consistent learning results regardless of students' socioeconomic status.[50] France and the United States, however, have below-average achievement scores and a wide performance variance.

Enhancing equity in Finland is accomplished through fair school funding, supporting the well-being and health of children, providing special education, and using a whole-child approach.[51] Finland's social and economic context provides a strong foundation for children. Finland ranks first on the Mother's Index, which measures the overall status of mothers in countries; second in the political empowerment of women; and fourth in overall child well-being. By contrast, the United States falls much farther down in rankings: thirty-first on the Mother's Index, fifty-fifth on political empowerment of women, and twenty-sixth on overall child well-being.

Hence, adopting the Finnish model may not be effective unless the United States addresses underlying equity issues.[52] Resolving equity imbalances would require fundamental changes in America's school systems, including creating equity in school funding, prioritizing the well-being of children, and providing education as a human right. Education in Finland serves as an equalizer in society, whereas in the United States, it tends to exacerbate disparities.

American schools with the least favorable conditions are often the ones that must educate students with the greatest academic challenges.[53] Students from impoverished communities attend schools that spend less per student, employ more inexperienced or unqualified teachers, and are most in need of physical renovation.[54] The Bureau of Indian Education (BIE) schools are an example of the severe inequities that exist in the United States. While 3 percent of public school facilities are in poor condition, 33 percent of BIE schools are in poor condition.[55] The lack of promised funding and support results in a "separate and unequal" system of education.

At the Bug-O-Nay-Ge-Shig School in northern Minnesota, teachers and students conduct school in a rodent-infested building with numerous other problems, including mold, a roof that caves in under heavy snowfall, a failing heating system, a sewer system that backs up during extreme cold, and an aging pole barn structure that has to be evacuated in winds over forty miles per hour.[56] These are the kinds of schools in which our Native American students, who have the lowest graduation rates at 67 percent,[57] must learn.

CHANGING HOW WE CHANGE EDUCATION

Our educational system is very effective at maintaining the system and the status quo. As such, current school reform efforts tend to reconfigure the same parts in an attempt to achieve different results. Effecting deep and systemic change requires more than just rearranging the pieces of the puzzle. For real change to happen, the underlying beliefs that sustain the present system must change, because education is ultimately driven by the beliefs and mental models that people have.[58] To radically change education requires changing the beliefs of enough people and creating the conditions where new and different beliefs can grow and thrive.

Change, particularly philosophical and cultural change, is difficult. It transcends curriculum and methodology changes. It requires educators to reexamine belief systems that have been intact and reinforced for a long time. Change is uncomfortable and comes with uncertainty. It requires significant intentionality, guidance, reinforcement, encouragement, and accountability. So what will help bring about change?

In order for systems to change, people must change. Policies, practices, and structures can be mandated, but ultimately, it is the people within the system who will determine whether change will be championed or stymied. People create culture; they create the conditions for effective engagement and learning. Policies, structures, and practices ought to align with and support those efforts, but it is the daily interactions among the people within the system that determine whether change will fail or succeed. So how do we proceed with educational change and innovation so that it will engage and support the people who are so critical to this process?

Systems-level educational innovation requires the right drivers to power the desired changes. Michael Fullan, international author and expert on educational reform, distinguishes between "right" and "wrong" drivers for educational systemwide reform.[59] To be considered effective drivers for change, potential drivers must meet four essential criteria: they must foster intrinsic motivation of teachers and students, engage educators and students in continuous improvement of instruction and learning, inspire collective or team work, and affect *all* teachers and students. In other words, intrinsic motivation, instructional improvement, teamwork, and *allness* are critical elements for successful change. Most importantly, people—educators and students—must be the driving force of reform.

Unfortunately, many school systems in the United States don't consider these crucial elements and, instead, use drivers that make matters worse.[60] Countries eager to move reform efforts forward (e.g., the United States and Australia) tend to choose wrong, ineffective drivers such as accountability (using test results and teacher appraisal to reward and punish teachers and schools); individual teacher and leadership quality (promoting individual solutions); technology (assuming that the use of technology takes precedence over instruction); and fragmented strategies (implementation of piecemeal solutions).

Not only do the wrong drivers demotivate the people—teachers and students—whose energy is required for success, they also fail to accomplish the desired results, and may even make matters worse.[61] Massive external pressure will not generate the intrinsic motivation necessary for reform. It's likely that countries that lead with these ineffective drivers will struggle to achieve whole-system reform. None of the top-performing countries in the world (e.g., Finland, Singapore, Korea) led educational reform with these drivers. Although the wrong drivers may still have some merit in the overall process, they are not effective for leading reform efforts. That is, they may be helpful, but they will not propel the system forward.

To implement whole-system reform, lead drivers must foster motivation and competency development of most educators. Effective or right drivers are policies and strategies that generate a concerted and accelerating force for progress toward reform goals, and ultimately, better measurable results with students.[62] The right drivers consist of the following:

- Capacity building (engagement, trust, collaborative practices, skill building)
- Group work (social and human capital; development of entire teaching profession)
- Instruction (quality pedagogy)
- Systemic solutions (in every school and district)

These drivers are effective because they directly change the culture (e.g., values, norms, skills, practices, relationships) of school systems, teaching, and learning, whereas the wrong drivers alter more formal attributes (e.g., structure, procedures) of the system without addressing the internal substance of reform.[63] The type of mind-set, policies, and strategies needed for whole-system reform are ones that generate individual and collective motivation, along with the necessary skills to transform the system.

In order to be effective, reform must also be approached in a systemic manner. Improving a portion of schools or starting new schools does not achieve whole-system reform.[64] The whole system must improve for schools to attain deep and lasting change. Countries that are successful with educational change have a pervasive belief that quality education for *all* is critical to their future. They also understand that everyone must be part of the solution. This approach to reform will likely present a challenge to the United States, with its strong cultural traditions of individualism and tendencies to focus on single, rather than systemic, solutions.

In addition to choosing the right drivers for educational transformation, implementation science is another effective systems change tool. Implementation science is the study of methods to promote systemic integration of research findings and other evidence-based practices into routine practice.[65] The powerful force of the status quo in systems can derail attempts to use new practices or interventions, but a purposeful investment in the implementation process can help ensure a successful outcome.

Ineffective implementation of new initiatives is a common occurrence. Examples of commonly used, yet ineffective, implementation include anything that is done or used in isolation, such as training; laws, mandates, or regulations; providing funding or incentives; dissemination of information; and implementation without changing supporting roles.[66] These strategies typically only produce 5 to 15 percent success rates.

Rather, what is needed is a strategic implementation process—one in which barriers and issues can be anticipated. Such a plan will maximize the benefits to those for whom the change was intended.[67] Experienced implementation teams can assist organizations with methodical implementation of new practices to improve success rates from less than 15 percent to 80 percent, and reduce time frames for successful use from seventeen years to three years.

SUMMARY

Doing more of the same is not serving our students well, nor is it empowering them to succeed in adulthood and life beyond school. Current attempts at reform tend to be more superficial solutions for what ails students and schools. Traditional reform efforts do not allow for the type of inquiry and changes that have the potential to move education in a different direction—one that puts students at the center, addresses their whole development, empowers them in the learning and educational change process, and provides for equitable education.

The questions we ask about young people and education are critical to the direction that education will take and the mental model(s) that will emerge. For new forms and new directions to take shape, we must ask different questions from those we have been asking. Along with asking change-producing questions, education needs to align with an ever-changing world and learner. Our schools must adapt to a new set of demands, a new generation of learners, and new evidence regarding what young people need to develop, learn, and prepare for success in life.

The United States has much to learn from high-performing countries, many of whom adopted some of their most effective and innovative practices from the United States. Educational transformation, however, is not easy. Educational transformation will require cultural, structural, power, relational, pedagogical, and other core changes in schools. It will require changing underlying belief systems, unlearning old patterns and practices, and working together in ways that contradict the usual ways of doing business in schools.

Moreover, educational transformation is much too important to leave to chance; rather, it must be done with care and systemic planning, using the right drivers and methodology to ensure successful adoption, implementation, and sustainability.

NOTES

1. *The Learning Compact Redefined: A Call to Action, A Report of the Commission on the Whole Child*, Association for Supervision and Curriculum Development (2007), accessed February 7, 2015,http://www.ascd.org/ASCD/pdf/Whole Child/WCC Learning Compact.pdf.

2. *Measuring Innovation in Education: A New Perspective*, Educational Research and Innovation, OECD Publishing (2014), accessed February 7, 2015, http://www.keepeek.com/Digital-Asset-Management/oecd/education/measuring-innovation-in-education_9789264215696-en -page1.

3. Pasi Sahlberg, "Five U.S. Innovations That Helped Finland's Schools Improve But That American Reformers Now Ignore," guest post on Valerie Strauss, *Washington Post*, July 25, 2014, accessed February 7, 2015,http://www.washingtonpost.com/blogs/answer-sheet/wp/2014/07/25/five-u-s-innovations-that-helped-finlands-schools-improve-but-that-american-reformers-now-ignore/.

4. Pasi Sahlberg, "Global Education Reform Movement Is Here!" *The Pasi Sahlberg Blog*, accessed February 7, 2015,http://pasisahlberg.com/global-educational-reform-movement-is-here/.

5. Joan Costello et al., "How History, Ideology, and Structure Shape the Organizations That Shape Youth," in *Trends in Youth Development: Visions, Realities, and Challenges*, eds. Peter L. Benson and Karen Johnson Pittman (Norwell, MA: Kluwer Academic Publishers, 2001), 191–229.

6. *Research on the Use of Khan Academy in Schools*, Research Brief (2014), accessed February 7, 2015, http://www.sri.com/sites/default/files/publications/2014-03-07_implementation_briefing.pdf.

7. Bernie Trilling and Charles Fadel, *21st Century Skills: Learning for Life in Our Times* (San Francisco: Jossey-Bass, 2009).

8. Joel Tolman, Patrice Ford, and Merita Irby, *What Works in Education Reform: Putting Young People at the Center*, International Youth Foundation (2003), accessed January 2, 2015,http://www.iyfnet.org/sites/default/files/WW_Education_Reform.pdf.

9. Don Tapscott, *Grown Up Digital: How the Net Generation Is Changing Your World* (New York: McGraw-Hill, 2008).

10. Trilling and Fadel, *21st Century Skills*.

11. Ibid.

12. Ibid.

13. Geoffrey Caine and Renate Nummela Caine, *The Brain, Education, and the Competitive Edge* (Lanham, MD: Scarecrow Press, 2001).

14. David H. Rose and Jenna W. Gravel, "Using Digital Media to Design Student-Centered Curricula," in *Anytime, Anywhere: Student-Centered Learning for Schools and Teachers*, eds. Rebecca E. Wolfe, Adria Steinberg, and Nancy Hoffman (Cambridge, MA: Harvard Education Press, 2013), 77–101.

15. *Profile of Teachers in the U.S. 2005*, National Center for Education Information (2005), accessed February 7, 2015,http://www.ncei.com/POT05PRESSREL3.htm.

16. Nicholas C. Donahue, foreword to *Anytime, Anywhere: Student Centered Learning for Schools and Teachers*, eds. Wolfe, Steinberg, and Hoffman.

17. Tolman, Ford, and Irby, *What Works in Education Reform*.

18. Wolfe, Steinberg, and Hoffman, *Anytime, Anywhere: Student-Centered Learning for Schools and Teachers*, 1–12.

19. Ibid.

20. "The Whole Child Approach to Education," The Whole Child, accessed February 7, 2015,http://www.wholechildeducation.org/about.

21. *The Learning Compact Redefined*.

22. "The Whole Child Approach to Education."

23. *The Learning Compact Redefined*.

24. Martin Blank and Amy Berg, *All Together Now: Sharing Responsibility for the Whole Child*, Coalition for Community Schools at the Institute for Educational Leadership, Washington, D.C. (2006), accessed January 25, 2015, http://www.ascd.org/ASCD/pdf/sharingresponsibility.pdf.

25. Eric Toshalis and Michael Nakkula, *Motivation, Engagement, and Student Voice*, Students at the Center (2012), accessed January 2, 2015,http://www.studentsatthecenter.org/sites/scl.dl-dev.com/files/Motivation Engagement Student Voice_0.pdf.

26. *Youth Engagement in Educational Change*, The Forum for Youth Investment (2005), accessed January 2, 2015, http://forumfyi.org/files/Youth%20Engagement%20in%20Educational%20Change.pdf.

27. "Principles of Student Voice in Schools," SoundOut, accessed February 8, 2015,http://www.soundout.org/principles.html.

28. *A Framework for Success for All Students*, Schools for a New Society Initiative and Carnegie Corporation of New York (2006), accessed January 2, 2015,http://annenberginstitute.org/pdf/SNS_cogs.pdf.

29. Francine Joselowsky, "Youth Engagement, High School Reform, and Improved Outcomes: Building Systemic Approaches for Youth Engagement," *NASSP Bulletin* 91, no. 3 (2007): 257–76, accessed January 2, 2015,http://www.leadingnow.org/sites/default/files/pdf/Youth_Engagement_High_School_Reform.pdf.

30. Alison Cook-Sather, "Authorizing Students' Perspectives: Toward Trust, Dialogue, and Change in Education," *Educational Researcher* 31, no. 4 (2002): 3.

31. Tolman, Ford, and Irby, *What Works in Education Reform*.

32. Marian C. Diamond and Janet Hopson, "Learning Not by Chance: Enrichment in the Classroom," in *The Jossey-Bass Reader on the Brain and Learning* (San Francisco: John Wiley & Sons, 2008), 70–88.

33. Tolman, Ford, and Irby, *What Works in Education Reform*.

34. Sobhi Tawil and Marie Cougoureux, *Revisiting Learning: The Treasure Within; Assessing the Influence of the 1996 Delores Report* (2013), accessed February 7, 2015,http://unesdoc.unesco.org/images/0022/002200/220050E.pdf.

35. Ibid.

36. Pasi Sahlberg, "What If Finland's Great Teachers Taught in U.S. Schools?" guest post on Valerie Strauss, *Washington Post*, May 15, 2013, accessed February 7, 2015,http://www.

washingtonpost.com/blogs/answer-sheet/wp/2013/05/15/what-if-finlands-great-teachers-taught-in-u-s-schools-not-what-you-think/.

37. Linda Darling-Hammond, "U.S. vs. Highest-Achieving Nations in Education," guest post on Valerie Strauss, *Washington Post*, March 23, 2011, accessed February 7, 2015,http://www.washingtonpost.com/blogs/answer-sheet/post/darling-hammond-us-vs-highest-achieving-nations-in-education/2011/03/22/ABkNeaCB_blog.html.

38. Linda Darling-Hammond, *What We Can Learn from Finland's Successful School Reform*, National Education Association (2010), accessed February 7, 2015,http://www.nea.org/home/40991.htm.

39. Pasi Sahlberg, *Finnish Lessons: What Can the World Learn from Educational Change in Finland?* (New York: Teachers College Press, 2011).

40. Darling-Hammond, "U.S. vs. Highest-Achieving Nations in Education."

41. Pasi Sahlberg, "How GERM Is Infecting Schools Around the World," guest post on Valerie Strauss, *Washington Post*, June 29, 2012, accessed February 7, 2015,http://www.washingtonpost.com/blogs/answer-sheet/post/how-germ-is-infecting-schools-around-the-world/2012/06/29/gJQAVELZAW_blog.html.

42. Pasi Sahlberg, Presentation for 2014 Education Minnesota Conference, October 16, 2014, accessed February 7, 2015, http://pasisahlberg.com/wp-content/uploads/2013/07/Minnesota-Talk-2014.pdf.

43. Sahlberg, *Finnish Lessons*.

44. Darling-Hammond, *What We Can Learn from Finland's Successful School Reform*.

45. Ibid.

46. Sahlberg, *Finnish Lessons*.

47. Sahlberg, "Five U.S. Innovations That Helped Finland's Schools Improve But That American Reformers Now Ignore."

48. Sahlberg, "How GERM Is Infecting Schools Around the World."

49. Sahlberg, "Five U.S. Innovations That Helped Finland's Schools Improve But That American Reformers Now Ignore."

50. Sahlberg, *Finnish Lessons*.

51. Pasi Sahlberg, "What Can the World Learn from Educational Change in Finland?" Presentation at NYSAIS Conference, Mohonk Mountain, New York, November 7, 2014, accessed February 7, 2015,http://pasisahlberg.com/wp-content/uploads/2013/07/NYSAIS-Talk-2014.pdf.

52. Pasi Sahlberg, "What the U.S. Can't Learn from Finland about Ed Reform," guest post on Valerie Strauss, *Washington Post*, April 17, 2012, accessed February 7, 2015,http://www.washingtonpost.com/blogs/answer-sheet/post/what-the-us-cant-learn-from-finland-about-ed-reform/2012/04/16/gIQAGIvVMT_blog.html.

53. *A Framework for Success for All Students.*

54. *The Learning Compact Redefined: A Call to Action, A Report of the Commission on the Whole Child*, Association for Supervision and Curriculum Development (2007), accessed February 7, 2015,http://www.ascd.org/ASCD/pdf/Whole Child/WCC Learning Compact.pdf.

55. Jill Burcum and the *Star Tribune* Editorial Board, "Separate and Unequal," *StarTribune*, December 10, 2014, accessed February 7, 2015,http://www.startribune.com/opinion/285613631.html.

56. Ibid.

57. Marie C. Stetser and Robert Stillwell, *Public High School Four-Year On-Time Graduation Rates and Event Dropout Rates: School Years 2010–11 and 2011–12* (2014), National Center for Education Statistics, U.S. Department of Education, accessed February 7, 2015,http://nces.ed.gov/pubs2014/2014391.pdf.

58. Caine and Caine, *The Brain, Education, and the Competitive Edge.*

59. Michael Fullan, *Choosing the Wrong Drivers for Whole System Reform*, Seminar Series 204, Center for Strategic Education (2011), accessed January 25, 2015,http://edsource.org/wp-content/uploads/Fullan-Wrong-Drivers1.pdf.

60. Ibid.

61. Ibid.

62. Ibid.

63. Ibid.

64. Ibid.

65. "When *Just Do It!* Doesn't Do It: Purposeful Implementation Increases Success Rates," *Early Developments* 14, no. 2 (2013): 6–8, accessed February 7, 2015,http://fpg.unc.edu/sites/fpg.unc.edu/files/resources/early-developments/FPG_EarlyDevelopments_v14n2.pdf.

66. Ibid.

67. Ibid.

Chapter Six

Valuing Our Youth, Valuing Our Future

Don't underestimate the youth, because we are the future!
Don't try and shoot our ideas down because we are younger than you
or have less life experience. Just trust in our judgment, because all in all,
we're the ones that are going to be managing your world.
—Josh

The previous chapter called for new forms of education for new learners and new times. However, before doing that, we must first address the underlying issue of youth devaluation discussed in chapter 3. It is essential that educators (and society) understand the importance of valuing our young people, including those who struggle with school. We need to value young people not only because as developing human beings they deserve it, but also because they are our future. Young people will be the ones who shape and manage the future, as Josh aptly noted.

Given the level of devaluation and oppression that young people experience, where do we even start? How do we begin to grow a mind-set and actions that reflect authentic youth valuation? What better place to model and practice the valuation of young people than one of the institutions most responsible for shaping culture in our society—our schools.

MORE THAN A SCORE

So how do we go about valuing youth within our schools and ultimately society? To answer that we first need to consider some very basic human needs. Valuation and validation are essential to the human spirit and personal growth. As human beings, we need to know that we matter, that we hold value to people around us and the world at large. When we have value, we have something to bring to the table, something we can offer to others. Our existence holds worth. This is especially important for developing children and adolescents.

Young people are vital members of our schools and community. By their mere existence as developing human beings, they hold value and deserve to be treated with dignity and respect, especially by the institutions in which they are required to participate. It is important that young people receive messages of worth and valuation from the adults around them early on and throughout their development. It is often easier for people to value babies and little children; however, as those same children become adolescents they tend to lose value in the eyes of society. They are perceived and treated as a problem or threat. Their valuation declines as a result of entering a developmental stage that is tainted by negative stereotypes and oppression.

This is particularly true within the school setting. Young people's humanity and individuality is often forgotten in the pursuit of standards of performance, grades, test scores, and graduation, as noted in students' comments below:

> It's important that the teacher cares about you, more than just gaining knowledge and finishing that grade. —Cassie

> Deal more with what's going on with them. Let them know you care about what's going on in their life. Ask what you can do to help them. I heard so many times in high school, "you have so much potential, but" . . . or, "if only you . . ." Focus on the positives, the successes, not just the performance goals. —Jacquelyn

Young people are not merely the test scores, grades, or diplomas they have earned. Each student has a unique personality and a distinctive set of talents, life experiences, and challenges. Accordingly, schools ought to be a place where young people can thrive beyond just academic achievement. As Lorenzo points out, school should be a place where students can aspire to reach their individual hopes, dreams, and aspirations:

> Every student is different. They should have the right to learn and fulfill their dream . . . You never know what that person might become; they might discover the cure for AIDS . . . if schools don't help them, they might miss that discovery.

An educator's first responsibility should be to recognize young people as whole, promising human beings—acceptable just as they are, apart from any expectations that may be placed on them. Likewise, before focusing on a young person's future, educators first need to meet young people where they are today. In other words, to help young people achieve their highest potential, educators must appreciate who students are now and provide nonjudgmental support, as Jacquelyn cautioned in her reflection:

> Don't tell them they have potential and they need to live up to it. Don't assume they don't care about not handing work in—they do. They are already putting pressure on themselves. They just felt poorly about themselves and couldn't pull it together, even though they wanted to.

Valuing young people also means they are not perceived as "problems." Oftentimes, when students seemingly don't cooperate or progress as schools have prescribed, they are labeled and treated as problems; Charlie described this experience in an earlier chapter. For young people to feel valued, it is important that educators view students as people who have challenges, not as people who are problems.

In addition to general devaluation of youth in schools, students who attend alternative or special education programs and schools have yet another layer of devaluation to deal with:

> Stop saying "those kids" at "those schools." Having a learning disability is not a crime and these students are not trash you can throw out! I want education to get better, dropout rates to go lower. This generation, they're the ones that are going to make the future. —Lorenzo

Students who struggle in school because of disabilities or other challenges often feel rejected by their home schools when they are recommended or required to attend a different program or school, as was the case with Ben in chapter 1. They are also aware that the programs or schools they attend are viewed negatively—that is where the bad kids or "losers" go. Alternative programs are often seen as "lesser-than" programs for "lesser-than" students. So not only do students at alternative schools have to reconcile being discarded by their previous school, they also have to grapple with the negative reputation associated with attending alternative or special education programs and schools.

MORE THAN A PAYCHECK

In addition to having their collective age group valued, young people also need to know that educators care about them as individuals. They need to be able to trust that adults in the school have a vested and personalized interest in them and their success, as Richard points out:

> At the end of the day, they [students] need to know that someone cares about
> them, their future, that they [teachers] care about their students succeeding, not
> just their paychecks.

A Midwestern district conducted action research in the form of Listening
Groups with students to learn what was helpful and meaningful for students.[1]
Students reported that they were motivated by staff who offered support,
advocated for them, and cared about them as people. One student remarked
about a teacher who demonstrated those traits:

> She is a wizard . . . genuinely cares about your education and you as a human
> being.

In other interviews with students, youth spoke about the need for educators to care about them as a person beyond their academics. Students want to
be considered as human beings, with lives outside of school first and as
students attending school second. When asked about the ideal learning environment, Kyle said that teachers would connect with students and provide
personal time up front (start of the day/class) to check in with students and
ask how their weekend was.

Research findings reveal that "caring" is essential for student valuation,
engagement, and progress.[2] Caring is critical, especially for culturally diverse students who may be at risk of failing or who may be disengaged from
school.[3] In a study that examined students' perceptions of teacher caring,
students identified teacher traits that represented caring to them.[4] The traits
fell into three main categories. The first, *validating student worth*, involves
respectful interactions and sincere regard for students as individuals and for
their welfare. It also includes perceiving students as human beings rather
than physical bodies in the classroom.

The second category of caring traits is *individualizing academic success*.
This category involves providing both cognitive and affective instructional
support and assistance to students, which in turn, helps to create a positive
and successful classroom experience for students.[5] *Fostering positive engagement*, the third category, includes teacher behaviors that encourage self-
esteem in the students. Educators spend time creating positive experiences
for students rather than discounting or labeling them as unmotivated when
they experience challenges. As a result, students feel that the teacher genu-
inely cares about their learning and success.

Other studies identified "teacher caring" as behaviors that enhance students' potential, foster self-esteem, value students' opinions, and respect
them as individuals.[6] Likewise, students do better in school when they perceive teachers as available, understanding, encouraging, respectful, listening,

and having a sense of humor. Teacher caring is a crucial element that impacts both students' success in school and their likelihood of remaining in school.

Although many educators believe their practices are caring in nature, students may not experience their teachers as caring. In one study, most teachers reported caring about their students; however, 40 percent of the students disagreed.[7] Differences can also exist between the actions and dispositions teachers identify as caring, compared with what students identify as caring.[8] So it is not enough for educators to just think they are caring about their students; they must ask students what caring means for them and whether they are experiencing it or not.

Students' perceptions of teacher caring also directly impact how students perceive the larger culture of the school.[9] Teacher behaviors that reflect caring and build relationships with students contribute to a sense of belonging and a culture of learning, especially for those students who feel disconnected from school. As a result, caring cannot be left to chance or to a few educators in a school; it must be an intentional, systemic process. "Care must be a deliberate focus, fundamental to the school's ideology, if schools are to create structures that enable caring relationships."[10]

Similar to the concept of caring is "Time to Teach," a program designed for at-risk and special needs youth that promotes the use of *unconditional positive regard* as one of its main components.[11] It differentiates between contingent and noncontingent interactions. At the upper grade levels, educators are more apt to use contingent interactions and reinforcement with students, such as "You did a good job on that assignment," or "I'm proud of how hard you have been working." These are examples of contingent interaction and reinforcement; they require that the student do something constructive to gain recognition or regard.

Contingent interactions are not a negative thing. They are, however, limiting for students if that is the only type of regard they receive. Students need noncontingent interactions and regard as well. Noncontingent regard says that you don't have to do anything in particular to gain regard or recognition; the person will just like you and care about you as you are.

In her interview, Jacquelyn was asked what the ideal learning environment would consist of. Her responses emphasized the importance of unconditional positive regard and valuation:

> Every student would have the opportunity to feel important and valued. You could do this by saying "we missed you," noticing them when they are there and when they are not, and having personal conversations as much as you can with them.

Another example of unconditional positive regard occurred when my students and I were presenting at a state conference. A former student who had previously participated in my Leadership class joined us for the session. Michael came from a background of numerous life challenges such as poverty, addiction, and criminal activity. He had survived a lot of adversities and had graduated from an alternative high school.

Usually students began workshop sessions by introducing themselves, sharing some of their struggles and accomplishments, and then a goal or dream they had. Audiences typically responded by applauding after each student shared his or her personal journey. However, at this particular workshop, the audience did not acknowledge individual students after they spoke. Michael was the last person to speak. He shared some of his background, and then for his final piece—his accomplishments—Michael simply said, "I'm alive." The audience erupted into loud applause. Somehow, they understood that was a huge achievement for him. It was valuation for a young man, simply because he existed and was present with us that day.

Unconditional positive regard is especially critical for students who have struggled in school. So often they are only provided attention, rewards, and the like if they are meeting expectations or following the rules. They are ignored, negated, or punished if they are not in compliance. It is not uncommon for educators to pull away and withdraw from students when they misbehave or act in ways that go against what is expected or required. The irony is that when educators do this, young people suffer, as that is when they need adult support the most.

Students need adults to stay the course when they are having their worst struggles. Educators don't need to reinforce harmful or disruptive behavior, but they also don't need to pull back their care and support until students come into compliance. It is the act of caring that will help them come back from less desirable places and behaviors, not the withdrawal of caring.

Throughout individual and group interviews with students, a pervasive theme revealed was the need for teachers to engage in relationship building with students. Students cited one-on-one relationships as being critical for trust, communication, and constructive interaction. They felt that teachers should have training and practice in relating to students.

R-E-S-P-E-C-T

Valuing young people also means that adults respect them. Young people need to be treated with dignity, even when they are not able to demonstrate respect themselves. Respect starts with educators—they are the adults who serve as role models. Richard spoke of the need for both respect and unconditional regard:

> Student respect is huge—mutual respect between students and teachers. Teachers need to earn the respect of the students, not just assume they're in

power and will get it [respect]. Instead of talking down, maybe pull them
aside, try [to] find out, figure out what's going on. Show unconditional care
even if the student rebukes you: "I'm still going to be here, you are, too, let's
get through this." Try to be as nice and sincere as you can.

Throughout the interviews and Listening Groups conducted with students, respect was a major concern brought up by students, especially as it pertained to how educators treated them. Students felt that respect was a one-way street; it was only required that students be respectful toward staff. Instead, students wanted a mutuality of respect between staff and students.

You have to give one respect to have one's respect. Don't be a total authority
figure. Everybody needs to have respect and dignity . . . Treat them with as
much respect as possible. They [students] are at a much more vulnerable age
and stage than adults realize. —Justin

Feliz also spoke about the importance of mutual, two-way respect:

The best teachers are the ones who have been working with youth and teens
many years and have built those relationships and have grown respect for us. If
they respect me, I respect them. You need a teacher or adult who works on the
level of the youth—someone who is not talking down, who has a perception of
youth that is more open-minded and understanding. That's a really big deal!

Likewise, when addressing difficult situations with students, young people still wanted to be treated in a dignified, respectful, and constructive manner:

Don't be the teacher, be the "person." Talk to them [students] like a person.
Don't scold or yell, 'cause you're implanting a negative image. They're more
apt to talk with you if your voice isn't raised. Have an understanding that the
anger isn't about you; it's misdirected anger, you're in the wrong place at the
wrong time. —Martin

Let the person know that you care—you're there to help them. Back up what
you say with your actions. Try not to demean or humiliate them. Don't call
attention to or be sarcastic about the situation or the person. —Kyle

In addition, Jacquelyn felt that using a solution-focused approach would be more helpful:

Approach situations with a constructive, problem-solving approach, versus
finger-shaking, blaming, and shaming . . . Deal more with what's going on
with them; let them know you care about what's going on in their life. Ask
what you can do to help them.

Anthony encouraged educators to consider the underlying causes of a young person's actions and to check their own dispositions so as to not make the situation worse:

> Some of the students may have other underlying issues you're not aware of at any given time. Certain conditions may arise, [so] take into consideration your own mood and state of mind. If you're having a bad day, don't let it affect the severity of the problem by making it worse.

Similarly, Richard recommended that educators respond in a professional, supportive, and uncontentious manner when addressing challenging issues with a student:

> Kill with kindness, help them through it, don't add fuel to the fire. Don't get at the same level of the student; that makes them more on edge and stressed. That will make them react by defending themselves, 'cause they will still feel you coming at them. How the teacher reacts will have a huge effect on the outcome! If the teacher wins every time, they really don't, 'cause in the end, you lose the student. The teacher needs to stay more professional than the student.

Which is more important—to win the struggle or to lose the student? As Richard so poignantly notes, if the teacher needs to win, that likely means the student is lost in the process. Instead, respectful, nonthreatening actions are much more productive.

On educators' toughest days of dealing with difficult situations, their ability to treat students with dignity and respect can be tested. That is why it is essential that staff are well trained and well supported. Educators need ongoing training, coaching, and support in multiple areas such as adolescent development, positive interventions, disabilities, and other relevant topics. In order for staff to be at their best with students, including students who struggle with school, they need to be equipped with the best training, tools, and support.

Similar to the unconditional regard and respect discussed earlier, young people also benefit from adults who are able to be nonjudgmental. Unfortunately, adultism is pervasive in school settings, and educators feel at liberty to make and pass judgment on students as a matter of course. This tendency for educators to judge happens on an individual level, in conversations with other staff, in teacher breakrooms or workrooms, and in school meetings.

Aimee encouraged educators to seek deeper understanding of students, rather than just making assumptions or judging them:

> Be understanding that people have lives beyond school; that affects how they're doing in school, and even physically. Have an understanding of what's really going on with people and their needs, not just thinking it's them being bad.

When adults can be nonjudgmental and open-minded, youth feel valued. These are essential qualities for building relationships and having an impact, as highlighted by Alyson:

> Don't always judge on the first encounter, someone may be at their worst. Treat people kindly, how you'd like to be treated . . . Be positive, keep an open mind, a level head, and just remember, at the end of the day you're making an impact on someone's life.

Jacquelyn encouraged teachers to withhold judgment and treat underperforming students with respect and valuation.

> You may not be that teacher who helps them find their potential, but you may still make a difference. They still need you to treat them as normal—ask about their weekend. You can still see them as having value, treat them like others in the class, they're valuable human beings. Keep believing in them and their potential. Let them know they are important to you.

Educators are confronted every day with situations and students that can present very challenging issues; however, withholding judgment of a young person is crucial. Doing so builds bridges and helps to validate students' evolving identities. Withholding judgment doesn't preclude having expectations, guidelines, and consequences. It just means that educators don't make assumptions, negative predictions, and hasty, foregone conclusions about students and that students aren't held hostage to beliefs and behaviors that are limiting, harmful, and often untrue.

Being judgmental can also be detrimental for educators. A negative and blaming mind-set does not cultivate an atmosphere of possibility and hope for learning and growth. Instead, it fuels discouragement and defeat, for both students and educators. It has the effect of depleting people's energy and motivation. What does engage and energize young people, and the staff who work with them, is working to envision success rather than failure.

DON'T GIVE UP ON US!

Valuing young people means educators don't give up on them. It does not serve young people to turn away from them. Throughout interviews and Listening Groups, students made a resounding plea not to give up on them, as in the case of Jacquelyn. She felt that teachers gave up on her when she didn't perform up to her potential:

> It can be easy to give up [on students], but you can't! When teachers realized I was smart and wasn't performing up to that, they treated me badly. Stick with every student, beyond them doing poorly. Students feel the negativity you put

out; when you've given up on them, they feel that. Don't judge or treat them
differently because they're not living up to their potential.

If adults are able to continue working with students despite the challenges, students often want to respond in kind, doing their best to succeed, as
in Andrew's case:

Even if they lost trust in you, they didn't kick you out as a bad student. Seeing
them teach like that made me want to succeed. I didn't want to be a bad
reflection of the teacher giving their all.

It can take a lot of patience, persistence, and a nonjudgmental mind-set to
support young people through challenging times, but the ability to persevere
with young people helps them to come out on the other side. Many of the
students who were interviewed appealed to educators: "Don't give up on us;
when you give up on us, we give up on ourselves." Young people want and
need adults to hold out hope for them, especially when they can't. Retaining
hope and possibility empowers both students and staff to take the steps
necessary to reach their goals.

EVOLVING ADOLESCENTS AND EMERGING ADULTS

Creating a caring, personalized educational environment in which students
are well known and accepted, and where they can experience unconditional
positive regard, helps to demonstrate valuation of young people. [12] Similarly,
understanding the developmental needs of young people is critical to their
success in school. [13]

All too often educators forget that adolescents are still going through a
developmental process that requires understanding and support beyond just
academics. Educators' knowledge and beliefs about the developmental needs
of adolescents affect their interactions with students, particularly marginalized students. [14] As such, educators need a strong and clear understanding of
adolescent development needs so that they can work with the "whole person."

Pittman and Wright define *youth development* as an ongoing process,
whereby young people attempt to meet their needs and develop the competencies perceived as valuable for both the present and future. [15] Basic needs
include safety and structure, belonging and membership, self-worth and contribution, independence and control over one's life, and closeness and relationships. Competencies include health and physical well-being; personal
and social development; and cognitive, creative, vocational, and citizenship
skills.

Adolescents are more likely to excel in schools that are structured in a way that supports rather than suppresses the needs of their students.[16] Adolescents experience empowerment when people and institutions create environments and experiences that help fulfill their basic needs and competencies. Conversely, when agents and organizations actively inhibit adolescents' ability to contribute, form close relationships, and master tasks perceived as important, they create disempowering environments for youth.

Development is an individualized process that is significantly influenced by the contexts in which it occurs.[17] Young people move among multiple settings every day, including familial, institutional, informal, virtual, and others. Adolescents' experiences in these varied settings affect their development. Excessive and prolonged exposure to negative life events, dangerous settings, and inadequate schooling can significantly impact an adolescent's development.[18] Any of these risk factors, occurring singularly or compounded, can impede a young person's ability to transition successfully through adolescence and perform in school.

In order to acquire and grow the personal and social assets that can counter negative impacts, adolescents need continued exposure to positive experiences, settings, and people, as well as opportunities to gain and refine life skills.[19] Consequently, schools should be places where students can build and reinforce assets, rather than places that add to the adversities already present in students' lives.

Adolescent development is not a lockstep, linear process; rather, it is fluid and specific to a particular individual.[20] No two young people are likely at the same developmental point as they transition from adolescence to adulthood. The development process is based in part on a person's physiological and cognitive abilities, earlier experiences, opportunities, and supports.

In addition, physical, cognitive, and social development each tends to progress at different rates for an individual adolescent.[21] So while a particular young person may exhibit physical or cognitive maturity, his or her social development might evolve at a slower pace. When adolescents experience delays in a given area, adults tend to blame young people for these delays and expect them to resolve the seemingly inadequate development. Instead of blaming adolescents for development issues, adults should address the matter by putting into place supports that can help develop these skills.

Educators, and adults in general, often expect that by a certain chronological age, all young people will have acquired and exhibit certain behaviors and thought processes. Instead, the reality of adolescent development is that it is more of a stop-and-start process. Adolescents are both evolving adolescents and emerging adults. Young people may exhibit an adolescent mind-set and actions in one circumstance and more adult thinking and behavior in another. Some of this uneven growth can be explained by brain development.

During adolescence, the brain undergoes a period of plasticity that entails a "rewiring" or brain changeability process that starts at the onset of puberty and continues into the twenties.[22] This rewiring is especially pronounced in the prefrontal cortex, which is considered to be the "CEO" of the brain. The prefrontal cortex is responsible for executive functions, such as focusing attention, planning, prioritizing, organizing, decision making, and impulse control.

Although the prefrontal cortex is critical to mature brain functioning, it is one of the last regions of the brain to fully develop. Adolescents' brains are still rooted in the amygdala, the emotional brain, which affects the ability to use good judgment in challenging life situations.[23] With time, however, the prefrontal cortex becomes increasingly connected with the limbic system (emotional center), allowing reason and emotion to be better coordinated.[24]

Certain factors, such as stress, impact adolescent brain functioning. The adolescent brain is more vulnerable to stress; it overloads the prefrontal cortex, making it more difficult to regulate emotions and thoughts.[25] Presently, adolescents are the most stressed age group of the various generations, with 31 percent of teens reporting they feel overwhelmed as a result of stress.[26] So not only does stress impact learning, it also short-circuits basic brain functioning, which affects how young people respond to their environment.

Each adolescent develops at an individualized pace and manner, depending in part on earlier life experiences, physiological factors, stressors, and personal and social assets. There is not a universal path through adolescence. Consequently, educators would better serve young people by recognizing, normalizing, and supporting the physiological, neurological, and socioemotional changes that adolescents go through, instead of labeling adolescence in negative and stereotypical manners. Students are both *evolving adolescents* and *emerging adults*. As such, they are deserving of care and protection as young people, and they are also worthy of consideration and participation as adults.[27]

In order to support adolescents' development, schools will need to provide ongoing education for staff about adolescent development, including the needs and challenges connected with that stage of development. Educators often maintain a focus on child development through the early elementary years; however, as young people age, educators tend to lose sight of the development process of young people. This is partly because inservice training for high school educators does not typically focus on adolescent development. Rather, learning and academic strategies are priority topics for the limited in-service time allotted each school year.

Along with physical, cognitive, emotional, and social support as they develop, young people also need opportunities to grow and shape their individual identities. This is often neglected in our school systems. As an institution and a system that needs to serve the masses in an efficient way, schools do not encourage or tolerate individualism very well. Andrew stressed the importance of educators taking the time and making the effort to really get to know their students as the unique individuals they are:

> Most mainstream teachers need to step back and see each student as an individual versus as a number. Granted, they have a lot of students, but they shouldn't only focus on those already-good students. They should spend more time bringing up the students who aren't quite up to speed . . . [Teacher] was great—she helped me get to school every day. She wasn't afraid to get to know students and recognize them for their individuality and uniqueness.

While it might be easier to communicate with the class as a whole, educators need to cultivate relationships with students as individuals.[28] Young people benefit from experiences that assist in developing their individual identities. They need experiences that help determine who they are, and who they are not—opportunities that can help them discover their interests, goals, and roles in the community so they can continue to grow and optimize their potential.

In one of his interviews, Andrew talked about the value of being able to speak openly to audiences about his personal journey as part of public presentations for his Leadership class. Through the experience of sharing and reflecting on his life experiences, he was able to form a clear and strong sense of identity.

> An accomplishment I am proud of is that I got out of that silence. If I hadn't come out of my shell, I don't know where I would be. Coming out of my shell led to everything of where I am now. I am proud of the presentations, the chance to tell my story, to be listened to, to have a chance to hear my own story and look back on what I did, who I became, and all the people I was in the process. Throughout high school, no one listens; they grade you and move on. You don't get the feedback, the involvement, enthusiasm, and the interest that people show when you tell your story. You feel like you matter, that people care about what you have been through.

Andrew felt as if he was at school to simply go through the motions of a predetermined academic agenda that allowed him no real identity or individual presence in the process or in the system. Many young people, especially those who have challenges or disabilities, do not thrive in a factory model of education. They become lost in an oversized, standardized system that doesn't allow for their unique needs and individuality. It becomes a matter of surviving, not thriving. In order to thrive, young people need experiences that help validate who they are, where they have been in life, and who they are becoming.

THE ANSWERS ARE IN THE QUESTIONS

In order to cultivate and uphold authentic and meaningful valuation of young people, we must begin by asking some key questions—questions that will help us move in a more positive direction of validating and supporting youth. And they must be youth-centered, not systems-centered, questions, questions like, "Where and how is valuation of all young people upheld in our schools?" and "Are students valued for who they are separate from academics?" And other questions such as, "If valuation exists, is it conditional, or is it withdrawn if a young person doesn't behave or perform according to expectations?" and "What do youth have to say about whether they feel valued, and what specifically helps them to feel valued?"

A prime starting place to investigate whether young people are valued in our schools is with the school's vision and mission statements. Most school districts have vision and mission statements along with articulated values and beliefs. If schools and educators truly value youth, school vision and mission statements would likely be worded differently than they are currently. Consider the difference in tone and messaging between these vision and mission statements by different schools in the same metropolitan area:

> School 1: Learners will achieve academic excellence and become productive.
>
> School 2: Our mission is to inspire and prepare all students with the confidence, courage, and competence to achieve their dreams, contribute to community, and engage in a lifetime of learning.

The first example emphasizes school achievement and productivity. There is no recognition of young people outside their limited role as learners. On the other hand, the focus and messaging in the second statement is very different. First and foremost, it emphasizes the individualized and holistic nature of students. The second statement recognizes students as human beings, young people who have identities and needs beyond just academics. It places importance on the developmental needs, life skills, and unique aspirations of each child, along with learning that extends beyond the school walls. The second statement is much more *student centered* or *youth centered* than the first example, which is more *systems centered*.

In reviewing numerous school vision and mission statements, it was much more common to see examples like the first vision statement, where the focus was on academic outcomes or a superior system, as opposed to a focus on the child and/or the development of the whole child:

> a) Every child college ready.
> b) [City] Public Schools will continue to be among the premier school districts both nationally and internationally. Our high expectations in

academics, arts, extracurricular activities and community involvement best prepare each learner to achieve success in college, career, and life.

While these vision statements are promoted with good intentions, they are still *systems centered*. Like the second example above, a number of schools assumed that their high expectations were the key to success, yet there is no mention of the supports that might be needed or provided to meet those high expectations. The next two vision statements don't even specify that they work with people or students. The second one is another clear example of a systems-centered vision:

a) Learning for life.
b) An innovative district modeling educational excellence.

Vision and mission statements are well intended, but they are only words on paper or a website. Even if those words are student centered and crafted to support and promote the valuation of all young people, schools still need to create the mechanisms (e.g., beliefs, culture, structures, policies, practices) to align with those intentions.

Shifting to a student-centered system is not easy. The vast majority of policy and practice conversations about youth well-being are still systems centered.[29] They are organized around, and constrained by, expertise and assumptions about systems, rather than about young people and their developmental needs. Moving toward youth-centered practices and policies means that schools must move away from what the system can and cannot do, and move toward what young people need to fully develop and maximize their potential.

THE PROOF IS IN THE BUDGET

A budget is a statement of our beliefs. If we truly valued young people, our national, state, and local budgets would reflect that. We will know we have begun to value youth more when adequate resources are provided to serve all students in an equitable and high-quality manner. Charlie's remark reflects current funding priorities in our nation and local communities:

We're cutting education, food . . . but we're building a new stadium. We need more incentives for education and for teachers because education is about molding our future.

Compared to other industrialized countries, America is first in gross domestic product and first in the number of billionaires, yet second to worst in child poverty rates, and the worst in protecting children against gun violence.[30]

Likewise, as noted in the previous chapter, the United States ranks twenty-sixth regarding child well-being, as compared to Finland, a high-performing country in the area of education, which ranks fourth. These disparities are reflective of a society that puts other concerns ahead of their children, which, in turn, has lasting consequences for our children, our country, and our future.

The amount the United States spends each year on corporate tax breaks for private jets would pay the salary of 6,400 high school teachers.[31] So where do we, as a nation, place our priorities? How do we change from being a country that underserves its children to one that provides equitable resources for children and for their education?

Investing in our children and education is an investment that will pay off in the long run. Funding education can help foster economic growth, enhance productivity, contribute to people's personal and social development, and help reduce social inequalities.[32] On the contrary, underfunding education can have negative consequences for both students and society, especially for students who struggle in school. Addressing those issues later, rather than up front, yields higher ultimate costs, such as students dropping out of school. The consequences are devastating for both the students and society.

The high school students who dropped out of the class of 2011 will cost the nation's economy approximately $154 billion in lost income over their lifetimes.[33] In addition, many of these undereducated students enter the "school-to-prison pipeline," going from school into the criminal justice system.[34] Paying for prison is much more costly than paying for education. Most states are spending three to four times more per capita incarcerating prisoners than they are educating students.[35] And in states like California, they expect to spend $62,000 per prisoner in 2014 to 2015, nearly seven times the $9,200 they will spend for each K–12 student.[36] We would be much better off as a society by significant investing in our youth through things like education than by applying punitive measures.

Another way to improve funding for students and education is by changing our perceptions of youth. Societal perceptions of youth are critical for driving funding toward youth and education.[37] A positive perspective of youth is more apt to encourage resource investment toward development efforts, whereas a negative perspective is more apt to result in funding for punitive measures. Hence, educators, researchers, and communities must work to change the negative images and stereotypes about youth currently held by society and reinforced by media.

OUR CHILDREN, OUR FUTURE

Our hope for the future lies in the encouragement of the unlimited talents, intelligences, skills, and attributes of our young people.[38] In order for our children to create a world of great opportunity and great outcomes, we must first recognize and treat them as the great members of our communities that they are. And then we must empower them and outfit them with the skills and capacity to act on their world. In her interview, Danielle stressed the importance of nurturing leadership and development early on in children's lives so that young people are well prepared and well positioned for the future:

> The fact that leaders don't just come in adults. They also come in children. In fact, once those adults die, you still have your children, who are going to be following leaders. So teach them at a very young age how to do what they are supposed to do, how to reach their dreams, how to score confidence and wisdom and the knowledge that they will need to do it.

Young people will have a powerful and lasting effect on everyone's future, as Josh noted in the opening quote, so what we do with and for them matters. And what we don't do with or for them also matters. We cannot, and should not, be surprised to see less-than-stellar results from young people as they emerge from high schools if society has put less-than-stellar efforts and resources toward our youth. We cannot expect exceptional results while investing minimal financial and other resources into the very people who will determine our future.

If we as a society don't provide what is needed for our children to thrive, it can be a lifelong struggle for them, our communities, and our future. What and how we invest in our young people will play out in our communities, economy, and future. So we can choose to invest now and reap the benefits, or we can pay later when the consequences are more costly.

How will we know whether young people are valued in our school communities and what helps them to feel valued? In addition to asking students directly, we will have evidence that youth are highly valued if the following conditions (and others) are commonplace in our schools:

- Young people are valued for who they are right now; they are well known, understood, accepted, respected, and cared for by the adults around them.
- Young people are recognized as developing adolescents and emerging adults and are supported in their developmental process.
- Young people's needs take precedence over the school's needs and political agendas.
- Young people aren't automatically blamed for the challenges they experience.

- Adults take time to listen and respond to youth in a respectful and appropriate manner.
- Young people want to be in the classroom and school.
- Adequate funding and resources are available to meet the varied needs of *all* students.

In addition to these factors, students also feel valued when someone in a position of power recognizes and honors them and their accomplishments, as Maria described in her remark:

> I think it's really cool that we're inviting mayors of our towns around us . . . they can hear and see what we've been trying to do and so that they begin to help make a difference. People listen to them and just knowing that they're actually interested in coming to see what we've done is amazing, because truthfully, I never would have thought they would have cared to come out here to do that.

Students were surprised when adults and people in power listened to them and showed up for them. That tells us that students are not used to adults, and those in positions of power, recognizing them and their accomplishments, and just how impactful it is when they do.

One of the best examples of an adult in power valuing young people was when the students in my Leadership class met with the local mayor to invite him to officiate at their Peace Pole dedication. He told them it would be an honor to do so and explained how meaningful their efforts were to the school and the city. When the students asked him about his availability, he responded, "No, what is *your* availability? This is an important event you are planning, so I want to work around *your* schedules."

The mayor's response is a potent example of someone in a position of authority and power who is able to recognize and reinforce the value of young people and their contributions. He engaged them with the underlying assumption that their efforts and time were as important as, if not more than, his time. He was responding in a youth- or student-centered manner, which carries an inherent tone of valuation for and about young people.

SUMMARY

Nelson Mandela once said, "There can be no keener revelation of a society's soul than the way in which it treats its children." In order to work with young people in a constructive and supportive manner, we have to *see* them as worthy and holding value. The students who are the most marginalized or disenfranchised likely experience the greatest devaluation in our schools and society, and consequently, they may benefit the most from valuation by the adults in their schools and communities. Valuing youth, however, benefits everyone, including young people, their families, the professionals who work with them, and society.

Although this work of valuing and supporting young people is needed throughout our communities and society, we can start with schools, as they are the primary institution for educating and socializing young people. Schools are instrumental in a child's development; they are the place where young people form their identity, self-worth, and place in society. For this reason and others, schools ought to be leaders and stewards of young people's development.

Valuing young people goes beyond understanding and supporting their development. It means that we put young people (students) at the center of education and align resources accordingly. Valuing young people means that schools become places and opportunities of learning where students can fully develop and flourish in all aspects, not just academically. Our future depends on it. In other words, what and how we invest in our young people will directly impact what our collective future looks like.

Although this chapter focused on the connection between young people and our future, it is also important to recognize that young people bring value to, and help create, our present reality. They do so by bringing their presence, ideas, and talents into our communities and schools every day, which in turn, helps shape who and what we are as a society.

NOTES

1. Maure Ann Metzger and Richard S. Scott, *Solution-Focused Practices: Listening Groups Summary Report,* Carver-Scott Educational Cooperative (2010).

2. Ruben Garza, Gail Ryser, and Kathryn Lee, "Illuminating Adolescent Voices: Identifying High School Students' Perceptions of Teacher Caring," *Academic Leadership Journal* 7, no. 4 (2009), accessed January 9, 2015,http://contentcat.fhsu.edu/cdm/compoundobject/collection/p15732coll4/id/420/rec/1.

3. Samuel Perez, "An Ethic of Caring in Teaching Culturally Diverse Students," *Education* 121, no. 1 (2000): 102–5.

4. Garza, Ryser, and Lee, "Illuminating Adolescent Voices."

5. Ibid.

6. Ibid.

7. Ibid.

8. Patricia King and Tak Cheung Chan, "Teachers' and Students' Perceptions on Teachers' Caring Behaviors," paper, Annual Meeting of Gera, 2011, accessed January 9, 2015,http://files.eric.ed.gov/fulltext/ED525290.pdf.

9. Ruben Garza, "Latino and White High School Students' Perceptions of Caring Behaviors: Are We Culturally Responsive to our Students?" *Urban Education* 44, no. 3 (2009): 297–321, accessed January 9, 2015,http://www.education.txstate.edu/ci/people/faculty/Garza/contentParagraph/03/document/Garza+2.pdf.

10. Deborah Schussler and Angelo Collins, "An Empirical Exploration of the Who, What, and How of School Care," *Teacher College Record* 108, no. 7 (2006): 1460–95.

11. Jennifer Nelsen, "At Risk Youth: Give Them the Knowledge to Shine," presentation at the Minnesota Social Services Association Annual Training Conference and Expo, Minneapolis, Minnesota, 2011.

12. Samuel Perez, "An Ethic of Caring in Teaching Culturally Diverse Students," *Education* 121, no. 1 (2000): 102–5; Deborah Schussler and Angelo Collins, "An Empirical Exploration of the Who, What, and How of School Care," *Teacher College Record* 108, no. 7 (2006): 1460–95.

13. Linda Kramer Schlosser, "Teacher Distance and Student Disengagement: School Lives on the Margin," *Journal of Teacher Education* 43, no. 2 (1992): 128–40.

14. Ibid.

15. Karen J. Pittman and Marlene Wright, *Bridging the Gap: A Rationale for Enhancing the Role of Community Organizations in Promoting Youth Development*, The Task Force on Youth Development and Community Programs at the Carnegie Council on Adolescent Development (1991), accessed January 24, 2015,http://files.eric.ed.gov/fulltext/ED364804.pdf.

16. Ibid.

17. Clea McNeely and Jayne Blanchard, *The Teen Years Explained: A Guide to Healthy Adolescent Development*, John Hopkins University (2010), accessed January 9, 2015,http://www.jhsph.edu/research/centers-and-institutes/center-for-adolescent-health/_includes/interactive%20guide.pdf.

18. *Community Programs to Promote Youth Development*, Institute of Medicine, National Research Council of the National Academies (2004), accessed January 9, 2015, http://www.iom.edu/~/media/Files/Report%20Files/2004/Community-Programs-to-Promote-Youth-Development/FINALCommunityPrograms8Pager.pdf.

19. Ibid.

20. McNeely and Blanchard, *The Teen Years Explained*.

21. Ibid.

22. Daniel R. Weinberger, Brita Elvevag, and Jay N. Giedd, *The Adolescent Brain: A Work in Progress*, The National Campaign to Prevent Teen Pregnancy (2005), accessed January 9, 2015,http://web.calstatela.edu/faculty/dherz/Teenagebrain.workinprogress.pdf.

23. "Adolescent Development E-Learning Module," Office of Adolescent Health, U.S. Department of Health & Human Services, accessed January 9, 2015,http://www.hhs.gov/ash/oah/resources-and-publications/learning/ad_dev/.

24. McNeely and Blanchard, *The Teen Years Explained*.

25. "The Teenage Brain, How Youth Learn: A Portfolio to Inform and Inspire Educators, Students, Parents & More," What Kids Can Do, Next Generation Press, accessed January 9, 2015,http://howyouthlearn.org/research_teenagebrain.html.

26. Carolyn Gregoire, "American Teens Are Even More Stressed Than Adults," *Huffington Post*, February 11, 2014, accessed January 9, 2015,http://www.huffingtonpost.com/2014/02/11/american-teens-are-even-m_n_4768204.html.

27. "Adolescence: An Age of Opportunity," Executive Summary in *The State of the World's Children 2011*. New York: United Nations Children's Fund, 2011.

28. Garza, "Latino and White High School Students' Perceptions of Caring Behaviors."

29. Nicole Yohalem and Karen Pittman, foreword to *The Teen Years Explained: A Guide to Healthy Adolescent Development*, by McNeely and Blanchard.

30. *The State of America's Children 2014*, Children's Defense Fund (2014), accessed January 9, 2015, http://www.childrensdefense.org/library/state-of-americas-children/2014-soac.pdf.

31. Ibid.

32. "Educational Expenditure Statistics 2013," European Commission, accessed January 9, 2015,http://ec.europa.eu/eurostat/statistics-explained/index.php/Educational_expenditure_statistics.

33. *The State of America's Children 2014*.

34. Linda Darling-Hammond, "From 'Separate but Equal' to 'No Child Left Behind': The Collision of New Standards and Old Inequalities," in *Many Children Left Behind: How the No Child Left Behind Act Is Damaging Our Children and Our Schools*, eds. Deborah Meier and George Wood (Boston: Beacon Press, 2004), 3–32.

35.   Elizabeth Prann, "States Spend Almost Four Times More Per Capita on Incarcerating Prisoners Than Educating Students," Fox News, March 14, 2011, accessed January 9, 2015,http://www.foxnews.com/politics/2011/03/14/states-spend-times-incarcerating-educating-studies-say-464156987/.

36.   Kathryn Hanson and Deborah Stipek, "Schools v. Prisons: Education's the Way to Cut Prison Population," *San Jose Mercury News*, May 16, 2014, accessed January 9, 2015,http://www.mercurynews.com/opinion/ci_25771303/schools-v-prisons-educations-way-cut-prison-population.

37.   James Youniss and Allison J. Ruth, "Approaching Policy for Adolescent Development in the 21st Century," in *The Changing Adolescent Experience: Societal Trends and the Transition to Adulthood*, eds. Jeylan T. Mortimer and Reed W. Larson (New York: Cambridge University Press, 2002), 250–71.

38.   William J. Mathis, "NCLB and High Stakes Accountability: A Cure? Or a Symptom of the Disease?" *Educational Horizons* 82, no. 2 (2004): 143–53.

Chapter Seven

The Power of Empowerment

Before, I was all about books. I loved to read them.
It really inspired me to read about all these people
changing their lives and the lives around them,
but now . . . I am definitely more about being the person
the books are being written about.
This was the perfect class for me to take right before graduation.
I really feel inspired to do something, something positive, with my life.
—Stephanie

Stephanie was asked to create a written or visual representation of her accomplishments in her Leadership class at a local alternative high school. She
had drawn two images: one of herself standing by a pile of academic and
other books, and a second image in which she had thrown all the books into a
trash can. In the first drawing Stephanie was smiling, in the second her
expression was bolder and more exuberant. When asked to explain her image, Stephanie shared the response noted in the opening quote. The class had
allowed her to move from being a passive audience member in her life to
being an active director of her future. Stephanie had gained a sense of confidence and efficacy to act on her world.

EMPOWERMENT

What does it take for students to move from being passive observers and
recipients of knowledge to being active decision makers and architects of
their lives? While valuing youth, as discussed in chapter 6, is critical for
helping young people to build a positive sense of self and their importance as
members of our schools and communities, it is not enough. Valuation must
be accompanied by a sense of personal efficacy that is also connected to a

larger, collective efficacy so that young people can see themselves as individuals and groups that matter.

Moving from a place of passivity to one of efficacy and agency does not happen easily for most young people in school settings. Although educators want students to be invested and responsible for their futures, schools provide few opportunities for students to practice the necessary skills and roles that help build a sense of mastery over one's life and future. The historical, institutional, and hierarchical nature of schools impedes the kind of empowerment that is essential for young people to build a much-needed sense of efficacy and agency.

So what is empowerment, and what does it mean for young people, especially within the school setting? Empowerment is a process that strengthens and activates an individual or group's capacity to satisfy their own needs, solve their own problems, and acquire the necessary resources to take control over their life.[1] It is a multidimensional social process that helps people to act on issues they define as important.[2] Relevant to youth, empowerment is defined as an attitudinal, structural, and cultural process whereby young people gain the ability, authority, and agency to make decisions and implement change in their own lives and the lives of other people.[3]

Empowerment does not just happen on its own. Certain conditions must prevail.[4] First, for empowerment to occur, power must be able to change. The fact that power is created within the context of a relationship between people or things makes it amenable to change. Second, the viability of empowerment depends upon the idea that power can expand, that it can be shared. People often associate power with control and domination. They perceive power as something that one person gains at the expense of another. But power can also be shared by, and mutually benefit, many people. This kind of power, "relational power," strengthens, rather than diminishes, the power of others. So if power is changeable and can be seen as something that is not finite, there is potential for empowerment.

Even if power is malleable and expandable, empowerment is not something all individuals or groups can easily attain. Groups that are either on the fringes of society or discriminated against often feel powerless. This is a result of being excluded from having a voice and decision-making capacity on issues that affect them. Young people are one such group. They are typically in one-down, authority-based relationships with adults who hold power over them. And when it comes to education, young people have little to no voice in the development of schools, classes, curriculum, staff, rights, and many other facets of their educational experience.

Individuals or groups who are disempowered can attempt to achieve empowerment themselves, or those who are not marginalized and who have access to empowerment opportunities can assist them.[5] Given society's adultism and oppression of youth, it is unlikely that young people can achieve empowerment on their own; more likely, they will need assistance from adults who are already empowered. That assistance includes proactive efforts to build in opportunities and mechanisms that will empower young people. Adults will also need to actively deflect actions that reinforce oppression or disempowerment of youth.

So how can adults help empower youth? Adolescents identified nine factors that influence whether they feel empowered: [6]

1. Nonauthoritarian adult leadership
2. Being able to experience and exercise power
3. Receiving education and training
4. Participating in critical analysis of issues
5. Experiencing an environment of safety, closeness, and appreciation
6. Being able to honestly express opinions and emotions
7. Accepting diversity
8. Developing a voice
9. Being able to take action

Youth are empowered when they feel they have choices, when they can make informed decisions freely, and when they can act on those decisions. [7] A key aspect of empowerment, the ability to engage in decision making, is often seen as a requirement for adult membership in society. This is problematic for adolescents as they remain marginalized in the adult community and are seldom invited to engage in collective problem solving. [8]

Within schools, there are few roles available to young people where they can take initiative or assume responsibility or authority. [9] There are very limited opportunities for students to make important plans or choices that are consequential for either the students themselves or the school as a whole. If we want young people to take responsibility, we must provide opportunities that support them in taking responsibility. "The way a child learns how to make decisions is by making decisions, not by following directions." [10]

Empowerment also involves recognizing, valuing, and using the knowledge, experience, and talents that already exist in young people. Such was the case when I asked Charlie what he had gained from being in his Leadership class. He initially said, "Nothing new, really." When I asked him what motivated him to stay in the class if he wasn't learning anything new, he responded, "I always knew I was a leader and that I could do the things we've been doing; I just never had the chance to show that before." In other words, Charlie felt he had the requisite skills and qualities for leadership, but nowhere in his school career was he granted meaningful opportunities to put them into action. Young people need environments where they can capitalize on their strengths and build skills that will help them in life.

Various terms and definitions are used to describe the concept of youth having an active role in education and decision making: youth engagement, youth voice, youth development, meaningful youth involvement, and participation. A common theme through all of the terms is a sense of agency and empowerment for students.[11] The term *empowerment* in this book encompasses the diverse terms used to discuss students' active and purposeful roles in education.

A PLACE OF DISEMPOWERMENT

Most schools are not structured in ways that encourage youth development, let alone empowerment. The Institute of Medicine identified "support for efficacy and mattering" as a key element for promoting positive youth development.[12] Support for efficacy and mattering entails youth-based empowerment practices that support autonomy, being taken seriously, responsibility granting, meaningful challenge, and making a difference in one's community. However, the opposite types of practices—those that are unchallenging, overcontrolling, disempowering, and disabling—represent how youth are typically treated in educational settings.

In addition to neglecting youth's developmental needs, schools are also guilty of keeping young people marginalized. Young people are seldom engaged in real decision making and power sharing in their schools.[13] That was not always the case. Student empowerment was strong in the 1960s and early 1970s when students were asserting their right to participate in decisions about their own education.[14] These efforts were about extending democracy and rights. Starting in the mid-1970s, student voice and power declined over time and students assumed a more passive role as recipients of education.

In stark contrast to the 1960s empowerment movement, current student voice efforts focus more on the benefits of student participation in order to improve reform outcomes, rather than to increase students' rights.[15] Focusing on student voice rather than empowerment, and linking it with successful school reform, is a less threatening concept of youth engagement than the empowerment of the 1960s. Today's politics require a justification of student voice as a means to increase student outcomes, especially test scores. Student voice for the purpose of individual rights is not legitimate in and of itself; it must serve the larger system.

Although current student voice efforts may serve as a catalyst for school change, engaging young people primarily for system-serving purposes is a statement of the continued devaluation and oppression of our youth. If schools were truly interested in empowering youth, they would do so solely because it helps emancipate young people and provides them with a much-needed voice in the institutions that serve them.

In the opening quote of chapter 3, Lorenzo advocated for youth voice in schools, emphasizing that young people should have more input with school matters as they get older. In actuality, engagement and leadership decline as young people age.[16] Young people are less likely to be involved in real decision making and power sharing in their schools as they age. In students' interviews regarding their Leadership class, it was apparent that they weren't used to having their voices and ideas heard and valued. When students spoke at a local conference, Ana was surprised that other people would listen to them and elicit their insights:

> We got to talk to some college people, people interested in a Leadership class, and we got to tell them about what we do. They were really cool and asked a lot of questions, and I liked how people asked for our advice and opinions. They actually asked for our advice!

It was also obvious that students weren't used to being treated as competent decision makers. Ana was astonished that students had full capacity to make and carry out decisions in her Leadership class, which was contrary to how she and her peers were typically treated:

> We students get to choose what we want to do. We get to decide on every-thing, like the design of our Peace Pole. I thought we were just going to design it and then somebody else was going to do it. It's always been like that. Nobody has ever given the students the chance to do things before, to let us do what we want to do and put their trust in us to do it.

Students have long been considered the least able and least powerful members of the educational community[17] and passive recipients of adults' decisions about education.[18] Education is something educators do *to* young people, not something they do *with* them. Many adults believe that young people are incapable of contributing to the development, implementation, and evaluation of services and programs.[19] Students who struggle with school are especially at risk for not being seen as people who can provide vital input into their education.

This belief of incompetency persists despite many young people being capable decision makers and actors outside the school walls. Young people often have multiple roles and responsibilities in their lives that they must navigate outside of school, yet within the confines of school they are not granted opportunities for responsibility or autonomy, as noted in Adrian's remarks about decision making in his Leadership class and the lack of it in his other classes:

> The teacher actually lets us make decisions. A lot of teachers, they say, "We're going to do this, we're going to do it this way"; especially at my old school, it was, "This way, this way, this way."

This kind of frustration plays out with students every day in our classrooms, where students remain largely voiceless. Even when adults are willing to hear what students have to say, adults still believe they are the experts—they are the ones who can best decide how to address students' needs or concerns.[20]

Empowerment of young people means that they can actively participate in the decisions that impact their lives. This includes schools, where students need opportunities to be decision makers and constructors of knowledge rather than passive recipients. Through her involvement in a Leadership class that supported youth voice, decision making, and action, Stephanie was able to move from being a passive bystander to being an active producer of her life and future.

YOUTH AS ASSETS AND RESOURCES

Before educators and schools can effectively empower students, they must first be able to view young people as assets and resources. William Lofquist, a noted practitioner in the field of youth development, asserts that young people are typically viewed in one of three ways:[21]

1. As *objects*: Adults believe they know what is best for youth. Adults make the decisions and generally believe that youth have little to contribute.
2. As *recipients*: Adults believe they must help youth prepare for the adult world. Youth are permitted to take part in decision making because it would be "good for them." Youth are not really expected to make contributions. Adults generally retain the power and control.
3. As *resources*: Adults believe that youth can make real contributions. Youth have an equal voice in decisions. It is recognized that both youth and adults have abilities, strengths, and experiences to contribute.

The first two views are largely representative of school settings. The third view is typical of community-based youth programs. Viewing youth as resources is critical as it is more apt to create and support a culture of empowerment than the first two widely-held beliefs.

Community-based youth programming is usually based on Positive Youth Development (PYD) principles, practices, and research.[22] PYD focuses on the strengths and potential contributions of youth and is a relatively recent shift in how adolescents are viewed and treated.[23] For about the first eighty-five years of scientific study of adolescent development, models and theories framed adolescence as a period of storm and stress, one of developmental disturbance. Adolescents were viewed through a deficit lens and were described as "broken" or in danger of becoming broken. Positive development meant the absence of negative or undesirable behavior: a youth who was *not* doing something—not taking drugs, not participating in crime, and such.

Collaborative interests of researchers, practitioners, and policymakers in the early 1990s led to a new vision and vocabulary that enabled youth to be viewed as resources to be developed, not problems to be managed.[24] Community programs began focusing on the strengths rather than the weaknesses of young people.[25] Programs were built on research, theories, and practices that promoted thriving in adolescence. The consistent, underlying principle was that youth need positive, nurturing environments in which to learn and grow. Another key principle of PYD is the understanding that all youth are developing, all youth have strengths, all youth have needs, all youth can contribute to their communities, and all youth are valued.[26]

Youth need positive and empowering experiences across the different domains in their life (e.g., home, school, community) in order to maximize their development and become healthy, productive adults. Youth programming that occurs in the community usually places a strong and intentional focus on positive youth development to ensure that young people successfully transition into adulthood. Schools, on the other hand, severely lack understanding and implementation of positive youth development principles and practices.

Educational institutions still tend to view students through a deficit-based lens. Educators often perceive students, especially those who struggle with school, as being broken and in need of fixing. This is not helpful, as defining students by perceived deficits, rather than strengths, marginalizes students and diminishes their hopes of getting an education.[27] The programs that are most effective at promoting positive outcomes for youth are formed around the positive assets they want to build, rather than the negative behaviors they want to avoid.[28] It is also more productive to engage young people as valuable resources who have the capacity to transform than as people who need to be "fixed."

Youth serve as assets and resources to adults and organizations (including schools) in multiple ways. Young people are typically motivated to explore issues of social justice and engage in cause-based action.[29] As a result, they often become the keepers of the vision, the ones who focus on the mission. Young people often speak their minds and bring a fresh perspective to organizational decision making. They change the content and quality of discourse for the better.

Young people provide other unique contributions through their interests, concerns, and passions, things that are not easily accessible to adults. [30] Youth bring valuable connections to other youth and can help leverage the participation and skill of their peers. They also bring underrepresented or marginalized groups into the organizational decision-making process. Another distinct contribution is youth's unique *insider* or *service user* perspective. Young people can provide firsthand information on what things are effective in the classroom and how they can be improved. [31]

In order for schools to empower youth, a key first step would be for educators to adopt and implement the PYD philosophy and principles within the school setting. However, implementing a PYD approach can be challenging for organizations for a number of reasons, including: organizational and cultural resistance to empowering young people; adults' reluctance to step back and let youth lead; young people lacking trust that they will be listened to or that they can impact the system; and logistical issues such as time, compensation, transportation, and scheduling that do not support youth involvement. [32]

Although they may face challenges and barriers to implementing PYD, schools can partner with community youth organizations that have successfully implemented PYD to grow their own PYD culture. Schools can also use information in the Resources section.

IT'S THE RIGHT THING TO DO

Although there are many benefits to empowering young people, first and foremost, it is the right and ethical thing to do. Young people should be granted basic human rights as valuable, deserving members of our communities, as Marie asserted in her interview:

> We have a say in things, too. We are human beings!

The signatories to the Convention on the Rights of the Child would agree with Marie. On November 20, 1989, the United Nations General Assembly adopted the Convention on the Rights of the Child (CRC). [33] It is the first legally binding international instrument to incorporate the full range of human rights for children (people under age eighteen). World leaders decided that children needed special care and protection; they also wanted to make sure that the world recognized that children had rights too. It is the most widely ratified human rights agreement in the world and in history. Currently, 194 nations have become States Parties to the CRC. Only Somalia and the United States have failed to ratify the CRC. The following are some of the key rights the CRC bestowed upon children: [34]

Article 3 (Best interests of the child):

The best interests of children must be the primary concern in making decisions that may affect them . . . When adults make decisions, they should think about how their decisions will affect children. This particularly applies to budget, policy, and lawmakers.

Article 12 (Respect for views of the child):

When adults are making decisions that affect children, children have the right to say what they think should happen and have their opinions taken into account . . .

Article 13 (Freedom of expression):

Children have the right to get and share information as long as the information is not damaging to them or others . . . The freedom of expression includes the right to share information in any way they choose, including by talking, drawing, or writing.

As they age, adolescents become increasingly capable of assessing their circumstances and making decisions on matters that affect their lives; hence, adolescents should be afforded opportunities that are congruent with their evolving capacities.[35] When youth are empowered, it helps them to become independent and better prepared for life, as Adrian experienced through his Leadership class:

> Another thing, with me being a senior now, that also helped me, 'cause like, so this is what decision making is . . . I'm not quite out there all by myself, but I'm kind of getting a sense for it, for self-fulfillment without actually being out in the world yet.

Society also benefits when young people are able to practice decision making, as noted in Adrian's remark:

> Your voice matters, and if generations before us want us to make their decisions, they need to let us practice, not just say, "Okay, you're an adult, make decisions now."

Similar to decision making, youth voice opportunities that support empowerment help create social capital for youth, which, in turn, can increase their opportunities to advance in life.[36] Kari's comment reflects the importance of enabling youth voice at an early age:

> I feel that if you don't use your voice, you're never going to be heard, and when you do try to use it and you haven't been using it, no one's going to listen. So you need to start using it while you're young so people can listen to you, because your voice, if nothing else, can get you farther.

Empowering young people through opportunities of voice, participation, decision making, and action holds significant benefits for young people, the adults who work with them, and the organizations that serve them. The benefits young people experience from having their voices heard and validated are not always quantifiable (e.g., grade points or attendance rates), yet they meet very important needs for young people.[37] They are the building blocks of development that help prepare young people for their future.

Including young people in the decision-making process allows them to experience gains in agency, competence, and attachment to social institutions.[38] Evidence of agency and competency was apparent with students who were able to use their voices and decision-making skills while completing service-learning projects in their Leadership class:[39]

> I believe we can. We can do whatever we want to do. —Shawn

> My confidence level has always been low, probably the smallest thing I've ever had in my life. I've gone through a lot of hard times in my life and this class has brought me so much confidence in myself, knowing that I can actually step up and do this. Before this, I didn't really think I could do anything. This class has just raised my confidence level. —Marie

> Know that things are going to happen. Even if you only have a $200 budget for a Peace Pole or to educate students, you will be able to do it because you have the power, you have the say, and you have the dedication. As long as you bring that energy, you're going to make a difference. —Marie

Empowerment is beneficial for learning and academic development. Young people learn best when they take on active roles, have opportunities for meaningful choice, and when they become contributors and change makers.[40] Likewise, when students have opportunities for voice, choice, control, and collaboration, they are also more likely to be motivated and engaged in learning.[41] Student voice and partnerships in classrooms also help reengage marginalized students and increase their academic achievement.

Higher-level cognitive skills are yet another benefit of student empowerment. In contrast to most curricula and pedagogy that seek to change the student in some way by increasing their knowledge, shifting their perspective, or modifying their behavior, student voice activities and programs position students as agents of change rather than targets of change.[42] As change makers, the ones who are creating change, students are able to develop higher executive skills. Situations that are highly prescribed require less executive skills, whereas activities in which students can explore, make decisions, and construct things involve higher-level executive skills.

Empowerment also impacts citizenship. Roles that allow young people to hold power and exercise influence are one of the strongest predictors of community connectedness.[43] When youth take on decision-making and leadership roles, it enhances their development and promotes civic engagement, which is important for effective citizenship in their communities.

Adults also benefit when youths' ideas, participation, and contributions are valued.[44] When adults work with youth on important matters, adults gain a better understanding of the needs of youth, a stronger connection with youth, more confidence in working with and relating to youth, and a renewed commitment and energy for their work.[45] Adults are also able to see youth as legitimate, important contributors rather than in negative, stereotypical ways.

In a study where student voice was implemented in their school, teachers' perspectives about youth changed.[46] Activities designed to build stronger student-teacher partnerships and improve communication led to decreased tension between teachers and students and increased informality. Both teachers and students identified one another as individuals rather than as stereotypes. Students were also able to partner with teachers to change classroom pedagogy.

Organizations benefit from youth empowerment as well. Including youth in the decision-making and change process creates a new power and synergy that can propel decision-making groups to greater innovation and productivity.[47] Student involvement helps to transform the attitudes and systems underlying the culture of schools and other organizations.[48] It can also help to bridge the achievement gap, engage diverse student populations, foster dynamic and supportive learning environments, and develop connections between schools and communities.[49]

Student involvement in school change and improvement efforts also produces benefits. When students have more formalized roles in school improvement, it ensures better and more sustainable outcomes.[50] Students can be engaged as decision makers, problem solvers, and change agents to help identify the issues and appropriate solutions.[51]

When involving students in school change, it is particularly important to engage those who have traditionally been excluded from the decision-making process. Including these students helps them feel more connected to their school, which increases participation, classroom attendance, and motivation to succeed, all of which contribute to improved academic success.[52]

IT'S THE DIFFICULT THING TO DO

Longtime practices and attitudes and political and economic barriers impede youth voice.[53] Minority youth, those who have disabilities, and other disadvantaged youth suffer even greater obstacles to having their voices heard. Empowering youth voice and participation will require eliminating legal, political, economic, social, and cultural barriers in order to create settings in which they can build their capacities and thrive.

Other obstacles inhibit empowering young people in our schools. First, organizations that serve youth are not necessarily structured to promote youth development.[54] Schools, for example, have mandates, goals, structures, funding sources, and accountability requirements that are in direct conflict with the needs of youth. Larger school and class sizes can be a deterrent for student participation, as can requirements for accountability of school effectiveness.[55] Hence, the needs or requirements of the system take precedence over those of the students.

Second, trying to change the traditional structures, practices, beliefs, and values of schools and educators is very difficult.[56] Teacher-student power and status differences in schools comprise yet another institutional constraint that is difficult to overcome.[57] Powerful norms that require deference to adult authority, separation of adult and youth roles, and the institutionalized roles of teachers and students make it difficult to implement student voice initiatives.

Granting youth power-sharing and decision-making roles may be difficult for educators if they believe that only one person or group can possess power. They might feel threatened by a shift to relational power whereby students have more decision-making capacity. Currently, the expectation is that the teacher is in control.[58] If students are allowed to make decisions, it is only under the condition that it won't disrupt the teacher's position of power and control.

Another challenge is one of trust. If adults have not had firsthand experience working with youth on change efforts, they may not be aware of, or may even doubt, young people's ability to be effective decision makers.[59] Adults might even believe that youth would obstruct the process. Or, in the case of educators, they may not know how to respectfully and effectively engage young people, or they may not have the necessary support to do so.[60]

Similarly, trust can be a major issue for young people who are not used to sharing or having power.[61] Given that young people's input, talents, and experience are not typically sought out in educational settings, students might not trust that educators have their best interests at heart. Student's reluctance to assume positions of power and influence may not be a matter of disinterest, but rather a need to build trust, confidence, and skills to assume newfound roles. Building trust and shifting the balance of power will take time on everyone's part.

Both structural and cultural barriers can deter youth voice in schools.[62] Structural barriers consist of formalized elements such as positions, policies, practices, and procedures. Culture barriers are more intangible; they are apparent in the attitudes, actions, interactions, and relationships of individuals in a school. Although structure and culture are interwoven, culture dictates structure. Student reluctance can also be a barrier. Most students have been conditioned to be passive at school as a result of years of being told what to do, so being asked to assume responsibility for one's self, peers, and the larger system can be uncomfortable and confusing.[63]

Moving to an empowerment model will also likely underscore the *isms* and inequalities that exist in the larger society. These issues may become even more intense as educators press forward with the difficult work of empowerment. Educators cannot allow themselves to be deterred, however, as it offers a much-needed opportunity to address the root causes of oppression and other social injustices that young people experience.[64] Addressing these tough issues helps counter the practice of blaming young people for problems arising from deeply rooted social inequities and institutional barriers.

For the sake of our young people and our future, schools must persevere despite the challenges, for if not now, when? Educators will not be alone in their efforts. Young people have enormous capacity to help create movement, but they cannot do it without the help and support of adults. Educators and policymakers must first unlock the gates and then invite youth to join them in creating more empowering environments.

YOUTH-ADULT PARTNERSHIPS

Youth-adult partnerships (YAP) are critical to the empowerment process; however, youth and adults working together in partnership is a fairly new phenomenon in the United States.[65] Relatively few adults have worked closely with youth in a sustained manner on matters of mutual concern or interest. The belief that youth and adults can and should collaborate on issues of importance contradicts prevailing policies, instructional structures, and community norms. As a result, there are few societal norms or institutions to support intergenerational partnerships.

Although YAPs are not common, especially in the school setting, it is important that adults cultivate opportunities to partner with youth as youth-adult partnerships have been found to strengthen the culture, structure, and programming of schools.[66] Youth-adult relationships mean that students and educators in schools will need to interact differently. Collaborating with youth means that adults must share the power they hold.[67] Respect, mutuality, and equality are important elements that can help bridge the power gaps.

Students who participated in a Leadership class spoke about the need for and significance of respect, mutuality, and equality:

> Respect and equality are very important. Even if you're forty-three and I'm seventeen, it doesn't mean you're better than me or that I don't know anything. You have to respect me and my ideas like an equal. —Lorenzo

... they [teachers] are going to be listening to us when we're talking, we're going to be listening to them when they talk. —Marie

... she's [teacher] helping out, she's one of us, she's learning from us, and we learn from her. —Jake

Using an empowerment model changes the power dynamics that define teachers as the sole authority and students as the recipients of what teachers have to offer.[68] In an empowerment model, teachers guide and support rather than direct students. Josh shared how the role of a teacher is different in a class that empowers students as compared with a more traditional class:

With Leadership class, it should be more about the students taking charge and doing what they are supposed to be doing instead of a teacher telling them what to do. It should be more the student's choice . . . I mean there are parts of the class that the teacher does need to step in, but with normal curriculum classes, the teacher is telling us what to do, guiding our paths on a strict route. With Leadership class, we lead; the teacher follows and points us in a direction if we get off course.

Despite the need and benefits of youth-adult partnerships, they are not easily attained in schools. Institutional constraints such as traditional and restrictive roles for students and teachers, power inequities, and institutional rules and norms make it difficult to develop partnerships that empower youth.[69] In order to succeed, YAPs need to be authentic, ensure meaningful roles for both youth and adults, and intentionally build trust and safety among members.

A study of thirteen high schools that worked on developing student voice initiatives revealed critical information about the conditions that enable or constrain student voice and youth-adult partnerships in the school setting.[70] The study found that establishing YAP in schools requires intentional efforts to push against institutional pressures to revert back to traditional teacher-student roles. Three specific strategies were found to help YAP persevere in aversive institutional climates.

First, it cannot be "business as usual"; explicit and clear expectations around youth-adult interactions must be established.[71] Second, accomplishing a quick and visible success can help establish legitimacy; and third, sufficient time and space must be allowed for relationships to develop and activities to be designed and implemented. Another consideration is that adults often have limited power themselves, so it is important that they are empowered. Research shows that the more empowered adults are, the greater they can enable power in others.

Youth-adult partnerships require significant cultural shifts that present challenges for both educators and students. Partnering effectively with youth requires a set of skills that must be learned.[72] Educators will need formal training and support to collaborate with students in ways that are different from the hierarchical relationships common in today's schools. Students will need training and support as well to help navigate new roles and to sustain their involvement.

ENVIRONMENTS AND EDUCATORS THAT EMPOWER

The most basic premise that educational policy and practice are based on is trust—whether or not adults trust young people.[73] Educational institutions and practices in the United States reflect a basic lack of trust in students and have worked to keep students under control and in their place as passive recipients of what others deem as education. Empowering young people calls for an environment in which young people are respected and trusted. Adrian felt empowered when teachers trusted and respected students as capable decision makers:

> When the teacher kind of stands aside and says the teams are going to do what they are going to do, it just gives some sense of self-respect; someone is trusting us. From what I've seen, a lot of teachers, the respect factor just isn't there. Once we actually have our decisions out there, just give self-respect to people who are willing to put their opinions out there.

In addition to trusting young people, adults must intentionally create the conditions and practices that will foster empowerment.[74] To do so, adults will need to change deeply held beliefs and take on new roles as allies and partners. Structures and processes must be revised and aligned with power-sharing beliefs and practices. Likewise, opportunities for youth voice, decision making, and leadership can help offset the institutional power inherent in schools.

One way to increase young people's power status in schools is to invite them to express their voices, ideas, and experiences. Youth voice is about expression, which is helpful for identity and self-development, but it is also about recognition by powerful others and inclusion in matters of importance.[75] In interviews with students, it was apparent that they felt empowered when adults really listened, engaged with them, and appreciated what they had to say:

> I'd really like people to know how really important it is and how much it means to the students, like I had a say in what we were doing and someone was listening. I think that is really important. For once, I felt like someone was listening to me. —Ana

Being truly heard can profoundly impact young people, validating that their ideas hold merit, as Jennifer experienced while on a Leadership class field trip:

> When we went to Best Buy we went and saw like the CEO or manager of that place and just her getting our input and caring about what we had to say made me feel really important and knowing that our opinions mattered. —Jennifer

School voice experiences range from expression and consultation to partnership, activism, and leadership.[76] Currently, most student voice activities fall at the less-intensive expression level. Students' roles at the lower levels of student voice consist of students primarily expressing their perspectives or serving as data sources. At the higher levels of student voice, students are collaborators, directors, organizers, and leaders. As the level of student voice increases, the need for adults to share authority, demonstrate trust, protect against co-optation, learn from students, and handle disagreement also increases.

Participating in higher levels of voice and participation, such as in leadership roles, empowers young people; it also helps to prepare them for future adult responsibilities. Danielle experienced this firsthand in her Leadership class:

> You walk away with intelligence and knowing what to do now. It helps you to grow up. Helps you to be responsible and teaches you how to reach your goals in a good way that you know is going to work, using step-by-step instead of expecting to go from A to Z in one leap.

Not only does the level of voice and participation matter, but the roles that students assume are also important. They can serve as decision makers and policymakers, organizers, advocates, leaders, philanthropists, service providers, educators, active learners, and researchers.[77] The more roles young people have, the more likely that a "youth-centered" approach is being used. When youth have few or no roles, it likely means they are being relegated to a peripheral or token role.

In addition to having diverse roles, it is also important that students' voices and participation are included at all levels within the school setting. Their contributions can help optimize educational practices and environments at the individual, classroom, and systems level. Some of the ways that youth voice and participation can be incorporated in schools include:

- Informing educators about what makes for successful experiences and learning in the classroom and school environment
- Identifying ways for learning to be more relevant to the needs and interests of students

- Assessing, planning, implementing, and evaluating youth empowerment efforts
- Partnering with educators to help drive school improvement efforts
- Assisting in developing the school's vision, mission, and values
- Planning, conducting, interpreting, and summarizing action research
- Speaking with teacher education classes at colleges or at other education-related workshops and conferences to help inform educators
- Informing policymakers

Other opportunities for youth voice and action include: preparing personal learning plans and goals; conducting student-led parent conferences; helping design discipline and classroom management policies; giving input into curriculum planning, design, and evaluation; evaluating teachers and classroom experiences; serving on hiring committees and interview panels; and joining the school board.[78]

Schools can also support young people to express their opinions through a common platform or adolescent-led organizations. These opportunities can help level inequalities and overcome discrimination, especially for adolescents with disabilities.[79] Examples of this include: youth councils and youth forums, community service initiatives, and online activism. Students and educators can also work together to organize an "Education Day at the Capitol," so that students can discuss their concerns with policymakers. This powerful opportunity enables lawmakers to hear firsthand from the people who are most impacted by their decisions.

Moving from a culture of disempowerment to one of empowerment, where students have voice, decision-making roles, and impact, is a significant shift and not easily constructed or implemented. It involves changing beliefs, relationships, learning strategies, and systems-level operations. Creating empowering environments requires careful consideration and intentional planning by educators. Policies, programs, practices, and leadership capacity will need to be reviewed and aligned to support student voice, participation, and decision making.

An example of successful student empowerment implementation is the Youth Engaged in Leadership and Learning (YELL) initiative at a struggling high school in California.[80] Students involved with YELL chose a topic to research and the methods to study it. Information students generated from their research efforts helped inform youth advocates and policymakers to create better programs and opportunities for youth. The first year of research focused on reforms needed at their high school. Students used surveys, documentary photography, and focus groups. Students shared their findings with a variety of audiences and participated in an educational forum in which students, school staff, neighborhood residents, and district officials came together to talk about the research and develop a plan.

As a result of their involvement in YELL, students increased their time-management, public-speaking, meeting-facilitation, collaboration, conflict-resolution, and critical-thinking skills.[81] They developed more self-confidence, community awareness, a sense of civic responsibility, and a stronger belief in their ability to make changes in their community. Students also broke down adults' negative stereotypes of youth, which led to greater youth voice in other important ways, such as the school reform process.

Educators and leadership were impacted as well. The high school's Leadership Team created two youth seats on the team to ensure student representation.[82] Student representatives joined the board of directors who were planning a new health center at the school, and one student was elected to the board of a local neighborhood improvement initiative. YELL is an example of how empowerment can have a far-reaching effect for young people.

Another effort to empower students and help teachers is Learning and Teaching Together, a project that is part of a teacher preparation course.[83] It brings together preservice and practicing teachers with high school students for the purposes of altering the power dynamics between students and teachers, preparing teachers to elicit and act on students' perspectives, and empowering students to assert their needs and wants as learners. The project is based on the premise that young people have unique perspectives on learning, teaching, and schooling—their insights warrant the attention and response of adults, and they should be provided opportunities to actively shape their education.

Creating a culture of empowerment also requires building the capacity of educators and school systems to engage and support young people in new ways. Although students can help create empowering environments, the adults in power are ultimately responsible for making this happen. Teachers, however, feel ill equipped to help students take on choice and autonomy in their own learning.[84] Staff at all levels of the school must be trained and supported on an ongoing basis to construct and foster opportunities and environments that welcome student voice, participation, action, and decision making.

Training teachers is not the only prerequisite to empowering young people. Educators must be empowered to act as change agents in the school.[85] They must be granted the same autonomy and decision-making opportunities as youth would be. Empowering educators allows them to recognize, value, and integrate the strengths, perspectives, experiences, and contributions that students bring to the school setting.[86] When teachers are empowered, they are more likely to empower their students.

Schools needn't start from ground zero to build empowering environments for their students. They can draw upon existing resources to learn about and cultivate youth empowerment. Community-based programs are adept at providing young people meaningful, active roles in learning and leadership.[87] With their experience and resources, community youth pro-grams can provide the necessary guidance and support for building school environments that empower young people.

Implementing Solution-Focused Practices (SFP) in schools is another means of setting the stage for beliefs and practices that empower young people. Solution-focused educators and school systems create environments that can foster change and competency and where students can become more responsible for their own actions and solutions.[88] Some of the same elements necessary for cultivating valuation and empowerment of young people in school settings are found in key principles and elements of Solution-Focused Practices:

- Students are seen as experts in their own lives and behaviors
- Students define their own goals
- The focus is on competencies, not deficits, of students
- Collaborative relationships between teachers and students are essential
- There is the belief that the problem is the problem, not that the student is the problem

Lastly, student empowerment efforts must include all students. In the past, student voice, decision making, and leadership have typically been limited to a small leadership or student government group or to those who have good grades, attendance, and behavior.[89] Lorenzo experienced this first-hand:

> Other schools had student council, but Lorenzo, yeah, no, Lorenzo doesn't lead. Not to take away from those kids, but at the same time, if you are not part of the popular crowd, you don't belong and you get degraded—it sucks! I know what it feels like to "be in the back." You do so much, but don't get recognized for that, only for trouble.

Schools need to ensure full participation of the traditionally underrepre-sented—those who are marginalized and disadvantaged. If schools only pur-sue students who are already active in positions of voice or leadership, schools are at risk for perpetuating existing patterns of power and privilege.[90] Similarly, empowerment cannot be limited to isolated activities in a class-room, or to a specific class, such as leadership or service learning. Empower-ment must take place at multiple levels—classroom, school, and district—and through a variety of strategies. Lastly, empowerment should be a well-planned and intentional process that is carried out by all staff in the school setting. It should be central to the mission, culture, and daily practices of the school.

HOW WILL WE KNOW?

How will schools and students know if young people are being provided meaningful opportunities and support for empowerment in the school setting? Resources for assessing whether schools are effectively empowering youth can be found in the Resources section. In addition, it will be evident that youth empowerment is an integral part of school culture and practices when the following conditions are present:

- Students are valued and treated with respect
- Students are considered the experts in their school experiences, and their input is critical to school planning
- Students are considered agents of change, rather than just sources of information
- Students have active, diverse, and influential roles within the school setting
- Students and teachers are collaborating on important matters
- School culture, practices, and curriculum are student centered rather than system centered
- Students, educators, and communities can see meaningful impact and tangible results of students' voices, participation, and leadership in schools
- Inviting young people to the table of decision making is no longer a novelty—their place at the table is expected
- All young people, including those who are most disenfranchised or marginalized, are empowered and considered essential to the educational process
- Empowerment is not an add-on or singular activity; rather, youth voice, decision making, and action are embedded in the school's culture, practices, and teaching methodology, and students receive regular school credit for their involvement in such activities

Attempts to empower students cannot be token or time limited. Empowerment must be ever evolving and far reaching. Most importantly, in their quest to empower young people, schools and educators must take great care to not compromise students' interests, replicate the status quo, or reinforce assumptions and approaches that undermine efforts to empower.[91] And whatever is put into action must be done for the sake of the students, not for the convenience of the school and its agenda.

SUMMARY

Keeping young people in a powerless, voiceless, one-down position is detrimental to youth, adults, and the community. Though it may be difficult to implement the cultures, practices, and structures needed to empower young people in our schools, educators must take the necessary steps to move schools in that direction. Despite the challenges, the benefits of doing this work are all encompassing, as youth empowerment builds the collective capacity of youth, schools, and communities. Empowerment allows young people to practice advocacy, collaboration, decision making, leadership, and other vital skills that help prepare them for adulthood and citizenship. School engagement, achievement, and connectedness also improve.

Youth empowerment is about valuing youth and recognizing them as assets and resources in our schools and communities. It entails a commitment to meaningful engagement of young people's voices, experiences, and skills solely for the sake of empowering them. Empowerment involves ongoing opportunities and roles for young people to be decision makers, problem solvers, leaders, and change agents.

All of this needs to happen in partnership—young people in partnership with educators and their schools—to create educational environments, cultures, and learning strategies that work best for students. Students need to become equitable partners and responsible decision makers for learning and for life. Furthermore, the most disenfranchised and marginalized students must be included in all these efforts, as they likely have the most to gain from learning and practicing skills that will help them advocate for and achieve their needs, goals, and places in society.

Schools have considerable work to do; empowerment cannot thrive in the oppressive environments characteristic of today's schools. Empowering youth must be an intentional and dynamic process of change that adults take on, with the help of youth, to improve the status and roles of students in our schools. Both educators and students will need training, support, and time to build and sustain empowerment efforts in schools.

NOTES

1. "Youth Voice Glossary," The FreeChild Project, accessed January 2, 2015,http://www.freechild.org/glossary.htm.

2. Nanette Page and Cheryl E. Czuba, "Empowerment: What Is It?" *Journal of Extension* 37, no. 5 (October 1999), accessed January 2, 2015,http://www.joe.org/joe/1999october/comm1.php.

3. "Youth Empowerment," Wikipedia, accessed January 2, 2015,http://en.wikipedia.org/wiki/Youth_empowerment.

4. Page and Czuba, "Empowerment: What Is It?"

5. "Empowerment," Wikipedia, accessed January 2, 2015,https://en.wikipedia.org/wiki/Empowerment.

6. A. DiBenedetto, "Youth Groups: A Model for Empowerment," *Networking Bulletin* 2, no. 3 (1992): 19–24.

7. *Facilitator's Guide*, ASPIRA Youth Leadership Development Curriculum, accessed January 2, 2015,http://www.aspira.org/sites/default/files/Facilitator%27s%20Guide 2012-V3. pdf.

8. Shepherd Zeldin et al., *Youth in Decision-Making: A Study on the Impacts of Youth on Adults and Organizations*, The Innovation Center for Community and Youth Development and the National 4-H Council (2000), accessed January 2, 2015,http://www.theinnovationcenter. org/files/Youth_in_Decision_Making_Brochure.pdf.

9. Joan Costello et al., "How History, Ideology, and Structure Shape the Organizations that Shape Youth," in *Trends in Youth Development: Visions, Realities, and Challenges*, eds. Peter L. Benson and Karen Johnson Pittman (Norwell, MA: Kluwer Academic Publishers, 2001), 191–229.

10. Alfie Kohn, "Choices for Children: Why and How to Let Students Decide," *Phi Delta Kappan* 75, no. 1 (1993): 11, accessed January 2, 2015,http://www.alfiekohn.org/teaching/cfc. htm.

11. Francine Joselowsky, "Youth Engagement, High School Reform, and Improved Learning Outcomes: Building Systemic Approaches for Youth Engagement," *NASSP Bulletin* 91, no. 3 (2007): 257–76, accessed January 2, 2015,http://www.leadingnow.org/sites/default/files/pdf/ Youth_Engagement_High_School_Reform.pdf.

12. *Community Programs to Promote Youth Development*, Institute of Medicine, National Research Council of the National Academies (2004), accessed January 2, 2015,http://www. iom.edu/~/media/Files/Report%20Files/2004/Community-Programs-to-Promote-Youth-Development/FINALCommunityPrograms8Pager.pdf.

13. Joel Tolman, Patrice Ford, and Merita Irby, *What Works in Education Reform: Putting Young People at the Center*, International Youth Foundation (2003), accessed January 2, 2015,http://www.iyfnet.org/sites/default/files/WW_Education_Reform.pdf.

14. Benjamin Levin, "Putting Students at the Centre in Education Reform," *Journal of Educational Change* 1, no. 2 (2000): 155–72.

15. Dana Mitra, "Student Voice or Empowerment? Examining the Role of School-Based Youth-Adult Partnerships as an Avenue Toward Focusing on Social Justice," *International Electronic Journal for Leadership in Learning* 10, no. 22 (2006), accessed January 2, 2015,http://iejll.synergiesprairies.ca/iejll/index.php/ijll/article/viewFile/622/284.

16. Tolman, Ford, and Irby, *What Works in Education Reform*.

17. Michael Fielding, "Radical Collegiality: Affirming Teaching as an Inclusive Professional Practice," *Australian Educational Researcher* 26, no. 2 (1999): 1–34.

18. Alison Cook-Sather, "What Would Happen if We Treated Students as Those with Opinions That Matter? The Benefits to Principals and Teachers of Supporting Youth Engagement in School," *NASSP Bulletin* 91, no. 4 (2007): 343–62.

19. *Positive Youth Development Toolkit: Engaging Youth in Program Development, Design, Implementation, and Service Delivery*, National Resource Center for Youth Services (2008), accessed January 2, 2015,http://www.nrcyd.ou.edu/publication-db/documents/2008-positive-youth-development-toolkit.pdf.

20. Francine Joselowsky, "Students as Co-Constructors of the Learning Experience and Environment: Youth Engagement and High School Reform," *Voices in Urban Education* 8 (Summer 2005), accessed January 2, 2015,http://vue.annenberginstitute.org/sites/default/files/ issuePDF/VUE8.pdf.

21. *Positive Youth Development Toolkit*.

22. Ibid.

23. Richard M. Lerner, *Promoting Positive Youth Development: Theoretical and Empirical Bases*, paper prepared for the Workshop on the Science of Adolescent Health and Development, National Research Council, National Research Council/Institute of Medicine, and the National Academy of Sciences, Washington, D.C., 2005, accessed January 2, 2015,http://ase. tufts.edu/iaryd/documents/pubPromotingPositive.pdf.

24. Ibid.

25. *Putting Positive Youth Development into Practice: A Resource Guide*, National Clearinghouse on Families & Youth on behalf of the Family and Youth Services Bureau (2007), accessed January 2, 2015,http://ncfy.acf.hhs.gov/sites/default/files/PosYthDevel.pdf.

26. *Positive Youth Development Toolkit.*

27. Ruben Garza, Gail Ryser, and Kathryn Lee, "Illuminating Adolescent Voices: Identifying High School Students' Perceptions of Teacher Caring," *Academic Leadership Journal* 7, no. 4 (2009), accessed January 2, 2015,http://contentcat.fhsu.edu/cdm/compoundobject/collection/p15732coll4/id/420/rec/1.

28. Thaddeus Ferber, Elizabeth Gaines, and Christi Goodman, "Positive Youth Development: State Strategies," *Strengthening Youth Policy—Research and Policy Report*, National Conference of State Legislators (October 2005), accessed January 2, 2015,http://www.ncsl.org/print/cyf/final_positive_youth_development.pdf.

29. Zeldin et al., *Youth in Decision-Making.*

30. Ibid.

31. Levin, "Putting Students at the Centre in Education Reform."

32. "Youth Engagement: Positive Youth Development," National Resource Center for Youth Development (NRCYD), accessed January 2, 2015,http://www.nrcyd.ou.edu/youth-engagement/positive-youth-development.

33. "Convention on the Rights of the Child: FAQs and Resources," UNICEF, accessed January 8, 2015, http://www.unicef.org/crc/index_30225.html.

34. *A Summary of the Rights under the Convention on the Rights of the Child*, UNICEF, accessed January 8, 2015,http://www.unicef.org/crc/files/Rights_overview.pdf.

35. "Adolescence: An Age of Opportunity," Executive Summary in *The State of the World's Children 2011*. New York: United Nations Children's Fund, 2011.

36. Mitra, "Student Voice or Empowerment?"

37. Dana Mitra, "Student Voice in School Reform: Reframing Student-Teacher Relationships," *McGill Journal of Education* 38, no. 2 (2003): 289–304, accessed January 2, 2015,https://www.bcps.org/offices/oea/pdf/student-voice.pdf.

38. Dana Mitra, "The Significance of Students: Can Increasing 'Student Voice' in Schools Lead to Gains in Youth Development?" *Teachers College Record* 106, no. 4 (2004): 651–88, accessed January 2, 2015,http://www.new.promente.org/files/research/ESPdocs/12633733.pdf.

39. Maure Ann Metzger, "An Appreciative Inquiry of Youth Perspective on Effective Youth Leadership Programming," EdD dissertation, St. Mary's University, 2007.

40. Tolman, Ford, and Irby, *What Works in Education Reform.*

41. Eric Toshalis and Michael Nakkula, *Motivation, Engagement, and Student Voice*, Students at the Center (2012), accessed January 2, 2015,http://www.studentsatthecenter.org/sites/scl.dl-dev.com/files/Motivation%20Engagement%20Student%20Voice_0.pdf.

42. Ibid.

43. Shepherd Zeldin, Brian D. Christens, and Jane L. Powers, "The Psychology and Practice of Youth-Adult Partnership: Bridging Generations for Youth Development and Community Change," *American Journal of Community Psychology* 51, nos. 3–4 (2012): 385–97, accessed January 2, 2015,http://fyi.uwex.edu/youthadultpartnership/files/2012/10/Am-Journal-of-Community-Psych-paper.pdf.

44. Barbara Cervone and Kathleen Cushman, "Moving Youth Participation into the Classroom: Students as Allies," in *New Directions for Youth Development* 26, eds. Benjamin Kirshner, Jennifer L. O'Donoghue, and Milbrey McLaughlin (San Francisco: Jossey-Bass, Winter 2002), 27–46.

45. Zeldin, *Youth in Decision-Making.*

46. Dana Mitra, "Increasing Student Voice and Moving Toward Youth Leadership," *The Prevention Researcher* 13, no. 1 (2006): 7–10, accessed January 2, 2015,https://eboardsecure.dcsdk12.org/attachments/080aee20-ba2b-4149-b28f-7d402eb4de1c.pdf.

47. Zeldin et al., *Youth in Decision-Making.*

48. Adam Fletcher, "What Is Student Voice About?" SoundOut, accessed January 2, 2015,http://www.soundout.org/article.107.html.

49. Adam Fletcher, *Meaningful Student Involvement: Guide to Inclusive School Change* (Olympia, WA: SoundOut, 2003), accessed January 2, 2015,http://www.soundout.org/MSIInclusiveGuide.pdf.

50. Toshalis and Nakkula, *Motivation, Engagement, and Student Voice.*

51. *Education Change and Youth Engagement: Strategies for Success*, Youth Leadership Institute (2009), accessed January 2, 2015, http://www.yli.org/media/docs/2648_Educationchangeandyouthengagement.pdf.

52. Ibid.

53. "Adolescence: An Age of Opportunity."

54. Joan Costello et al., "How History, Ideology, and Structure Shape the Organizations That Shape Youth," in *Trends in Youth Development: Visions, Realities, and Challenges*, eds. Peter L. Benson and Karen Johnson Pittman (Norwell, MA: Kluwer Academic Publishers, 2001), 191–229.

55. Dana Mitra, "Amplifying Student Voice," *Educational Leadership* 66, no. 3 (2008): 20–25, accessed January 2, 2015,http://www.academia.edu/2005795/Amplifying_student_voice.

56. Toshalis and Nakkula, *Motivation, Engagement, and Student Voice.*

57. Dana Mitra, Stephanie Serriere, and Donnan Stoicovy, "The Role of Leaders in Enabling Student Voice," *Management in Education* 26, no. 3 (2012): 104–12, accessed January 2, 2015, http://www.academia.edu/2005772/The_role_of_leaders_in_enabling_student_voice.

58. Kohn, "Choices for Children."

59. Zeldin et al., *Youth in Decision-Making.*

60. *A Framework for Success for All Students*, Schools for a New Society Initiative and Carnegie Corporation of New York (2006), accessed January 2, 2015,http://annenberginstitute.org/pdf/SNS_cogs.pdf.

61. Kohn, "Choices for Children."

62. Adam Fletcher, "Overcoming Barriers to Student Voice," SoundOut (2007), accessed January 2, 2015, http://www.soundout.org/overcoming-barriers-to-student-voice/.

63. Kohn, "Choices for Children."

64. Shawn Ginwright and Taj James, "From Assets to Agents of Change: Social Justice, Organizing and Youth Development," *New Directions for Youth Development* 26, eds. Benjamin Kirshner, Jennifer L. O'Donoghue, and Milbrey McLaughlin (San Francisco: Jossey-Bass, Winter 2002). 27-46

65. Zeldin et al., *Youth in Decision-Making.*

66. Ibid.

67. Mitra, "Student Voice in School Reform: Reframing Student-Teacher Relationships."

68. Cook-Sather, "What Would Happen If We Treated Students as Those with Opinions That Matter?"

69. Dana Mitra, "Strengthening Student Voice Initiatives in High Schools: An Examination of the Supports Needed for School-Based Youth-Adult Partnerships," *Youth & Society* 40, no. 3 (2009): 311–35.

70. Ibid.

71. Ibid.

72. *Youth Engagement in Educational Change*, The Forum for Youth Investment (2005), accessed January 2, 2015, http://forumfyi.org/files/Youth%20Engagement%20in%20Educational%20Change .pdf.

73. Alison Cook-Sather, "Authorizing Students' Perspectives: Toward Trust, Dialogue, and Change in Education," *Educational Researcher* 31, no. 4 (2002), accessed January 2, 2015,http://repository.brynmawr.edu/cgi/viewcontent.cgi?article=1017&context=edu_pubs.

74. Cervone and Cushman, "Moving Youth Participation into the Classroom: Students as Allies."

75. Zeldin, Christens, and Powers, "The Psychology and Practice of Youth-Adult Partnerships."

76. Ibid.

77. Tolman, Ford, and Irby, *What Works in Education Reform.*

78. *Putting Positive Youth Development into Practice: A Resource Guide.*

79. "Adolescence: An Age of Opportunity."

80. Yolanda Anyon and Sandra Naughton, *Youth Empowerment: The Contributions of Youth-Led Research in a High-Poverty, Urban Community,* Issue Brief, John W. Gardner Center for Youth and Their Communities (2003), accessed January 2, 2015, http://gardnercenter.stanford.edu/resources/publications/JGC_IB_ContributionsChallengesYouthLedResearch2003.pdf.

81. Ibid.

82. Ibid.

83. Cook-Sather, "What Would Happen If We Treated Students as Those with Opinions That Matter?"

84. Tolman, Ford, and Irby, *What Works in Education Reform.*

85. *The Promise of Urban Schools: In Search of Excellence,* Senior Fellows in Urban Education, Annenberg Institute for School Reform (2000), accessed January 2, 2015, http://annenberginstitute.org/pdf/Promise.pdf.

86. *A Framework for Success for All Students.*

87. Tolman, Ford, and Irby, *What Works in Education Reform.*

88. Linda Metcalf, *Teaching Toward Solutions: Improve Student Behavior, Grades, Parental Support and Staff Morale* (Norwalk, CT: Crown House Publishing, 2005).

89. Joselowsky, "Youth Engagement, High School Reform, and Improved Learning Outcomes."

90. Barry Checkoway, *Adults as Allies,* School of Social Work, University of Michigan, W. J. Kellogg Foundation (2001), accessed January 2, 2015, https://ppoe.at/scoutdocs/yi/Adults%20as%20Allies.pdf.

91. Michael Fielding, "Students as Radical Agents of Change," *Journal of Educational Change* 2, no. 2 (2001): 123–41, accessed January 2, 2015, http://www.edugains.ca/resourcesSV/StudentVoiceResearch/StudentsasRadicalPartnersofChange.pdf.

Chapter Eight

Real Learning for Real Life

In the real world, they don't want someone
that can just follow, do this, be this way . . .
they want someone that can step up, stand out,
and bring what you are that makes a difference!
—Andrew

After seeing how many credits he had left to earn, Andrew began working on his GED. He continued attending his regular classes while working full time and was able to complete his GED and enter the workforce before his class graduated. After transitioning into the professional work environment, Andrew realized that the traditional school experience does not prepare you for the competitive world of employment. In fact, it does quite the opposite:

Right now school is about "get them in, teach them everything they need to know (from an intellectual standpoint) and get them out." They don't actually tell you how to use that information. They give you food, but they don't give you a platter to carry it on. They don't really prepare you for the workforce. In the workforce, you have to come up with your own ideas, your own practices; however, in school it's the opposite—they tell you what your ideas should be, what your practices should be—it's totally backwards.

As Andrew discovered, being able to stand out and act independently is what gives someone that much-needed edge in today's marketplace.

FUTURE READY

Our economy and marketplace have shifted substantially in recent years. The world has moved from an Industrial Age manufacturing and production

139

economy to a Knowledge Age economy that is information- and data-driven and globally networked.[1] Instead of creating products, a knowledge economy converts information, expertise, and technological innovations into needed services. Accordingly, what is required to be successful in today's world is different from what it was fifty, even twenty-five years ago. In the early twentieth century, 95 percent of jobs were low skilled and primarily required employees to follow prescribed procedures.[2] In the present century, however, employees need to be able to communicate, collaborate, research ideas, and collect and process information.

Daniel Pink claims that we are now moving beyond the Information Age to the Conceptual Age, an economy and society built on inventive, empathic, big-picture capabilities.[3] The new way of thinking and approaching life requires *high concept* and *high touch* aptitudes. The upcoming Conceptual Age calls for people who differ from the knowledge workers of today—they will be creators, empathizers, pattern recognizers, and meaning makers.

With a new age comes a demand for new mind sets, skills, tools, and learning. Higher-order skills such as critical thinking, reasoning, problem solving, communication, collaboration, digitally based learning, and citizenship will be the new normal for the future.[4] Not only are these skills needed, but students like Ben also value them when given the opportunity to learn and apply them in the context of the real world:

> [The] most important learning in my school was Leadership class. It got me out in the business world, it showed me I could do more than sit in a classroom and do worksheets. Going to Los Angeles I learned business skills, marketing, networking, communication, public speaking. That's what school should be about, doing things like that.

The Partnership for 21st Century Skills (P21) brings together the business community, education leaders, and policymakers in a collaborative partnership to help ensure that all students are twenty-first-century ready.[5] P21's *Framework for 21st Century Learning* guides schools in providing the necessary knowledge, skills, and expertise that students need to succeed in work and life (see Resources section for the complete P21 framework). In addition to core subjects and twenty-first-century themes, the P21 framework focuses on three sets of skills most in demand for the twenty-first century and essential for success in college, career, and life:[6]

- Learning and innovation skills (creativity and innovation, critical thinking, problem solving, communication, and collaboration)
- Information, media, and technology skills
- Life and career skills

A significant gap exists between the knowledge and skills students need for success in their twenty-first-century communities and workplaces and the knowledge and skills students acquire in school today.[7] To prepare students for rigorous higher education coursework, career challenges, and a globally competitive workforce, schools must align classroom environments with real-world environments.

Academic competence is not enough to ensure success in life. Only three in ten seniors are college ready, and only four in ten high school graduates are work ready.[8] Success in adolescence and adulthood requires diverse skills and competencies—physical, vocational, civic, emotional, social, and cultural.[9] The demands of the future also require young people to be effective at innovating, making decisions, collaborating, and taking action.

REAL-WORLD LEARNING—WHAT STUDENTS WANT AND NEED NOW

Given the needs of the changing economy and marketplace, the traditional, one-size-fits-all factory model of education does not bode well for current and upcoming generations of learners.[10] In the present educational model, students must respond within confining, teacher-determined parameters (e.g., raising their hands while sitting in their desks), and their responses must match a specific, prescribed answer. Although unintentional, educators are teaching and reinforcing passivity, rote learning, external motivation, and compliance. Ironically, these traits are the very opposite of what is needed to be successful in the real world.

Students are also expected to learn a disproportionate amount of information through pencil and paper activities that have limited value in the real world, as Charlie noted:

> You do everything paper and pencil in school and then you get a piece of paper that represents all your paper and pencil work instead of having real-life experiences and receiving acknowledgement for that.

The learning needed to effectively prepare young people for the future, and real life cannot be limited to paper and pencil tasks and passive information acquisition. Students need authentic learning experiences in order to practice the roles and responsibilities necessary for adulthood, citizenship, and success in a world that is increasingly complex, diverse, global, and technologically focused. Real-world preparation requires students to be acting in, and experimenting with, the world around them both inside and outside the school.

Many young people have an inherent sense that what they're currently learning in school does not always transfer to the skills and knowledge needed for real life, as Charlie discovered:

> School should be about learning that general knowledge plus much more of a focus on preparing students for the future. Elementary prepares you for middle school and middle school prepares you for high school, but that's all about "school." That doesn't prepare you for "life."

Students value and understand the importance of acquiring life skills that have a direct bearing on their future. In response to the interview question, "What were the most valuable learning experiences you had in your school career?" Feliz was quick to cite the class that she felt had best prepared her for life:

> Leadership—speaking in front of people, you had to have people skills. I got those skills there and I use them. They helped me for the better and for the long run. I developed social skills that I needed to and wouldn't have made it without them. They helped me mature and I will use them for my future—job, college . . . I will have those forever.

Schools typically exist separately from authentic, lived experience.[11] School comes first, and life experience follows. The challenge is to integrate the two. Research shows that students learn more and perform better on complex tasks when they can engage in "authentic learning" that involves applying classroom knowledge to real-world problems.[12]

Students, especially those who struggle with school, want to see immediate and relevant benefits from what they are learning. They want and need real-world connections. Most of the students interviewed for this book and my doctoral research on youth leadership valued classes, programs, and projects with a vocational, leadership, or service learning focus. These classes were highly valued because they were connected to real life and real-world learning. Students were learning skills they could apply and use in their life, both now and in the future. They also considered these experiences to be meaningful because they involved active, hands-on, project-based learning that was engaging, empowering, and rewarding. Such was the case with Ana:

> I think I enjoyed this class [Leadership] more than any other class just because it's about what we have to say and what we want to do, more like hands-on. We go out and learn things instead of being in a classroom all day. We go out and listen to speakers and do things that are really awesome that we've never had a chance to do before.

Similarly, Adrian distinguished between book learning and the real-life learning he experienced in his Leadership class:

> Just like, you know, throughout the entire school period you read about it, [you] read about homelessness and you do research on it and you get information on it, but none of the teams are actually getting out there and seeing it. They're not seeing the effects of it, they're just reading about it. They don't have it right in front of them, people right in front of them, showing them!

Many students prefer hands-on learning to paper-pencil type learning because the community's real-life setting allows for a greater understanding and appreciation of the subject matter. Motivation is also higher when students are problem solving and applying new knowledge to real-world problems than when they are using textbooks and worksheets to learn.[13]

It was also important for students in the Leadership class to have immediate and tangible results, and to be able to apply their learning to both the present and the future:

> It's different than all my other classes, 'cause it's like you're going to use this eventually, and here it's like you get out there . . . You don't have to wait for your results, and it's just different, and you'll use it now, not just someday. — Jennifer

LEARNING IS AN ACTION VERB

Active learning is a powerful learning method. It has a more significant impact on academic performance than any other variable, including student background and prior achievement.[14] While content knowledge is important, students learn material and advanced skills best through active learning experiences.[15] Students compared their active learning experiences of Leadership class with their more passive learning experiences in the traditional classroom. They described their traditional classes as boring, monotonous, and book and seat based. Students preferred to be up out of their seats "doing," as Jennifer related below:

> It's more get out of your seat and do something, whereas in other classes they lecture and then they give you an assignment and you hand it in. It's monotonous and boring.

Jake shared a similar experience:

> It's like I learned more from Leadership than I learned in my other classes. Other classes you are sitting down doing work; Leadership class I'm up and doing something instead of doing paperwork or bookwork.

Accumulating or processing information is of limited value without action.[16] Thoughts and ideas must be tested out in the real world. Experiential, action-based learning enables students to learn by doing, by experiencing. In active learning, students are doing things and thinking about what they are doing. Active learners do more than just listen; they are engaged in higher-order thinking such as analysis, synthesis, and evaluation.[17]

Not only is active learning preferred by and advantageous for students, it is also a crucial aspect of brain function related to learning. Neuroscience research indicates that active engagement is necessary for learning.[18] Active engagement is a prerequisite for the changes in brain circuitry that underlie learning. As such, passive sitting in a classroom while listening to a lecture may not prime the brain for learning, whereas active, relevant learning experiences inside or outside the school enhance brain functioning that supports learning.

How can active, real-world learning be incorporated both inside and outside of the school building? Inquiry-based and collaborative learning methodologies provide real-world practice to learn the skills that students will need as they leave high school and transition to higher learning, training, and the workforce. Students involved in this type of learning are able to develop content knowledge and build the important twenty-first-century skills noted earlier, such as teamwork, problem solving, communication, and innovation.

There are a variety of inquiry-based learning approaches. In their article, "Teaching for Meaningful Learning,"[19] Dr. Barron and Dr. Darling-Hammond discuss three methods that are typically used for inquiry-based learning: project-based learning, problem-based learning, and designed-based learning. Inquiry-based learning also typically entails a great deal of cooperative, small-group learning, which can help students prepare for future work.

Project-based learning (PBL) is a dynamic learning approach in which students explore real-world problems and challenges and develop cross-curriculum skills while working in small, collaborative groups.[20] When using PBL, students complete complex tasks that result in some type of product, event, or presentation to an audience. Research studies validate numerous benefits of PBL over traditional instruction, such as gains in factual knowledge, the ability to transfer learning to new situations, the ability to use knowledge more proficiently in performance situations, higher levels of critical thinking, and increased confidence.

Project-based learning was one of the most inspiring and engaging teaching and learning methodologies for students who were interviewed for this book and my doctoral research on youth leadership. When Feliz was asked in her interview, "When were you most inspired or engaged in school?" she replied:

> When I was doing projects—I was excited for those. I wanted to be at school for the planning process and doing those. They made me feel important because you're going to be able to give your input, people will listen, you're

doing something good for the community and having fun. It's selfless work, but you do have fun, too. I love projects; I loved hearing about a new thing that we could have a part in helping out with. Something in me just makes me want to step up and help out when I hear about issues now.

Feliz's comments confirm that empowerment and engagement are important for students to thrive in school. Not only did Feliz like the technical components of project-based learning (e.g., planning process), she also felt empowered in the process. There were opportunities for voice, her input mattered, she felt needed (importance), she could contribute, and she was able to become an active agent both in her learning and the community. Feliz's reference to "fun" is also indicative of someone who is intrinsically motivated. Her interest and enthusiasm for learning transferred beyond the school and was integrated into Feliz's own life, of her own volition.

Project-based learning is a significant component of schools that focus on preparing young people for life, future education, and careers. The Partnership for 21st Century Skills has identified, studied, evaluated, and celebrated *Exemplar Schools* that successfully use 21st Century educational practices and structures to help students master the skills needed for success in life. [21]

The specific models and implementation processes for the P21 Framework for 21st Century Learning vary considerably among Exemplar Schools; each school is unique. [22] Despite the individual variances, one of the most common and transformational approaches among Exemplar Schools is project-based learning (PBL). Exemplar Schools that are engaged in PBL incorporate authentic learning—learning that focuses on problems or projects centered on issues that are important to students, the school, and/or the community. This, in turn, makes learning more relevant for students.

Other schools, such as High Technology High School, Expeditionary Learning, and Envision Schools, also integrate project-based learning on a schoolwide basis. Innovation Tech High School in New York, one of more than 130 New Tech schools in the country, uses project-based learning that engages students in authentic learning and meaningful collaboration. [23] Students work in teams to creatively solve problems in collaboration with businesses in the community. Students earn college credit and participate in internships and service learning. Learning is relevant, student driven, and takes place in an empowering learning culture. Students become self-directed learners who no longer depend on teachers and textbooks to search for a specific, right answer.

Project-based learning helps New Tech students gain the knowledge and deeper learning skills they need to succeed in life. [24] Students use critical thinking, creativity, and communication to answer challenging questions or solve complex problems. More information about how these and other schools use project-based learning can be found in the Resources section.

In design-based learning, another common inquiry approach, students are asked to design and create an artifact that requires understanding and application of knowledge.[25] Design-based learning is ideal for developing technical and subject matter knowledge. It calls for collaboration and allows for students to have specific roles, which enables them to become "experts" in certain areas. Skills used in design-based learning (e.g., teamwork, problem solving, creativity) align with twenty-first-century skills deemed necessary for success.

Design-based approaches can be used in many disciplines, including science, technology, art, engineering, and architecture, and are especially beneficial for developing students' understanding of complex systems.[26] FIRST robotics and ThinkQuest competitions are examples of design-based learning. Learning by design, in general, was found to produce better learning outcomes than traditional instruction.

In the third approach to inquiry learning—problem-based learning—students learn by solving problems.[27] Students work in small groups to investigate meaningful problems, identify what they need to learn to solve the problem, and generate solutions. Students then implement the solution(s), evaluate their results, and continue to develop new strategies until the problem is solved. Problems are realistic and have multiple solutions. Problem-based learning surpasses traditional instruction for supporting flexible problem solving, applying knowledge, and generating hypotheses and explanations.

A familiar and popular form of problem-based learning is service learning. Although service learning usually includes elements of project-based learning, it is fundamentally a problem-based approach to learning. Service learning consists of the following steps: identifying and investigating a community problem, planning ways to solve it, providing action through service, reflecting on the experience and what was learned, and demonstrating the results.[28]

Through service learning, students acquire twenty-first-century skills that prepare them for life such as collaboration, communication, and critical thinking.[29] Students are able to connect to the community and their peers in ways that are more powerful than basic cooperative learning in the classroom. They are able to learn twenty-first-century skills in real-world settings by engaging in service projects that address real-world problems. Students can see the value and impact of their efforts and contributions. This is especially rewarding and empowering for students who may not have experienced much success or satisfaction in school. Jennifer shared the impact of her service learning projects:

> Having mattered . . . making a Peace Pole and making our generation better and encouraging other schools to do the same. It's going to be there for a long

time and knowing that it was my year that helped put that in there, I want to be like, "Yeah, I helped with that," or "Yeah, I contributed to that," and be proud of it!

A unique model of education, the EAST (Environmental and Spatial Technology, Inc.), combines both project-based learning and service learning. The EAST model and EAST Core classes support students to work in a collaborative manner to develop twenty-first-century and STEM (science, technology, engineering, math) skills through student-driven service projects using the latest technology.[30] Research proves that the EAST model produces strong, scientifically valid student gains in STEM and twenty-first-century skills.

Another learning approach—cooperative small-group learning—is common in inquiry-based learning. Also known as collaborative learning, it consists of students working in pairs or groups to design a product, complete a project, or solve a problem.[31] Students benefit from cooperative group learning, as studies confirm that teams outperform individuals on learning tasks. Students also experience social and behavioral gains such as improved self-concept, social interaction, time on task, and positive feelings toward peers. In addition, learning to collaborate helps prepare students for the workplace.

Research shows that certain groups of students experience even greater gains from cooperative group work.[32] Low-income students benefit more than high-income students, urban students benefit more than suburban students, and racial and ethnic minority students benefit more than nonminority students. Students from alternative schools and special education programs who were interviewed for my doctoral study on youth leadership were asked what they valued about the group of students they worked with on service learning projects. One of the students, Marie, responded:

> Well, when we work as a team, it's really a bigger contribution because the more people that we have, the better to work on those issues in the world.

Marie elaborated on why it was helpful to work as a team:

> They [peers] are also very dedicated and try really hard. Having them also by my side and having us all work together, we do such an amazing job, and when we all just say we are going to do this, everybody gets it done. We just make sure that it happens.

When asked the same question, Kimberly perceived collaboration as a vital life skill:

> Because if you can't work with other people, you aren't going to get nowhere, because there are other people everywhere in the world, so you have to be able

to work. Even if you don't like the person, you have to be able to work and talk
to them and being able to be respectful and respect that person.

Implementing inquiry and collaborative learning approaches requires si-
multaneous changes in curriculum, instruction, and assessment practices.[33]
Teachers' responsibilities and roles change as well, and are potentially more
challenging and time consuming. Instead of "sages on the stage," teachers are
more of "guides on the side," serving as facilitators and coaches. The group-
based aspect of inquiry learning also requires teachers to be able to manage a
different kind of classroom dynamic that supports multiple groups of students working independently.

Although changes in teaching and learning are needed, existing barriers
can obstruct instructional change. Bonwell and Eison identified several challenges that can impede implementation of new teaching strategies: the powerful influence of educational tradition, faculty self-perceptions and self-
definition of roles, discomfort and anxiety that change creates, and limited
incentives for faculty to change.[34]

Some of the most significant barriers to implementing methodologies like
active learning involve risk taking: the risk that students will not participate,
engage in higher-order thinking, or learn sufficient content; or the risk that
faculty will feel a loss of control, lack necessary skills, or be criticized for
teaching in unorthodox ways.[35] To overcome barriers and challenges, supporting philosophies, beliefs, structures, and practices will need to align with
new ways of thinking and operating to avoid sabotaging innovation. Likewise, educators will need the training, tools, and ongoing support necessary
to implement new ways of teaching.

BRIDGING TO THE FUTURE

Teachers and parents often tell students that they aren't ready for, or that they
lack a good sense of, the demands of the real world. This is partly because
artificial yet solid boundaries exist between schools and life on the outside.
We confine students inside schools all day, releasing them when the last bell
of the day signals that they are free to return to their lives outside the school
walls. This routine repeats every day until graduation, when we release them
to their future, whatever that might be. The question must be asked, "Does
this model of learning and daily routines adequately prepare students for
what lies beyond?" The serious consequences of inadequately preparing students for adulthood are reflected in Lorenzo's remarks:

Students gave up twelve years of their life. Graduation is supposed to be the
end of the childhood road and the beginning of adult life, real life, but for so

many kids it is not that. They get let down by school and when school lets you down, what else do you have to turn to?

There must be accessible pathways that move young people from preparation to full participation and action in the community, workplace, and larger society.[36] In order to be prepared for life and roles in the real world, young people need learning opportunities in the real world. Schools must begin to create more flow between learning inside and outside the school—fewer brick walls and more blurred lines between learning that happens in the school, community, workforce, and college.

Schools like the School Without Walls High School (SWWHS), located on the campus of George Washington University in Washington, D.C., blur the lines between learning in the traditional school and learning beyond the school walls. SWWHS eliminates the physical and programmatic boundaries between an urban high school and a research university.[37] It uses its partnership with the university and its location in an urban setting to maximize learning for students. Using the city as a classroom, SWWHS taps into a wealth of resources for learning, creating a quality, student-centered, urban learning environment that emphasizes integrative, interactive, and experiential learning. One of the students who attends the schools says this:[38]

> We always have a connection back to reality, back to life, back to the other disciplines inside the school. That makes a big difference. If you don't have something tying it all together, it just seems like you're going to eight different teachers, learning eight different lessons. —Delonte Briggs, high school senior

Several other schools that have expanded learning outside the school walls into the community are featured in a documentary, *Schools That Change Communities*.[39] Featured schools consist of K–12 public schools in economically and environmentally challenged urban and rural areas.[40] Some of the schools and projects include high school students in South Dakota who built an interdisciplinary curriculum around a plan to save the town's struggling economy; Appalachian elementary school students who helped clean up a stream polluted by acid mine drainage from former coal mines; California high school students studying Roosevelt's New Deal who tried to create a New Deal for their farming community; and Oregon students who helped create a sustainable environment while learning valuable science, engineering, and math lessons.

The local community became the classroom for these schools, and real-life problems and issues became the curriculum and foundation for learning.[41] Schools integrated with local communities using an interdisciplinary, hands-on approach that engaged students, built civic responsibility, and benefited the community. In the process, students use critical-thinking and problem-solving skills to help create meaningful solutions for real-world issues.

The Build San Francisco Institute (Build SF) is another school program that takes place both at school and in the community.[42] Students are involved in a yearlong design program cosponsored by the school district and the Architectural Foundation of San Francisco (AFSF). Students learn subjects such as math, history, and writing in the broader context of compelling, real-world projects. Basic subjects become vital tools for conceptualizing, understanding, sketching, and building their projects. By integrating academic skills into a real-world setting, Build SF creates a bridge between education and the business sector.

The Build SF curriculum was designed to promote student interest in architecture-related fields, but it also serves as a vehicle for students who have no community context to gain voice and insight into the public process.[43] The noise level in the studio where students go every afternoon is much higher than would be tolerated in a high school classroom; however, the AFSF's program director characterizes it as "the real sound of learning."

When core academic curriculum is connected to the community, and the artificial boundary between the classroom and real world is removed, student outcomes improve.[44] As learning spills out into the community, it allows for deeper and more meaningful learning, lessons that cannot be learned and contained within a fifty-minute time slot in a traditional classroom. Moving learning from within the school into the larger community broadens students' options and possibilities for learning, training, jobs, and life.

Creating fluidity between schools and communities is not the only change that must be made to optimize students' learning and future preparation. The American educational system does little to prepare high school graduates who will transition directly into the workforce.[45] Other postindustrial societies (e.g., Germany) provide strong links between school and work; however, American students must find their way into the labor force primarily on their own.

Students with secondary school credentials in Germany have a much more orderly entry into the labor force, primarily because the majority of students participate in the dual system of schooling and job training (apprenticeships) related to specific areas of employment.[46] Students leave high school well prepared and well trained for specific areas of employment.

Finland is also proactive about preparing students for the workforce and higher learning. In Finland, students spend two weeks in a selected workplace as part of the overall career guidance curriculum.[47] In addition, ongoing career guidance at both the lower and upper secondary levels helps students choose whether to participate in general upper secondary school, in vocational upper secondary school, or enter the workforce. Other forms of learning, such as alternative workshops, apprenticeship training, and virtual learning, are commonplace in upper secondary education and help prepare students for occupations in the workplace.

Students in the United States need opportunities to bridge from high school to work and careers by "trying-on" potential areas of interest through job shadowing, internships, apprenticeships, vocational classes, or similar possibilities. Research indicates that students who participate in structured programs that link schooling with careers can achieve higher levels of education and better labor market outcomes.[48]

Some schools in the United States have developed links between high school and the world of work and careers. A recent reform strategy of creating schools with occupational themes helped to make curriculum more relevant and personally meaningful to students.[49] Occupational-themed schools typically provide a broad occupational focus to encompass a wide range of learning options (e.g., health occupations vs. nursing; industrial production vs. welding). Themes are not always limited to occupations; they can also focus on the arts, science, technology, international trade, aviation, and so forth.

In a theme-based model, academic content is integrated with occupational applications so students can see how various subjects are related, as opposed to traditional courses that are independent and disconnected from one another and future goals.[50] In addition to content-area relevancy, theme-based programs place a strong emphasis on preparing students for both careers and college after high school. They do so, in part, by including learning opportunities outside the school such as projects in the community or work world, job shadowing and internships, and cooperative education that integrates work-based learning into the curriculum. These experiences help blur the lines and close the gap between school and life beyond school.

MetWest, one of forty Big Picture Learning schools, is another example of schools that help students to bridge to real life by incorporating experiential learning and internships.[51] At MetWest, learning is based on the interests and goals of each student and is relevant to the real world. Students have individualized learning plans and work with mentors at community internships they chose. The school commits to educating one student at a time by using mentors and resources inside and outside the school.

The same absence of transitional bridges between high school and the workforce is also apparent between high school and higher education or training. Not only are struggling students sometimes dissuaded from pursuing postsecondary learning, they also have difficulty with the steps and process, which are not made explicit or accessible to them. Counselors with caseloads of a thousand students have insufficient time to effectively help high school students—especially those who struggle with school—move on to college and careers. The transition process cannot be left to chance, nor can students be left to navigate it on their own. If they are, students must overcome yet more obstacles in order to succeed in life, as Charlie experienced:

> I didn't have any goals for college. I didn't think I could. Yeah, I wanted to go
> to college to play football, but had no idea what that meant, "to go to college,"
> what that all meant. I don't remember that anyone at the [high school] ever
> talked to me about college. I got a sense about it since I have been doing
> research on my own at age twenty-one. I checked into the [university] and took
> the SAT test, but didn't have a high enough score.

Richard was also left to pursue postsecondary education on his own while trying to overcome his previous negative history and self-image with school:

> After I graduated, I told myself, "never again!" It [high school] was so bad,
> then going to college and doing so well, now I can't learn enough. I am like a
> sponge; it feels so good and gives me a huge sense of accomplishment! I only
> got six wrong out of 200 questions on the entrance test to college. That made
> me feel so good about myself. I had it in my head that I was stupid, I thought I
> would end up in jail and all that bad stuff. But now, if I keep setting the bar
> high, and helping myself advance, I will do well.

American students are expected to make the transition from high school to college, training, or the workforce largely on their own. Like other countries, preparing students for life beyond high school ought to be a critical component of U.S. high school curriculum. Preparation should start as early as ninth grade by developing education and career plans and outlining paths to graduation.[52] Building career education, planning, and practice into high school curriculums could include strategies such as researching different jobs, careers, colleges, and training options; field trips to various postsecondary options, including vocational, community, and four-year colleges; and community-based visits to a diverse range of potential job and career areas.

High school graduates who are pursuing careers and college can be invited back to speak with students about potential training, careers, and higher-learning options. Hearing from former students who are working or attending college helps build linkages that make the future more real and accessible for students still in school. Former students have credibility—they are similar in age, not too far removed from high school, and are doing what it takes to reach their goals.

Bringing students out into the community to learn about careers in different sectors of the workplace—business, trades, nonprofit, government, and others—is another valuable future-planning and preparation strategy. Students are able to learn firsthand about the career options within a given field, the daily functions of the job, and the requisite schooling or training.

The knowledge that students gain from these experiences is important; however, it is not enough. It is not sufficient to just know one's options and the required steps to pursue post–high school careers or education, it is also critical that students are able to actually complete the steps, which requires action and performance. Action- or performance-oriented preparation for college consists of activities like spending quality time at places of career or college interest, completing a (sample) college application and entrance exam, meeting with a college counselor, completing a financial aid application, shadowing a college student, or working with a mentor.

Likewise, job- or career-based preparation consists of things like completing real applications, creating a resume, job shadowing in an area of interest, and going through mock interviews with real employers. Internships and apprenticeships provide additional, in-depth opportunities for students to acquire practical, hands-on experience in the workplace.

When students enter and engage in the actual environments where future learning and careers occur, it becomes practice for real life. It breaks down barriers and makes the process more known, more accessible, and less intimidating for when students pursue future goals after high school. Interacting with their future in the present builds a bridge to the future, a bridge that can support and guide them forward. This type of preparation, however, cannot be limited to a one-time career class. Nearly every class that a student takes during high school should introduce potential jobs, careers, experts, and professionals who work in that particular field.

In addition to making the steps and processes to work and college much more explicit for students, schools must also broaden the options deemed worthy and viable for students, such as vocational schools, community colleges, and formalized training. As a culture, Americans tend to define educational attainment primarily in terms of high school and four-year college degrees.[53] Other postsecondary education and training options are not considered to be as valuable, leaving a large gap between the most common credential (high school diploma) and the next-most-commonly recognized level of attainment (four-year college diploma). Students need other viable options beyond just these two credentials.

SUMMARY

Although change and innovation are the new normal, educational methodology has not been able to keep pace with either the content or type of learning needed to function in today's world. While academic skills are still important, they are not enough for success in the twenty-first century. Students must be able to collaborate, think creatively, and solve problems.

A critical aspect of twenty-first-century learning is being able to learn in relevant, real-world contexts. Students need opportunities to engage in the classroom and community with the real-world issues, jobs and careers, data, tools, and experts they will encounter later in work, college, training, and life. Integrating real-world and community-based learning into curriculum allows for authentic learning and provides the much-needed relevance factor that is important for engagement and future preparation. Active, collaborative, and community-based learning, along with inquiry-based methodologies, are "real learning" for real life.

Students also need opportunities to practice transitioning to their future. This calls for linkages that directly connect high school with future employment, training, or higher-level education. These linkages require fluidity between schools, communities, and real life. Schools must make the processes for bridging between school and the (future) world of work and higher education or training more tangible, transparent, and accessible. Schools and communities also need to expand legitimate options for students after high school graduation, including formal training, apprenticeships, vocational schools, community colleges, and such.

NOTES

1. Bernie Trilling and Charles Fadel, *21st Century Skills: Learning for Life in Our Times* (San Francisco: Jossey-Bass, 2009).

2. Brigid Barron and Linda Darling-Hammond, *Teaching for Meaningful Learning: A Review of Research on Inquiry-Based and Cooperative Learning*, Edutopia, The George Lucas Foundation (2008), accessed January 25, 2015,http://www.edutopia.org/pdfs/edutopia-teaching-for-meaningful-learning.pdf.

3. Daniel H. Pink, *A Whole New Mind: Why Right-Brainers Will Rule the Future* (New York: Riverhead Books, 2006).

4. Michael Fullan, *Choosing the Wrong Drivers for Whole System Reform*, Seminar Series 204, Center for Strategic Education (2011), accessed January 25, 2015,http://edsource.org/wp-content/uploads/Fullan-Wrong-Drivers1.pdf.

5. "Our History," Partnership for 21st Century Skills, accessed January 25, 2015,http://www.p21.org/about-us/our-history -SkillsMaps.

6. "Framework for 21st Century Learning," Partnership for 21st Century Skills, accessed January 25, 2015,http://www.p21.org/about-us/p21-framework.

7. "FAQ," Partnership for 21st Century Skills, accessed January 25, 2015,http://www.p21.org/about-us/p21-framework.

8. Karen J. Pittman, "College and Career Readiness," *The School Administrator* 67, no. 6 (2010): 10–14, accessed January 25, 2015, http://forumfyi.org/files/School%20Administrator%20Article%206-10.pdf.

9. Karen Pittman, Merita Irby, and Thaddeus Ferber, "Unfinished Business: Further Reflections on a Decade of Promoting Youth Development," in *Trends in Youth Development: Visions, Realities, and Challenges*, eds. Peter L. Benson and Karen Johnson Pittman (Norwell, MA: Kluwer Academic Publishers, 2001), 3–50.

10. Trilling and Fadel, *21st Century Skills*.

11. Geoffrey Caine and Renate Nummela Caine, *The Brain, Education, and the Competitive Edge* (Lanham, MD: Scarecrow Press, 2001).

12. Barron and Darling-Hammond, *Teaching for Meaningful Learning*.

13. National Research Council, Institute of Medicine, *Engaging Schools: Fostering High School Students' Motivation to Learn* (Washington, DC: The National Academies Press, 2004).

14. Barron and Darling-Hammond, *Teaching for Meaningful Learning*.

15. Christina Hinton, Kurt W. Fischer, and Catherine Glennon, *Mind, Brain, and Education*, Students at the Center (2012), accessed January 25, 2015,http://www.studentsatthecenter.org/sites/scl.dl-dev.com/files/Mind%20Brain%20Education.pdf.

16. James E. Zull, *From Brain to Mind: Using Neuroscience to Guide Change in Education* (Sterling, VA: Stylus Publishing, 2011).

17. Charles C. Bonwell and James A. Eison, *Active Learning: Creating Excitement in the Classroom*, ASHE-ERIC Higher Education Report No. 1, The George Washington University, School of Education and Human Development (Washington, DC: 1991).

18. Rebecca E. Wolfe, Adria Steinberg, and Nancy Hoffman, eds., *Anytime, Anywhere: Student-Centered Learning for Schools and Teachers* (Cambridge, MA: Harvard Education Press, 2013).

19. Barron and Darling-Hammond, *Teaching for Meaningful Learning*.

20. Ibid.

21. "About the 21st Century Learning Exemplar Program," Partnership for 21st Century Skills, accessed January 25, 2015,http://www.p21.org/exemplar-program-case-studies/1255-about-the-exemplar-program.

22. Christopher Brown, *Patterns of Innovation: Showcasing the Nation's Best in 21st Century Learning*, Pearson Foundation, Partnership for 21st Century Skills (2013), accessed January 25, 2015,http://www.p21.org/storage/documents/exemplars/P21_Patterns_of_Innovation_Final.pdf.

23. "Innovation Tech High School," OCMBOCES, accessed January 25, 2015,http://www.ocmboces.org/teacherpage.cfm?teacher=2445.

24. "Project-Based Learning," New Tech Network, accessed January 25, 2015,http://www.newtechnetwork.org/about/project-based-learning.

25. Barron and Darling-Hammond, *Teaching for Meaningful Learning*.

26. Ibid.

27. Ibid.

28. John M. Bridgeland, John J. Dilulio Jr., and Stuart C. Wulsin, *Engaged for Success: Service-Learning as a Tool for High School Dropout Prevention*, A Report by Civic Enterprises in association with Peter D. Hart Research Associates (2008), accessed January 25, 2015,http://civicenterprises.net/MediaLibrary/docs/engaged_for_success.pdf.

29. National Coalition for Academic Service-Learning, *Engaging Students Through Academic Service-Learning: National Guide to Implementing Quality Academic Service-Learning*, Learn and Serve America National Service-Learning Clearinghouse (2012), accessed January 25, 2015,http://ncasl.org/wp-content/uploads/Engaging-Students-Through-Academic-Service-Learning-Implementation-Guide.pdf.

30. "EAST Initiative," EASTCore, accessed January 25, 2015,http://core.eastinitiative.org/home/EAST-Initiative.aspx.

31. Barron and Darling-Hammond, *Teaching for Meaningful Learning*.

32. Ibid.

33. Ibid.

34. Bonwell and Eison, *Active Learning*.

35. Ibid.

36. Pittman, Irby, and Ferber, "Unfinished Business: Further Reflections on a Decade of Promoting Youth Development."

37. "A New Approach to Schools," The School Without Walls High School, accessed January 25, 2015,http://www.swwhs.org/.

38. *Learning Opportunities for Children and Youth: Expanding Commitments, Blurring the Lines*, Forum for Youth Investment (2002), accessed January 25, 2015,http://forumfyi.org/files/Expanding%20Commitments%20Blurring%20Lines.pdf.

39. *Schools That Change Communities*, DOCMAKERonline.com, accessed January 25, 2015,http://www.docmakeronline.com/schoolsthatchangecommunities.html.

40. *Schools That Change Communities*, The Video Project, accessed January 25, 2015,http://www.videoproject.com/schoolschange.html.

41. Ibid.

42. Barron and Darling-Hammond, *Teaching for Meaningful Learning*.

43. Ibid.

44. Martin Blank and Amy Berg, *All Together Now: Sharing Responsibility for the Whole Child*, Coalition for Community Schools at the Institute for Educational Leadership, Washing-

ton, DC (2006), accessed January 25, 2015, http://www.ascd.org/ASCD/pdf/sharingresponsibility.pdf.

45. Alan C. Kerckhoff, "The Transition from School to Work," in *The Changing Adolescent Experience: Societal Trends and the Transition to Adulthood*, eds. Jeylan T. Mortimer and Reed W. Larson (New York: Cambridge University Press, 2002), 52–87.

46. Ibid.

47. Pasi Sahlberg, *Finnish Lessons: What Can the World Learn from Educational Change in Finland?* (New York: Teachers College Press, 2011).

48. John M. Bridgeland, et al., *Raising Their Voices: Engaging Students, Teachers, and Parents to Help End the High School Dropout Epidemic*, A Report by Civic Enterprises in association with Peter D. Hart Research Associates (2010), accessed January 25, 2015, http://www.civicenterprises.net/MediaLibrary/Docs/raising_their_voices.pdf.

49. National Research Council, Institute of Medicine.

50. Ibid.

51. "About MetWest," MetWest, accessed January 25, 2015, http://www.ousd.k12.ca.us/domain/1996.

52. Francine Joselowsky, "Youth Engagement, High School Reform, and Improved Learning Outcomes: Building Systemic Approaches for Youth Engagement," *NASSP Bulletin* 91, no. 3 (2007), 257–76, accessed January 25, 2015, http://www.leadingnow.org/sites/default/files/pdf/Youth_Engagement_High_School_Reform.pdf.

53. Kerckhoff, "The Transition from School to Work."

Chapter Nine

Engaged for Learning

No, because the Leadership teacher is always in a positive attitude
and she's trying to share that attitude and trying to teach us things,
and with other classes, we just sit like a stick of mud, of drying mud,
bored and tired and wanting to get to our next class and get the
day over. But in Leadership class, the day just flies by.
—Shawn

Shawn provided the above response when asked if his Leadership class was like his traditional classes. It is apparent that Shawn was highly engaged in his Leadership class, a positive environment in which opportunities for voice and choice and service learning projects were the norm. His class engagement was so strong that when he transferred to another school, Shawn continued to call and inquire about how "our" project was going.

Not only does success in the twenty-first century call for different types of learning that can better prepare young people for life beyond high school, it also calls for approaches that effectively engage young people in the learning process. How schools and educators engage students matters. Engagement is a vital strategy for involving students in their own learning in ways that nurture a desire to learn, take initiative, and seek opportunities to grow.[1]

Student engagement is a strong predictor of achievement and behavior in school, regardless of socioeconomic status.[2] When students are engaged in school, they tend to have higher grades and test scores and are less likely to drop out of school. Conversely, students with low levels of engagement are at risk for a variety of negative consequences, including disruptive behavior, absenteeism, and dropping out. Research shows that young people who are engaged emotionally, cognitively, and behaviorally in learning also have higher school connectedness.[3]

Engagement is essential as it leads to sustained interaction and practice.[4] When students are engaged for longer periods of time, they are more likely to build skills and achieve success. This increases their confidence and competence, which in turn, motivates them to engage and attempt increasingly complex academic tasks, which ultimately leads to improved learning and achievement. It creates a positive self-perpetuating cycle of engagement and competence.

UNPLUGGED FROM SCHOOL

Although research links higher levels of school engagement with improved academic performance, engaging students within traditional, bureaucratic school structures is a challenge.[5] Results from the 2013 Gallup Student Poll revealed that 55 percent of students surveyed considered themselves to be engaged in school, which is down from the 63 percent of students who reported being engaged in school in 2009.[6] That means that currently, 45 percent of all students are not engaged in school.

High school students who report decreased engagement are more likely to be male, not White or Asian, lower in socioeconomic status, and receiving special education.[7] Students disengage from school when they cannot identify with school.[8] Identifying with school can be difficult if a student's background doesn't coincide with the White, middle-class values that exist in most schools. Students can end up feeling alienated and disengaged.

Disengagement is a serious matter. It can have a cascading effect on attendance, participation, behavior, and success in the classroom, eventually leading to dropping out, the ultimate form of disengagement.[9] So along with relevant, quality educational content, schools must be able to effectively engage students.

Studies of student engagement typically focus on traditional, measurable aspects of student behavior, including time on task, attendance/truancy, and suspension or discipline rates.[10] The High School Survey of Student Engagement (HSSSE), on the other hand, views student engagement as a deeper and broader construct, one that goes beyond traditional behavioral indicators.

The HSSSE addresses three dimensions of engagement.[11] The first, Cognitive Engagement, also referred to as *engagement of the mind*, involves students' effort and engagement during instructional time and activities. The second, Social Engagement or *engagement in the life of the school*, refers to students' actions, interactions, and participation within the school community separate from instructional time and tasks. The third, Emotional Engagement, also known as *engagement of the heart*, focuses on students' internal experiences about school—their feelings of connection or disconnection from school.

Schools that have effectively used the results of the HSSSE to inform their planning, professional development, and dialogue to improve academic performance, teaching, and learning environments in their schools are making progress.[12] One such example, Chesterfield County Public Schools in Virginia, used their engagement data to strengthen academics by focusing on relationships. Programs were created that focused on the needs of at-risk students to connect to the learning environment. Their investment paid off—student engagement rates rose within two years of implementing engagement strategies.

Shawn was quite graphic in expressing his boredom with traditional classes in the opening quote. Boredom, a temporary form of disengagement, is a common phenomenon in our schools, as 66 percent of students are bored at least every day in class in high school.[13] Of the students who are bored, 81 percent cited "material wasn't interesting" as a reason for their boredom, while 42 percent claimed lack of relevance of the material being learned as the cause of their boredom. Other major reasons for boredom included work not being challenging enough or too difficult, and a lack of interaction with the teacher. So what does excite or engage students in learning and remaining in school?

When asked to rate the degree to which certain instructional methods excite or engage them, 61 percent of students rated those methods that involve working and learning with peers (e.g., discussion, debate) the highest.[14] Group projects were also highly rated by 60 percent of the students. Other methods that excited or engaged students included learning opportunities in which they had an "active" role (e.g., presentations, role-play, art, drama) and projects and lessons involving technology. Students reported being least excited or engaged about the "teacher lecture" instructional method.

Students who had dropped out of school provided similar responses. The far majority of former students (81 percent) said they would likely have stayed in school and graduated if there were more opportunities for real-world learning (e.g., internships, service learning) that would make classroom learning more relevant.[15] In addition, 81 percent of respondents wanted teachers who would keep classes interesting, and 71 percent said that smaller class sizes would have allowed for more individualized attention and instruction.

Educators often blame students for a seeming lack of motivation and engagement, but students' abilities and efforts are not necessarily to blame.[16] Often, it is more a matter of the school failing the student rather than the student failing school. In order to help students, teachers must be able to identify and address the institutional barriers that keep students from being engaged in school. Teachers also need to know what factors support and promote engagement.

WHAT STUDENTS WANT AND NEED

The sheer numbers of students, formalities, and bureaucracies associated with a school system can make it difficult for students to obtain the individualized attention and support they need to feel connected to school. Consequently, students who are disconnected, marginalized, or alienated at school may need to be engaged personally and socially before they develop motivation to achieve academically.[17] Engagement requires a personalized learning environment in which educators take into account each students' unique blend of interests; cultural, social, and economic backgrounds; past experiences; and needs.

Along with a personalized, individualized approach to learning, various other key elements impact engagement in the classroom and school: relevancy of learning, teachers' role, school climate, class/school size, fun, novelty, emotions, decision making, methodologies, and voice/choice. While the following discussion addresses several important elements of engagement, it is not intended to be an all-inclusive list of influential factors.

Relevancy of Learning

In order to invest time and energy in the present, young people need to believe that there is a viable future.[18] Students need to be able to link what they do in the classroom today to future education and careers. If students can identify that a class or activity is a means to achieve an unrelated or long-term goal, they may be more likely to engage.[19] Charlie felt that it was important to build linkages between current learning and the future:

> Make sure there is more motivation. Make sure people know about what matters. I didn't really think ahead, like to the future, so building the "sheer importance" of your high school diploma.

As Charlie noted, utility value in education requires a future time perspective, an understanding of the connection between current tasks and long-term goals, and a belief that the goals are linked to school and obtainable.[20] Unfortunately, the utility value of courses and activities are often not made explicit for students. As such, establishing identifiable connections between content, required classes, and future goals can provide purpose and meaning for what students do in school.

Teachers Who Care, Connect, and Expect

Teacher support, as part of personalized learning environments, is fundamental to student engagement.[21] Research indicates that a caring, personalized learning environment is conducive to academic performance. Students who experience caring and supportive interpersonal relationships in school report more positive academic attitudes and values, more satisfaction with school, and more engagement in school.

In a study of students who were at risk for dropping out but continued to attend school, committed and caring teachers were more important to students' persistence than academic support or counseling programs.[22] Committed and caring teachers made a difference by seeking to understand students' behavior, believing in students' ability to succeed, and accepting students as they were. Another study revealed that students felt cared for when they experienced respect, flexibility, family atmosphere, belonging, and opportunities to succeed.[23]

Caring connections are particularly important for students who are disconnected from school.[24] Likewise, caring behaviors are important for culturally diverse students who may be at risk of failing or who are disengaged from school.[25] Culturally diverse students need mutually caring and respectful relationships with their teachers. They must like their teachers, and they must believe that their teacher cares for them as well.

Other teacher-related factors impact engagement as well. Students need teachers who hold them to high standards and who provide the necessary support to achieve those standards.[26] When teachers were observed to determine which teaching styles had the most impact on Native Alaskan students, four types of teachers emerged.[27] However, only those belonging to the fourth group—*warm demanders*—were successful with students. They consisted of teachers who demonstrated high personal warmth along with high active demandingness. Students in classrooms of warm demanders were willing to work hard for teachers with whom they had developed mutually respectful rapport.

Belonging

In addition to caring connections with educators in their school, students also need to feel connected to peers and the school as a whole. Strong relationships with both adults and peers in school function as strong predictors of student engagement.[28] When students feel that they are important and valued members of their school community, they are more likely to be invested in school.[29] On the 2009 High School Survey of Student Engagement, 57 percent of students agreed or strongly agreed that "I am an important part of my high school community." That means that 43 percent of high school students do not feel they are an important part of their schools.

Although feeling socially connected to school (teachers and peers) in and of itself does not guarantee engagement, it is a necessary element for many students.[30] When students feel they belong, it helps them identify with the values and goals of the school. Students who do not feel respected, or that they belong, are less likely to function effectively in school. Likewise, students whose values and culture conflict with that of the institution, or who do not find meaning in their schoolwork, may also feel they don't belong.

Class and School Size Matter

School and classroom size matter. Smaller classes and schools are more conducive to the success and engagement of students, especially students who struggle with school. Smaller classes and schools positively impact school achievement, likely because of the increased personalization and individualized attention that helps students to feel more connected, valued, and cared for.[31]

Two critical elements of school engagement and success—teacher-student relationships and individualized support—are difficult to achieve under our current school paradigm of time-limited classes with too many students. In a fifty-minute class with thirty students or more, if the teacher lectures or provides direct instruction for twenty minutes, that leaves one minute or less per student for teacher interaction and support. So on an average day of six fifty-minute classes, students will receive six minutes or less of individualized attention. The reality is that some students will receive more time, and many will receive none at all.

Smaller classes and schools help make a difference. In a small-schools initiative conducted in New York in 2002, students enrolled in the small schools (about one hundred students per grade) had higher graduation rates than students in a control group.[32] The benefits were apparent early on as 69 percent of ninth-graders in the small schools were on track to graduate compared to 58 percent of their peers in the control schools. Success in the small schools was not solely due to size, but rather to the personalized environments in which students were more likely to be known and teachers being able to provide the necessary academic and socioemotional supports.

Similar to the New York initiative, some schools have created schools-within-a-school (SWAS) as a way to capitalize on the benefits of small school size.[33] Some of these small learning communities are organized around an academic or vocational theme. Studies of SWAS and schools that have "houses" of 250 students show increases in achievement test scores, attendance, grades, reading comprehension, student responsiveness, and student satisfaction.

School size can be especially beneficial for economically disadvantaged students.[34] Small school size has been found to reduce the impact of poverty on student achievement. Smaller-size schools are beneficial in low-income communities, while larger-size schools are harmful. Small schools appear to be advantageous for students most at risk; they may also support greater equity in achievement outcomes.

So the true value of small schools and classrooms is not merely size, but what teachers can do when they can provide more time and individualized support in the classroom. Smaller schools enable educators to create a climate that cultivates engagement.[35] Educators are more able to have meaningful student-teacher connections, create a sense of belonging and attachment, and individualize instruction.

Climate

School climate is an important factor, especially for disconnected youth. Learning and engagement are cultivated by a school climate that promotes caring and supportive relationships, respect, fairness, trust, and shared responsibility by teachers for student learning.[36] School climate refers to the quality and character of school life. It is based on patterns of experience of school life and reflects the norms, goals, values, interpersonal relationships, teaching and learning practices, and organizational structures of the school.[37] A positive school climate fosters youth development and the learning necessary for a productive, contributing, and satisfying life. An engaging school climate also includes decision-making power for students and a sense that every student is essential to the process.[38]

Suspension and expulsion policies, on the other hand, can negatively impact engagement and school climate.[39] Though they may enhance the climate for remaining students, suspension and expulsion exacerbate the disengagement of students who were removed. Alternative approaches that can help keep students engaged include: discipline strategies that emphasize collaboration versus authoritarian-based punishment, democratic classroom principles and student responsibility, and climates of trust. Two other approaches, restorative practices and solution-focused practices, also provide constructive alternatives to suspension and expulsion.

The "F" Word: Fun

Quiet, orderly, disciplined classrooms are often assumed to be ones where students are learning; conversely, classrooms where young people are out of their chairs, interacting, and noisy are assumed to be "out of control" and places where students are not learning. Neither assumption is necessarily true. A few years ago at a national alternative education conference, a session was offered on "How to have the noisiest classroom in the school and be proud of it!" This would seemingly require a courageous educator, one who was willing to challenge the traditional notion of what it means to have students engaged in learning.

"Fun" is actually beneficial, not detrimental, to learning. When homogeneity and conformity replace joy and spontaneity, students' brains are more removed from effective information processing and long-term memory storage.[40] Despite this, many high school educators are reluctant to associate fun with learning. The invalid assumption is that if learning is fun, students must not be engaged in substantive learning.

At a national Service Learning conference, teachers were sharing stories of success and how fun the projects had been for both students and staff. However, one teacher shared that when preparing to present their project to the school board, she instructed the students to avoid using the word *fun* as they described their experience. She was fearful that the school board would think that they hadn't been engaged in quality learning.

As Jake points out below, fun and learning can go together:

> You can have fun learning . . . in a class, it shouldn't be just teaching, it should
> be having fun while you're learning . . . You're having fun while you're doing
> your work.

Incorporating humor and fun in the classroom has positive emotional and physical effects. The human brain and physical body react positively to laughter.[41] Laughter releases positive chemicals, increases oxygen levels, and builds community. Incorporating humor in lessons also helps to connect learning to a positive emotional event. Students appreciate teachers who use humor; having a sense of humor is viewed as another form of caring by students.[42]

Novelty

Both students and brain research affirm the benefits of introducing novelty and variety into learning. People consistently seek new experiences and behaviors as the brain is naturally inclined to pursue novelty and curiosity.[43] This is because discovery and action bring pleasure and activate reward centers in the brain.[44] New cognitive development is often accompanied by feelings of fulfillment and joy. When Kimberly was asked why she valued certain experiences in her Leadership class, she replied:

> It was like something that I haven't heard of before; it was a different idea. I
> like new ideas, so I thought it was interesting.

Surprise, novelty, and variation also help to gain and maintain students' attention so that the brain can engage and activate executive functioning and higher-order thinking skills.[45] As such, variety and the introduction of new things can help counter some of the routine or repetitive learning that many learners find boring.

Risk Taking and Decision Making

In order to build their decision-making skills, young people need opportunities to practice—to engage in real experiences that entail choice and negotiation.[46] A sense of emotional safety, however, is critical for risk taking as students are more likely to take educational risks when they feel safe in the school setting.[47] This type of safe risk-taking and decision-making environment was apparent in Lynn's classroom when they moved from a reward and points system of managing students' behaviors to one that used Solution-Focused Practices (SFP):

> Big difference—much more focused on what kids did well and their strengths versus deficits . . . It was much more positive for staff and it created a safer place for kids to take risks both academically and emotionally . . . [It] really seemed to show kids we were working together to help them, instead of an us versus them dynamic. It was tricky at first to understand how to hold kids accountable for behaviors, but once we understood, kids really started connecting their behavior to outcomes instead of feeling like adults were punishing them . . . We spent most of our time focusing on what they did well in a frustrating situation and celebrated the small steps of success which really helped them own their behavior and make real behavior change instead of an adult needing to "manage" their behavior.

Using an approach that encouraged students to take healthy risks in a safe environment, staff were able to support students to grow their skills and capacity. Students were able to take responsibility and ownership for their actions. Additionally, the SFP approach kept the focus on what students could, rather than could not, do. It kept the problem as the problem, not the student as the problem. Working with students in this manner led to more positive and energizing student-adult partnerships for creating change that benefitted both students and staff.

Learning Is an Emotional Experience

The emotional aspects of learning are as important as the nonaffective elements.[48] Optimal brain activation occurs when people are in positive emotional states or when the material holds personal meaning or is connected to their interests.[49] Engaging students' emotions in learning is also beneficial for memory. Emotions help activate and chemically stimulate the brain, which increases recall ability.[50] The more intense the amygdala arousal, the stronger the imprint. Students are much more likely to remember a field trip or science experiment than a lecture. Positive emotions help students to both engage and remember what they learned.

Learning Approaches

Learning is active, engaging, and social.[51] In order to apply high-order, crea-
tive-thinking skills, students need to be engaged and motivated. Students are
most engaged when they are constructing meaning rather than when teachers
are doing it for them. Learning methodologies and strategies that help engage
students, as discussed in chapter 8, include project-based, community/ser-
vice-focused, experiential, cooperative, and expeditionary learning.

Students who struggle with traditional instruction frequently excel in a
project-based learning context because it is a better match for their learning
style or preference for collaboration and activity type.[52] Studies also indicate
that students experience positive changes in motivation and attitude toward
learning when they engage in project-based learning.

The "active, doing" aspect discussed in the previous chapter is effective
not only for real-world learning but also for engaging students in the learning
process. Students enjoy school and put forth more effort when they are
active, rather than passive, participants.[53] Students are more likely to engage
when they are asked to conduct experiments rather than read about them,
participate in a debate or role-play as opposed to listening to a lecture, and
complete projects rather than answer questions about how a process works.

Service learning is another powerful way to engage students in learning.
Service learning is an educational technique that integrates community service into the academic curriculum.[54] In addition to the benefits of preparing
students for twenty-first-century skills, service learning also promotes school
engagement. Of students involved with current or past service learning
classes, 77 percent report that service learning has a very or fairly large
influence on motivating them to work hard and do their best in school.
Likewise, 65 percent of all students find service learning appealing, with
African American students reporting the highest level of appeal at 70 percent.

Studies demonstrate positive impacts on academic, civic, personal, social,
ethical, and vocational development for students who participate in service
learning.[55] Specific findings and benefits of students who were involved with
service learning include: higher interest and motivation for learning and engagement in school; reportedly, more learning in service learning classes
than other classes; improvements in reading, language arts, math, science,
and history; and higher gains in knowledge and political efficacy.

Voice and Choice

Much of what goes on in school creates and encourages dependency.[56] Students are dependent on teachers for instructions, assignments, behaviors, and
information. Dependency is counterproductive to learning. It places the focus

on the educator and not so much on the student. Dependency also impedes higher-level brain functioning. The front integrative cortex in the learner is not engaged, and as such, neither ownership nor problem solving are supported. This is important, as ownership greatly enhances learning.

One of the most powerful tools for developing ownership and influencing academic achievement is student voice and choice, which was discussed in chapter 7. Motivation to engage and do something is greater when people have a voice in the process or event.[57] Research confirms that the more educators give students choice, control, and opportunities for collaboration, the more their motivation and engagement are likely to increase.

As evidenced with Lynn's class, students do better when they are cocreators of their school experience. Hence, educators need to find out what is important to students individually, and use their goals, strengths, and resources to cocreate solutions that are student centered.[58] Doing that requires building relationships with students and treating them as experts in knowing what they need, setting goals, and finding solutions. The benefit is that when educators honor students' goals, educators achieve their goals much faster.

MOTIVATION FROM THE INSIDE OUT

Intrinsic motivation is the willingness to do an activity for the inherent satisfaction of the activity itself, such as seeking out novelty and challenges, extending and exercising one's capacities, and exploring and learning.[59] Although intrinsic motivation is inherent, maintaining and enhancing it requires conditions that support self-determination.

For students to be self-determined, they must experience three things: feelings of competence, a sense of autonomy, and relatedness.[60] When students trust that they can do what is being asked of them with some level of capability (competence), when they feel they have some control over an activity (autonomy), and when they experience meaningful connections to those around them while performing (relatedness), students are considered to be self-determined. Ben's remark about why he valued his Leadership class suggests self-determination:

> Why was it valuable? 'Cause "I" did it. It's something you went out and did and proved you could do it. [You] did it 'cause it was important, [you're] not just doing it to get a grade out of it.

Ben speaks of competence ("proved you could do it"); autonomy ("I" did it); and intrinsic motivation ("not just doing it to get a grade"). He likely also experienced "relatedness" during the course of his Leadership involvement. When these basic elements are present, young people experience self-determination.

Two other points are important to keep in mind. First, people's *own* perceptions of their competence, autonomy, and relatedness matter more than someone else's perceptions.[61] Second, the frequency with which self-determined experiences occur matters—the more frequent they are, the higher and more lasting motivation tends to be.[62] Given that self-determination (intrinsic motivation) is crucial for engagement and success in school, how can the essential elements of competency, autonomy, and relatedness be supported and encouraged in the learning process?

People experience competence and motivation when they take on and meet optimal challenges. Optimal challenges means being able to do something that requires effort and work but is also achievable.[63] It must hold challenge, yet it must be within reach to be motivating. Doing something that is relatively easy does not promote competence; people must perceive that it requires work. And for best results, the challenge must be linked with autonomy support, rather than control. Jennifer's comment represents the optimal challenge concept:

> I like to be challenged . . . I like to be challenged like that and being able to make something great when we basically came in with nothing.

Likewise, Marie's comment speaks to the value of achieving something difficult:

> It's just an honor to be able to contribute to something that is so hard to do.

Educators can set the stage for competency by providing learning opportunities that require students to expend optimal effort to accomplish a task but that is also within their reach. Finding that critical balance of requisite effort, yet reachable outcome, takes time, patience, and experience. If effort is minimal, students will likely be bored; if it is beyond reach, students may not even attempt the task. Competency experiences are especially important for students who have experienced a lot of failure in school. They need opportunities to use their strengths and to experience success on tasks that require substantial but not overwhelming effort.

Autonomy, another element of self-determinedness, entails free will.[64] When people experience autonomy, they are acting from a place of self-governance rather than from a place of being controlled or pressured. Autonomy is consistent with a perceived internal locus of control, whereby behavior is the result of one's own volition.[65] Motivation is enhanced by a sense of autonomy. While working on uninteresting tasks, students who were provided autonomy persevered compared with those who were deprived of autonomy.[66]

Autonomy support differs substantially from the more traditional, controlling, and hierarchical approach common in today's schools.[67] It requires that teachers change some of their beliefs and behaviors. Providing autonomy support involves building an alliance with students and being able to understand how they see the world. Lynn, the teacher quoted earlier, achieved this by implementing more autonomy-supported practices in her classroom.

Behaviors of autonomy-supportive teachers differ from those of controlling teachers. Autonomy-supportive teachers are responsive (spend time listening), supportive (praise mastery), flexible (give students time to work in their own way), and motivate through interest.[68] Controlling teachers, on the other hand, take charge, give directives, command, shape students toward a right answer (teacher-dominated problem solving); evaluate (criticize); and motivate through pressure (demanding and controlling).

Teachers tend to impose more controls with students who are more passive or defiant; however, they are the ones who need autonomy support the most.[69] The more students are controlled, the more likely they are to act as if they need to be controlled. Even though it seems to contradict what teachers might think, educators must refrain from the tendency to control, as doing so can actually intensify students' defiance or passivity.

Although a controlling approach is not helpful, even detrimental, autonomy support does not mean a free-for-all permissiveness; neither complete permissiveness nor rigid, harsh controls is productive.[70] What is more effective is helping young people master difficult situations. Autonomy support means being clear, consistent, and setting limits in an understanding but empathetic manner.

Students benefit more when teachers are autonomy supportive versus controlling. Studies revealed that students who had more autonomy-supportive teachers were more curious, mastery oriented, and had higher self-esteem.[71] Students with autonomy-supportive teachers also experience higher levels of academic achievement, perceived competence, positive emotionality, self-worth, creativity, and retention.[72]

A key element of autonomy support is providing *choice*. Danielle stressed the importance of choice and autonomy support in her remarks about an autonomy-supportive teacher:

> Most teachers will tell you what to do, and with ADD students, they're never going to do it; they're going to have to want to do it. And like with you, you stand by our sides and give us ideas. You let us choose what we want to do and when we figure out what we want to do, you help us achieve that goal.

Creating classrooms and school environments in which students have more choice requires more, not less, work on the part of educators.[73] It is much more demanding of an educator than the traditional, autocratic approach of simply telling or directing students common in today's classrooms. An autonomy-supportive teacher's role is more like that of a facilitator.

Similar to other new learning and empowerment approaches, teachers will need training and support to shift to a different role within the classroom and learning process. It is also critical that teachers are empowered in this process, as they are likely recreating the conditions they themselves have been subjected to.[74] Likewise, providing autonomy support for students doesn't mean that they will automatically gravitate toward it and feel comfortable with it; they are used to control and limited choice. It will take time to build trust, comfort level, and skills in this area.

While autonomy-supportive teachers and environments enhance intrinsic motivation, certain factors can undermine intrinsic motivation, including nonoptimal challenges, a lack of connectedness, tangible rewards, and praise. A meta-analysis of reward effects revealed that all expected tangible rewards contingent on task performance undermine intrinsic motivation.[75] As an external reward, praise can also have negative effects.[76] Praise that is controlling and that involves expectations and social comparisons decreases the natural desire to feel competent. Conversely, praise that is not controlling, that simply states, "You've done very well," supports a high level of interest and persistence.

In addition to tangible rewards and controlling praise, threats, deadlines, directives, pressured evaluations, and imposed goals also lessen intrinsic motivation because they are perceived to originate from outside the person (external causation).[77] In one study, the more students were externally regulated, the less interest, value, and effort they demonstrated for achievement and the more likely they were to not take responsibility for negative outcomes.

Meaningful change happens when there is a readiness for change; pressuring someone is not helpful and usually produces negative effects.[78] When people feel pressured, compliance or defiance often results. While compliance might seem desirable, it produces only short-lived change and adverse consequences, including extreme anxiety and maladaptive patterns of coping with failure. Defiance is also not helpful because it is an obstacle to change. Meaningful change occurs when people accept themselves, are interested in what they are doing, and decide to change on their own terms.

In addition to feeling competent and autonomous, people also need to feel connected with others.[79] Relatedness is the third key element of self-determinedness. The intrinsic need for relatedness opens people up to being part of a group and being socialized, which in turn can help shape identity. Teacher behaviors that support a sense of belonging for students help to reinforce the other two elements—competency and autonomy. In fact, these two factors need to be experienced within the context of relationships in order for students to feel self-determined.

MOTIVATION FROM THE OUTSIDE IN

With all the requirements and high standards mandated in education and the pressure to meet them, educators forget that these are not the students' goals—they are the school's goals for them. They are imposed requirements from people and systems far removed from the student.

> Much of education is about trying to coerce students into something they don't care about. Although adults are not likely to do things they aren't interested in, they expect young people to engage in and do things they care little about. — Doug Anderson[80]

Students likely won't put forth effort unless they see a valid reason for doing so.[81] Reasons for engagement can vary and are affected by the degree to which the students feel that the reasons come from within self (self-determination—doing it because they *want* to) or that they are being imposed externally (coercion—doing it because they *have* to). The degree to which students feel self-determining and autonomous, as opposed to coerced and controlled, impacts the quality of the effort and learning.

While intrinsically motivated (self-determined) performance is largely superior to externally controlled performance, many learning requirements in school are not designed to be intrinsically interesting.[82] The challenge, then, is to motivate students to value and engage in such activities without external pressure. For this to happen, students must be able to understand the meaning of what is being required and connect it to their own goals and values. Because much of school consists of external expectations and social mores imposed by others, it is important that educators know what helps students to move from compliance to more self-regulated behavior.[83]

The process of *internalization* can help young people accept responsibility for activities that are important but not intrinsically motivating.[84] The lesser form of internalization is known as *introjection*. This involves taking on the values and rules of a group by internalizing the "shoulds" and "oughts" of the group—the voices that come from outside the person, typically in the form of orders. However, this produces a superficial level of internalization and does not usually result in someone fully integrating the values or requirements. Attending classes and completing schoolwork only to avoid negative consequences is an example of introjection.

A deeper and more optimal level of internalization is *integration*.[85] Integration occurs when someone has internalized the value or behavior on a personal and authentic level. In order to integrate things that may be uninteresting but necessary for development and success in life, people need to feel autonomous and in charge of themselves. When the need for autonomy is met, people are more likely to integrate a given value or regulatory process into themselves.

In a study on motivation, people were given an uninteresting task to do. Those who were provided a rationale for doing the uninteresting activity, whose feelings were acknowledged (that they may not want to do the task), and who were given the request in the form of an invitation rather than a demand (emphasizing choice and minimizing pressure) exhibited more internalization than those who were not provided with autonomy support. [86]

External motivation can also come from important people in students' lives. [87] Students' beliefs and values, and the quality of a given relationship, affect the influence of other people as motivators. The deeper the connections between students and the motivators (people), the more likely students will internalize the motivations. Extrinsic motivation rarely becomes internalized separate from the context of meaningful, supportive relationships; hence the need for caring, supportive, relationship-based educators.

Students' motivation to persist with tasks is also impacted by their mindset. While it might seem that students who exhibit low effort might lack motivation, they may in fact be experiencing a fixed mindset and protecting themselves from being perceived as a failure by not trying. [88] Carol Dweck identified two types of mindsets that were important to students' efforts: The first consists of a *fixed mindset*, which entails the belief that people's qualities, such as intelligence, personality, or moral character, are fixed and limited in capacity. As such, people must prove that they have enough of these qualities or they risk feeling or looking deficient. The other mindset, a *growth mindset*, is based on the belief that people can cultivate or improve their basic qualities through effort.

Mindset is critical because it dictates how a student will respond to difficult tasks and failures. [89] A fixed mindset limits achievement. In a study where seventh-graders were asked how they would respond to a poor test score in a new course, students with a growth mindset said they would study harder for the next test, whereas students with a fixed mindset said they would study less for the next test. Further, students with a fixed mindset said they would even consider cheating. So instead of trying to learn from their failures, students with the fixed mindset may simply try to repair their self-esteem by assigning blame or making excuses.

How educators provide feedback matters, depending on the student's mindset. In one study, students praised for their *ability* relative to a task rejected new, subsequent challenging tasks that could expose their flaws. [90] Ability praising resulted in students taking on a fixed mindset. On the other hand, 90 percent of the students who were praised for their *efforts* of doing whatever it took to succeed wanted the additional challenging task.

Consequently, educators must help students understand that their achievements result from their having worked at something (which they can control), instead of having derived from an innate ability (which is perceived as unchangeable).[91] Despite past achievement history, if students can believe, or are taught to believe, that they can gain new skills and improve existing skills through focus and effort, their motivation to try will increase.

In addition to students having a growth mindset, it is also beneficial for teachers to have a growth mindset. Teachers with a fixed mindset tend to prejudge their students' abilities and achievement, whereas those with a growth mindset view achievement as changeable—something that is the result of hard work—and treat their students accordingly.[92]

Finally, while it is critical for students to be engaged and motivated, it is also important for teachers to be engaged as well. This was pointed out by Joseph, a thirteen-year-old student who was asked to represent a youth perspective at an educational conference on Finnish education in the United States during the summer of 2014. He summed up the kind of teachers students need in his "4 E's for an Excellent Teacher" presentation:

Experienced: Teachers that are experienced can understand, consider, and evaluate situations given to them, thus, they are able to better care for the needs of the child/adolescent.

Engaged: Not only should the students pay attention and be engaged with the teacher, but the teacher should also be engaged with the students. When this situation happens there is a mutual, beneficial relationship with the teacher and the pupil. The classroom becomes a better place. The teachers should be engaged with the students and the curriculum. Then, work turns to play. (For it is [through] the relationship between the teacher and the student that learning and true education is accomplished.)

Educated: All I can say for this one is where would we be without education? With it, we can open doors for the future. What makes teaching so important is that teachers and parents can shape the world of tomorrow. Educated teachers that know how to teach, and how to play, are a formidable combination.

Energized: There is no doubt that the teacher that is fun and exciting is the teacher kids would most likely learn and be interested in. Now, this is not an incentive to be crazy, but to find a balance between, if you will, Good Cop and Bad Cop. You need a balance between being fun and engaging and responsible and serious. It might be hard for some people but not impossible.

Like much of the current research, Joseph emphasizes elements that are important for engagement such as the importance of the "relationship factor" between teachers and students and the importance of "fun"—turning work into play. The wisdom of Joseph and other students provides valuable insights as to what students need for successful experiences in school.

SUMMARY

Engagement is essential to students' success in school and their motivation to remain in school. In order to be engaged, students need to understand the purpose and relevancy—the present or future value or application—of what they are learning. Connections between what students are learning and their culture, personal lives, and past experiences are also important.

Cultivating engagement in learning and school, especially for those who are disengaged, is about relationships—supportive and caring teachers who can personalize and individualize education. A sense of belonging and the social climate of the school are also important factors for student engagement and motivation. All of this needs to take place in a community-type environment that is better fostered in small schools and programs where educators can create the necessary conditions for nurturing motivation and engagement.

Students are more likely to be engaged in safe learning environments that offer a balance of support and freedom to assume responsibility and make decisions. Moreover, when students are self-determined—when they experience competency, autonomy, and relatedness—they are more likely to be motivated and engaged. Students are also more likely to be engaged and motivated when they and their teachers have a growth mindset.

All students, especially those who struggle with school, need engaging and empowering learning strategies and environments. When schools and educators are able to provide settings, relationships, and strategies that promote engagement, students have one less barrier to learning.

NOTES

1. *A Framework for Success for All Students*, Schools for a New Society Initiative and Carnegie Corporation of New York (2006), accessed January 2, 2015,http://annenberginstitute.org/pdf/SNS_cogs.pdf.
2. Adena M. Klem and James P. Connell, "Relationships Matter: Linking Teacher Support to Student Engagement and Achievement," *Journal of School Health* 74, no. 7 (2004): 262–73, accessed January 16, 2015,http://ceep.indiana.edu/hssse/Klem.pdf.
3. *Youth Engagement in Educational Change*, The Forum for Youth Investment (2005), site accessed on January 2, 2015, http ://forumfyi.org/files/Youth%20Engagement%20in%20Educational%20Change.pdf.

4. Judith L. Irvin, Julie Meltzer, and Melinda S. Dukes, *Taking Action on Adolescent Literacy: An Implementation Guide for School Leaders* (Alexandria, VA: Association for Supervision & Curriculum Development, 2007).

5. Klem and Connell, "Relationships Matter."

6. *2013 Gallup Student Poll: Overall U.S. Results*, Gallup Student Poll (2014), accessed January 16, 2015,http://www.gallupstudentpoll.com/174020/2013-gallup-student-poll-overall-report.aspx; Shane J. Lopez, *Youth Readiness for the Future: A Report on Findings from a Representative Gallup Student Poll Sample*, Gallup Student Poll, accessed on January 16, 2015,http://www.gallup.com/poll/141842/youth-readiness-future.aspx.

7. James J. Appleton, Sandra L. Christenson, and Michael J. Furlong, "Student Engagement with School: Critical Conceptual and Methodological Issues of the Construct," *Psychology in the Schools* 45, no. 5 (2008): 369–86.

8. Linda Kramer Schlosser, "Teacher Distance and Student Disengagement: School Lives on the Margin," *Journal of Teacher Education* 43, no. 2 (1992): 128–40.

9. Klem and Connell, "Relationships Matter."

10. Ethan Yassie-Mintz, *Charting the Path from Engagement to Achievement: A Report on the 2009 High School Survey of Student Engagement*, Center for Evaluation & Education Policy, Indiana University (2010), accessed December 21, 2014,http://ceep.indiana.edu/hssse/images/HSSSE_2010_Report.pdf.

11. Ibid.

12. Ibid.

13. Ibid.

14. Ibid.

15. John M. Bridgeland, John J. Dilulio Jr., and Karen Burke Morison, *The Silent Epidemic: Perspectives of High School Dropouts*, A Report by Civic Enterprises in association with Peter D. Hart Research Associates (2006), accessed January 16, 2015,http://files.eric.ed.gov/fulltext/ED513444.pdf.

16. Daniel Princiotta and Ryan Reyna, *Achieving Graduation for All: A Governor's Guide to Dropout Prevention and Recovery*, National Governor's Association Center for Best Practices (2009), accessed January 16, 2015,http://www.nga.org/files/live/sites/NGA/files/pdf/0910ACHIEVINGGRADUATION.PDF.

17. Eric Toshalis and Michael Nakkula, *Motivation, Engagement, and Student Voice*, Students at the Center (2012), accessed January 2, 2015,http://www.studentsatthecenter.org/sites/scl.dl-dev.com/files/Motivation%20Engagement%20Student%20Voice_0.pdf.

18. Francine Joselowsky, "Youth Engagement, High School Reform, and Improved Learning Outcomes: Building Systemic Approaches for Youth Engagement," *NASSP Bulletin* 91, no. 3 (2007): 257–76, accessed January 2, 2015,http://www.leadingnow.org/sites/default/files/pdf/Youth_Engagement_High_School_Reform.pdf.

19. National Research Council Institute of Medicine, *Engaging Schools: Fostering High School Students' Motivation to Learn* (Washington, DC: The National Academies Press, 2004).

20. Ibid.

21. Klem and Connell, "Relationships Matter."

22. Kimberly Knesting, "Students at Risk for School Dropout: Supporting Their Persistence," *Preventing School Failure* 52, no. 4 (2008): 3–10.

23. Deborah L. Schussler and Angelo Collins, "An Empirical Exploration of the Who, What, and How of School Care," *Teachers College Record* 108, no. 7 (2006): 1460–95.

24. Ibid.

25. Samuel A. Perez, "An Ethic of Caring in Teaching Culturally Diverse Students," *Education* 121, no. 1 (2000): 102–5.

26. National Research Council Institute of Medicine, *Engaging Schools*.

27. Judith Kleinfeld, "Effective Teachers of Eskimo and Indian Students," *School Review* 83, no. 2 (1975): 301–44.

28. Yassie-Mintz, *Charting the Path from Engagement to Achievement*.

29. Knesting, "Students at Risk for School Dropout."

30. National Research Council Institute of Medicine, *Engaging Schools*.

31. *A Summary of Research on Using Student Voice in School Improvement Planning*, The Education Alliance, Business and Community for Public Schools (2004), accessed January 16, 2015,http://maaikerotteveel.pbworks.com/f/UsingStudentVoice+soort+literatuurstudie.pdf.

32. Bryan Goodwin, *Simply Better: Doing What Matters Most to Change the Odds for Student Success* (Alexandria, VA: ASCD, 2011).

33. National Research Council Institute of Medicine, *Engaging Schools*.

34. Ibid.

35. Ibid.

36. Ibid.

37. "School Climate," National School Climate Center (2015), accessed January 16, 2015,http://www.schoolclimate.org/climate/.

38. James McMillian and Daisy Reed, *Defying the Odds: A Study of Resilient At-Risk Students*, Virginia Commonwealth University (1993), accessed January 16, 2015,http://files. eric.ed.gov/fulltext/ED389780.pdf.

39. National Research Council Institute of Medicine, *Engaging Schools*.

40. Judy Willis, *Research-Based Strategies to Ignite Student Learning: Insights from a Neurologist and Classroom Teacher* (Alexandria, VA: ASCD, 2006).

41. Ibid.

42. Ruben Garza, "Latino and White High School Students' Perceptions of Caring Behaviors: Are We Culturally Responsive to Our Students?" *Urban Education* 44, no. 3 (2009): 297–321, accessed January 16, 2015,http://www.education.txstate.edu/ci/people/faculty/Garza/ contentParagraph/03/document/Garza+2.pdf.

43. Eric Jensen, *Teaching with the Brain in Mind* (Alexandria, VA: ASCD, 1998).

44. James E. Zull, *From Brain to Mind: Using Neuroscience to Guide Change in Education* (Sterling, VA: Stylus Publishing, 2011).

45. Willis, *Research-Based Strategies to Ignite Student Learning*.

46. Alfie Kohn, "Choices for Children: Why and How to Let Students Decide," *Phi Delta Kappan* 75, no. 1 (1993), accessed January 2, 2015,http://www.alfiekohn.org/teaching/cfc.htm.

47. Knesting, "Students at Risk for School Dropout."

48. Zull, *From Brain to Mind*.

49. Willis, *Research-Based Strategies to Ignite Student Learning*.

50. Jensen, *Teaching with the Brain in Mind*.

51. "Engaging Learning Strategies," What Works, The Whole Child, accessed January 16, 2015,http://www.wholechildeducation.org/what-works.

52. Brigid Barron and Linda Darling-Hammond, *Teaching for Meaningful Learning: A Review of Research on Inquiry-Based and Cooperative Learning*, Edutopia, The George Lucas Foundation (2008), accessed January 16, 2015,http://www.edutopia.org/pdfs/edutopia-teaching-for-meaningful-learning.pdf.

53. National Research Council Institute of Medicine, *Engaging Schools*.

54. Bridgeland, Dilulio Jr., and Wulsin, *Engaged for Success*.

55. Andrew Furco and Susan Root, "Research Demonstrates the Value of Service Learning," *Phi Delta Kappan* 91, no. 5 (2010): 16–20, accessed January 16, 2015,http:// nmcommunityservicelearning.wikispaces.com/file/view/research+demonstrates+value+of+csl. pdf.

56. Zull, *From Brain to Mind*.

57. Toshalis and Nakkula, *Motivation, Engagement, and Student Voice*.

58. Doug Anderson, PhD, LP, Trainer and Consultant, Solution-Focused Practices, interview with the author, April 8, 2014.

59. Richard M. Ryan and Edward L. Deci, "Self-Determination Theory and the Facilitation of Intrinsic Motivation, Social Development, and Well-Being," *American Psychologist* 55, no. 1 (2000): 68–78.

60. Toshalis and Nakkula, *Motivation, Engagement, and Student Voice*.

61. Edward L. Deci and Richard Flaste, *Why We Do What We Do: Understanding Self-Motivation* (New York: Penguin Books, 1995).

62. Toshalis and Nakkula, *Motivation, Engagement, and Student Voice*.

63. Deci and Flaste, *Why We Do What We Do*.

64. Ibid.

65. Ryan and Deci, "Self-Determination Theory and the Facilitation of Intrinsic Motivation, Social Development, and Well-Being."

66. Kohn, "Choices for Children."

67. Deci and Flaste, *Why We Do What We Do*.

68. Johnmarshall Reeve, "Self-Determination Theory Applied to Educational Settings," in *Handbook of Self-Determination Research*, eds. Edward L. Deci and Richard M. Ryan, (Rochester NY: The University of Rochester Press, 2002). 183–203

69. Deci and Flaste, *Why We Do What We Do*.

70. Ibid.

71. Ibid.

72. Reeve, "Self-Determination Theory Applied to Educational Settings."

73. Kohn, "Choices for Children."

74. Ibid.

75. Ryan and Deci, "Self-Determination Theory and the Facilitation of Intrinsic Motivation, Social Development, and Well-Being."

76. Deci and Flaste, *Why We Do What We Do*.

77. Ryan and Deci, "Self-Determination Theory and the Facilitation of Intrinsic Motivation, Social Development, and Well-Being."

78. Deci and Flaste, *Why We Do What We Do*.

79. Ibid.

80. Doug Anderson, PhD, LP, Trainer and Consultant, Solution-Focused Practices, interview with the author, April 8, 2014.

81. National Research Council Institute of Medicine, *Engaging Schools*.

82. Richard M. Ryan and Edward L. Deci, "Intrinsic and Extrinsic Motivations: Classic Definitions and New Directions," *Contemporary Educational Psychology* 25, no. 1 (2000): 54–67, accessed January 16, 2015,http://www.selfdeterminationtheory.org/SDT/documents/2000_RyanDeci_IntExtDefs.pdf.

83. Toshalis and Nakkula, *Motivation, Engagement, and Student Voice*.

84. Deci and Flaste, *Why We Do What We Do*.

85. Ibid.

86. Ibid.

87. Toshalis and Nakkula, *Motivation, Engagement, and Student Voice*.

88. Carol Dweck, *Mindset, The New Psychology of Success: How We Can Learn to Fulfill Our Potential* (New York: Ballantine Books, 2006).

89. Ibid.

90. Ibid.

91. Toshalis and Nakkula, *Motivation, Engagement, and Student Voice*.

92. Dweck, *Mindset*.

Chapter Ten

Partnerships That Transform

Key partnerships begin within classrooms and schools. When teachers collaborate, students and staff reap powerful benefits. One way for teachers to collaborate is by coteaching. An investment in coteaching led to significant student academic gains for a school in Minnesota. Students at Valley View Elementary School consistently produce some of the best scores on the Minnesota Comprehensive Assessments when compared to other schools in the state with high poverty levels.[1]

Leadership and staff attribute students' success in large part to teacher collaboration—having multiple teachers in the classroom.[2] Teachers felt that coteaching made them better teachers—working with another teacher helped them to continually improve their own practice. Another factor contributing to success is the shared responsibility that teachers feel, as noted by a Valley View teacher: "We see each kid as our own . . . I'm responsible for the fourth-graders in my class, but I feel equally as responsible for the kindergartners and the fifth-graders." Her remarks reflect the "shared responsibility" that Finland uses to achieve educational success.

In addition to collaborating in the classroom, teachers can work together within and between schools to address students' needs and improve learning. This helps build the social capital needed for successful educational reform. Social capital consists of the relationships among educators—the patterns of interaction among teachers and between teachers and administrators that focus on student learning.[3] This contrasts with human capital, which consists of teachers' individual abilities, knowledge, and skills.

Both human capital and social capital are beneficial and necessary, but social capital is a more powerful tool because it can be used to leverage human capital.[4] High social capital increases individuals' human capital, but human capital cannot increase social capital.[5] Hence, building trust levels and improving the quality and frequency of collaboration among educators is what will most improve educational outcomes. In one study, even low-ability teachers performed as well as average-ability teachers if they had strong social capital in their schools.[6]

Countries that succeed in educational reform use strategies that leverage the whole group, rather than just individual teachers.[7] In Finland, education policies focus more on school effectiveness rather than teacher effectiveness. This means that everyone in the school, working together rather than as individual teachers, is responsible for the intended outcomes. In order to collaborate, however, teachers need dedicated time for such a purpose, similar to teachers in Finland and other European and Asian countries, where nearly half of teachers' school time goes toward collaboration and refining their practice.[8]

Strategies that build collective capacity dramatically accelerate the pace and effectiveness of change.[9] This is partly because collective capacity is more than the sum of individual capacities. It is a powerful strategy that compounds individual efficacy into collective capacity and impact. In fact, only collective action (versus individual) is strong enough to change systems. Collective capacity makes knowledge about effective practice more widely available and accessible on a daily basis. It also makes it possible for all teachers, individually and collectively, to become better, which in turn, produces more quality teachers working in unison.

Not only is it advantageous for teachers to collaborate, but it is also beneficial for schools to collaborate. Lateral capacity—the widespread adoption of effective practices and experimentation with innovative approaches across the system—helps schools to learn from each other.[10] When schools collaborate, they increase their ability to successfully implement change.

Student-teacher partnerships are also important within the school. They are instrumental to students' engagement, empowerment, and success in school. Students, teachers, and the larger system all benefit when students are enlisted as partners in learning and school improvement efforts. Building quality and sustainable student-teacher partnerships, however, takes time, training, and a willingness to learn. Creating a "culture of partnership" can help ensure success for youth-adult partnerships. A successful partnership culture requires certain shared values and beliefs: that youth-adult partnerships are a core priority; youth and adults will learn from each other; and the organization will explicitly address issues of trust, power, and authority.[11]

Parents are another key partnership. Research is clear that parental involvement is one of the most critical factors in a child's school performance, yet parental involvement decreases significantly during middle school and high school.[12] Low-income, lesser-educated, single, and minority parents have relatively lower rates of involvement in their children's schools. School practices may be partly responsible for the lower participation of parents with children who are most at risk of school failure.

Educators may view uninvolved parents as being uninterested in their child's schooling. Seeming disinterest may actually be the result of a single parent who is limited by inflexible work and home responsibilities. Other times, it may be a matter of transportation or issues with mental health, addiction, or incarceration. Some parents experienced school as a negative part of their own life history, while others may be overwhelmed from battling the system on behalf of their child. For many, contact with and from the school means only "bad news."

Marquel had been in my Leadership class for a couple of weeks. One morning I called Marquel's mom to let her know how he was doing in the class. After a few rings, a voice said, "Hello?" I asked if she was Marquel's mom. She hesitated a bit before saying, "Yes." I explained who I was and that Marquel had recently joined the Leadership class. I proceeded to share that I appreciated having him in the class and that he had a lot of natural leadership abilities. I paused and waited for a response. After a bit of silence, I said, "Are you there?" She replied, "Yes." I went on to describe how Marquel's ideas and speaking skills were an asset to the projects we were working on and how he was able to motivate other people. Once again, there was silence at the other end, so I asked, "Are you still there?" She responded again with a tenuous "yes . . . "

Given the limited response I was encountering, I said, "Well, that's basically all I called about, to tell you what a delight it is to have Marquel in Leadership and how much I appreciate what he brings to the class." Another pause, and then came her stunning response: "Nobody, nobody has ever called me in sixteen years to tell me something positive about my son!" I apologized for her previous experience and assured her that her son had many positive attributes.

As I hung up the phone, I was saddened and angered to think that this parent (and likely many others) had only received negative reports about her son throughout his school career. No wonder she hesitated to engage in conversation. She was bracing herself for what she likely anticipated to be another negative report on Marquel's behavior at school. Often, by the time students who struggle with school reach high school, their parents are tired and battle weary, having dealt with one difficult occurrence after another with the school. They hold their breath, like Marquel's mom, hoping they don't get that dreaded phone call from the school.

Considering the importance of parental involvement, it is essential that schools and educators keep parents engaged. Parents, as engaged partners, are powerful allies. Their involvement benefits their child's progress in school. So educators need to do all they can to engage parents, and not just on the school's terms. Although connecting with some parents may require special efforts, research indicates that the efforts are worthwhile. [13]

To gain parental involvement, it is important that parents feel welcomed. Language and culture can impede parental involvement, so communicating to parents in their language is important. [14] Making sure that schools are physically and socially hospitable to parents and families can also be helpful. Offering transportation or childcare may assist parents in attending school meetings and events. Schools can assess the needs of their particular parent community and identify potential resources to minimize obstacles to school involvement.

Parents need to be informed about how their child is doing—both the positives and the challenges. Communication and meetings should, however, engage parents as a partner in problem solving, not as an enforcer or target of blame. Hope, not blame or another prediction of failure, is what parents and students need. Even if circumstances are bleak, educators can collaborate with students and parents to develop a feasible plan of recovery to move forward.

Partnering with parents is about relationship building. In order to build bridges with parents, educators need time and support to do that. At the end of the school day, teachers still have meetings to attend, papers to correct, lesson plans to develop, and crises to resolve. That leaves staff little or no time to call or visit parents at home. School staff needs the allotted time and support to make this a priority in their work, as is the case in other countries.

BREAKING WALLS, BUILDING BRIDGES

Partnerships must begin in the school but cannot end there. Schools need allies and external partners to transform education. [15] Core community partners can help leverage action within schools and districts while also building engagement and support for policy, practices, attitudes, and behavior changes. Partners have the potential to produce increased capacities, new accountabilities, greater trust, and stronger commitments to young people in the community.

Communities can serve as extensions of the learning environment. They offer a network of people, places, and events that provide opportunities for students to learn, gain experience, be mentored, and become more connected with their communities. Many of the strategies discussed in chapter 8 require a variety of partnerships. Schools can tap into the full array of resources available in the community—businesses, libraries, museums, nonprofit organizations, advocacy groups, environmental organizations, colleges, and other community organizations—to meet active and real-life learning needs.

Likewise, schools can partner with key professionals and leaders in the community as learning resources either inside or outside schools.

Schools can also benefit from partnerships with external change catalysts—intermediary organizations that are deeply connected to education but that have an independent base of resources and support.[16] In addition to serving as bridge builders between researchers and practitioners, intermediary organizations can serve as policy advocates, network builders, and resource brokers. External catalysts can help create learning environments rooted in youth-centered principles. They can also help build peer-learning networks and youth-serving networks that span the private, public, and nonprofit sectors. Catalysts are often most useful as bridge builders between researchers and practitioners who put the knowledge into action.

Universities and colleges offer yet another partnership opportunity. They can disseminate current research, help schools design and carry out action research, and assist schools with systems change efforts using implementation science. Moreover, given their key role in educating new teachers, universities can partner with schools to train new teachers, as was done in the Learning and Teaching Together initiative discussed in chapter 7.

Current and previous school and community or organizational partnerships serve as examples for others. In years past, Gonzalo Garza Independence High School held a Youth Action for Education Change class to research educational issues and join with other young people and community members to organize youth-led projects.[17] A partnership emerged between Garza and Austin Voices for Education and Youth, a local nonprofit that engaged youth, parents, community members, and policymakers to improve educational and other opportunities for youth. As a result of this effort, students were more empowered and school-community connections were strengthened.

Another major partnership effort, the Carnegie Corporation of New York's Schools for a New Society, sought to reinvent urban high school education by building partnerships between school districts and their communities. The initiative, Schools for a New Society (SNS), focused on creating working partnerships between schools and businesses, universities, parent and student groups, and community organizations committed to high school reinvention.[18] Schools and partner organizations worked together to transform "factory model" schools into schools that meet the individual learning needs of each student.

Other school-community partnerships have addressed nonacademic needs. Community Schools were created to address students' nonacademic needs by bringing the community into the school and by the school tapping into the community as a resource.[19] The 102 Community Schools in Chicago have lead agencies such as the YMCA, the Children's Home and Aid Society, and the Logan Square Neighborhood Association, all of which work with schools to develop the whole child. [20]

The P21 exemplar schools noted in chapter 8 partner with local organizations and businesses to participate in service learning, project-based learning, internships, and college and career academy opportunities. [21] Similarly, many schools that use inquiry-based strategies, such as Eagle Rock, High Tech High, The Met, Schools for Environmental Studies, and Rocky Mountain Schools of Expeditionary Learning, partner with local businesses and organizations to provide real-world learning opportunities, including internships.

Partnerships clearly benefit students and schools, but forming and sustaining them is not without challenge. Practitioners in youth-related fields all have unique philosophies, mental models, and practices. [22] Overcoming these sometimes divergent perspectives can be challenging, yet when people learn more about each other during their professional training, barriers between groups are more likely to dissipate.

Collaborative learning and coalition building among different youth-based organizations and disciplines can be implemented through interdisciplinary conferences, forums, or working groups. In addition to learning from one another, groups can develop shared advocacy and coalitions to help advance young people's causes. It is also critical that staff who provide direct services to youth are involved in this process, not just those in leadership positions.

Foundations and other entities that have forged school-community partnerships can offer their experiences, knowledge, and lessons to those who follow. Several key findings about partnerships emerged from the Schools for a New Society reform initiative: [23]

- Successful partnerships are a product of positive relationships that develop over time; are infused by trust; and respond to, and foster, opportunity for collaboration.
- Trust between partners is critical to an effective relationship, but it is tenuous and can easily dissipate in the wake of supervening events or as the result of erroneous assumptions.
- Partnerships are shaped and developed by districts' evolving perceptions of the need for and value of them.

In addition, a formal contract or memorandum of understanding may help school and community partnerships to develop and sustain. [24] A contract or memorandum can define the roles for designing, managing, and implementing the work, and it can clarify the roles and responsibilities of each organization and staff member. It can also help limit or remove the bureaucratic constraints that might impede the impact and role of external partners.

Lastly, schools alone cannot compensate for the economic and social inequalities that impact young people and their ability to learn; they need policies and resources to address these issues.[25] Those who influence policy formation and resource availability—policymakers and lawmakers—must first attain a deep understanding of what young people need to maximize their success in school and life. Next, policymakers and lawmakers need to partner both with students and educators, and with other entities that serve youth, to help meet those needs.

One such group, the Interagency Working Group on Youth Programs (IWGYP), is composed of seventeen federal departments and agencies that support youth programs and services, including the U.S. Departments of Education, Health and Human Services, and Justice.[26] The primary function of the IWGYP is to support coordinated federal activities focused on improving outcomes for youth. Their specific goals are to promote collaboration and coordination at the federal, state, local, and tribal levels; identify and disseminate innovative and evidence-based strategies; promote youth engagement and partnerships to strengthen programs and benefit youth; and produce a federal interagency website on youth.

Working collaboratively, federal agencies can maximize what they are able to accomplish. While this is a significant step in the right direction, there is much work yet to do. Given the diversity of programming for youth within each field, considerable effort will be needed to build collaboration within each field and then to learn and collaborate with other fields, both locally and nationally. This, however, is the type of capacity building called for by Pasi Sahlberg and Michael Fullan.

It will take powerful and strategic partnerships across all entities—students, educators, parents, communities, researchers, policymakers, and others—to design and implement the educational transformation needed for students now and in the future. No one person or group can do it alone, but working together, individuals and organizations can bring the expertise, energy, and commitment necessary to do this valuable work.

NOTES

1. Kim McGuire, "Valley View Elementary Students Beat the Odds," *Star Tribune*, September 20, 2014, accessed February 15, 2015,http://www.startribune.com/local/north/275902881.html.

2. Ibid.

3. Michael Fullan, *Choosing the Wrong Drivers for Whole System Reform*, Seminar Series 204, Center for Strategic Education (2011), accessed January 25, 2015,http://edsource.org/wp-content/uploads/Fullan-Wrong-Drivers1.pdf.

4. Ibid.

5. Ruth Nelson, "Andy Hargreaves Discusses the Importance of Professional Capital in School Improvement Efforts," HOPE Foundation, November 19, 2012, accessed February 15,

2015,http://www.hopefoundation.org/andy-hargreaves-discusses-the-importance-of-professional-capital-in-school-improvement-efforts/.

6. Fullan, *Choosing the Wrong Drivers for Whole System Reform*.

7. Ibid.

8. Linda Darling-Hammond, *What We Can Learn from Finland's Successful School Reform*, National Education Association (2010), accessed February 7, 2015,http://www.nea.org/home/40991.htm.

9. Michael Fullan, *All Systems Go: The Change Imperative for Whole System Reform,* (Thousand Oaks, CA: Corwin and Ontario Principals Council, 2010).

10. Darling-Hammond, *What We Can Learn from Finland's Successful School Reform*.

11. Shepherd Zeldin and Julie Petrokubi, "Youth-Adult Partnership: Impacting Individuals and Communities," *Prevention Researcher* 15, no. 2 (2008): 16–20, accessed January 2, 2015,http://fyi.uwex.edu/youthadultpartnership/files/2011/07/Zeldin-Petrokubi-Prevention-Researcher-2008.pdf.

12. National Research Council, Institute of Medicine, *Engaging Schools: Fostering High School Students' Motivation to Learn* (Washington, DC: The National Academies Press, 2004).

13. Ibid.

14. Ibid.

15. *A Framework for Success for All Students*, Schools for a New Society Initiative and Carnegie Corporation of New York (2006), accessed January 2, 2015,http://annenberginstitute.org/pdf/SNS_cogs.pdf.

16. Joel Tolman, Patrice Ford, and Merita Irby, *What Works in Education Reform: Putting Young People at the Center*, International Youth Foundation (2003), accessed January 2, 2015,http://www.iyfnet.org/sites/default/files/WW_Education_Reform.pdf.

17. Francine Joselowsky, "Students as Co-Constructors of the Learning Experience and Environment: Youth Engagement and High School Reform," *Voices for Urban Education* 8 (Summer 2005), accessed January 2, 2015,http://vue.annenberginstitute.org/sites/default/files/issuePDF/VUE8.pdf.

18. *Schools for a New Society Leads the Way*, Schools for a New Society, Carnegie Corporation of New York (2004), accessed February 15, 2015,http://carnegie.org/fileadmin/Media/Publications/PDF/SNS-BrochureForWeb.pdf.

19. National Research Council, Institute of Medicine, *Engaging Schools*.

20. Martin Blank and Amy Berg, *All Together Now: Sharing Responsibility for the Whole Child*, Coalition for Community Schools at the Institute for Educational Leadership, Washington, DC (2006), accessed January 25, 2015,http://www.ascd.org/ASCD/pdf/sharingresponsibility.pdf.

21. Christopher Brown, *Patterns of Innovation: Showcasing the Nation's Best in 21st Century Learning*, Pearson Foundation, Partnership for 21st Century Skills (2013), accessed January 25, 2015,http://www.p21.org/storage/documents/exemplars/P21_Patterns_of_Innovation_Final.pdf.

22. Martin Blank et al., "Reforming Education: Developing 21st Century Community Schools," in *Applied Developmental Science: An Advanced Textbook*, eds. Richard M. Learner, Francine Jacobs, and Donald Wertlieb (Thousand Oaks, CA: 2005), 227–46.

23. Robert A. Kronley and Claire Handley, *Sustaining Partnerships: Emerging Lessons from the Carnegie Corporation's Schools for a New Society Initiative*, Kronley & Associates (2006), accessed February 15, 2015,http://www.kronley.com/documents/SustainingPartnerships-Carnegie.pdf.

24. Francine Joselowsky, "Youth Engagement, High School Reform, and Improved Learning Outcomes: Building Systemic Approaches for Youth Engagement," *NASSP Bulletin* 91, no. 3 (2007), 257–76, accessed January 25, 2015,http://www.leadingnow.org/sites/default/files/pdf/Youth_Engagement_High_School_Reform.pdf.

25. National Research Council, Institute of Medicine, *Engaging Schools*.

26. "Pathways for Youth: Draft Strategic Plan for Federal Collaboration," Interagency Working Group on Youth Programs (2013), accessed February 15, 2015,http://www.findyouthinfo.gov/docs/Pathways_for_Youth.pdf.

Conclusion

You can't sugarcoat this,
and it's going to take a lot to get it fixed,
'cause everyone knows it needs to be.
—Charlie

Education is important for all students, yet for many, the educational journey can be overwhelming and fraught with obstacles. Students with disabilities, preexisting challenges that often reflect life or societal circumstances, or other barriers enter an institution that is meant to serve the masses in an efficient, standardized manner. The depersonalization and disempowerment of the system further intensifies those challenges, and school becomes yet another stressor, barrier, and failure in students' lives.

School can be a place of success for those who can navigate a standardized system in a relatively easy manner. It works for the "succeeders," as Charlie put it. However, *all* students need to be "succeeders." All students need to know how to thrive and succeed in school and life beyond school. Helping students to succeed means that educators do not blame students for the system's failure to meet their myriad needs. It is not students' responsibility to figure out how to survive the system; rather, it is educators' responsibility to figure out how to meet the diverse needs of students.

In a new and better model of education, young people will be valued for who they are and who they are becoming, they will have voice and meaningful roles in their schools, and learning will be designed around their needs. Learning will be active, relevant, engaging, personalized, and connected to real life. Students will have segues, pathways, and more direct preparation for their next steps in life.

As the world and learners evolve, so should education. Education must become more agile and adaptable to students' needs and marketplace demands. Education must be both forward looking and forward acting, because the investment we make in young people is an investment we make in ourselves and our future as a society. If young people flourish, we all flourish. If they struggle, we all struggle.

This book calls for transformation, rather than reformation. To transform education, we must remember that the system exists for the student, not the adults and not the system. Focusing on the students means that schools must create learning environments and experiences that empower and equip learners for school and life success, including those proposed in this book: valuing young people; fostering a positive youth development approach in classrooms and schools; empowering young people through voice, decision making, action, and youth-adult partnerships; incorporating active, inquiry-based learning in and about the real world; and using strategies that welcome, engage, and sustain learners in the learning process.

These changes are needed, but transformation may not be easy. The educational system is what it is, and does what it does, to sustain itself and to carry on an efficient, yet ineffective and obsolete, factory model of delivering education. Even with help from students, changing education will be difficult given its current biases, hierarchical structure, lockstep proceedings, and entrenched history.

The types of educational transformation proposed in this book require deep change—different ways of thinking about young people, their development, and their learning. It requires new ways of working with young people, ways that are more egalitarian, respectful, engaging, motivating, and real-life oriented. It means embracing young people as actors, contributors, and stakeholders in their own education. It means valuing what students bring—their wisdom, experiences, and aspirations. New ways of thinking and doing will likely be messy at times. It will take time and practice for everyone to figure out their parts. Schools might be louder, livelier places. But they will also be places of heightened empowerment, engagement, and learning.

There is hope. Schools and districts highlighted in various chapters are making progress by designing learning around how students want and need to learn. By implementing meaningful cultural and programming changes, these schools are supporting students to become empowered, engaged, and better prepared for life beyond high school.

Although pioneering efforts with some of the proposed changes are underway in some schools, the challenge is to bring them into systemwide implementation in order to ensure deep and sustainable change. The learning cultures, strategies, and environments proposed in this book cannot be limited to one class or one teacher; instead, they must permeate all boundaries for educational change to succeed. Like the bellows in figure 2, chapter 2, we must leverage change in order to transform a seemingly unchangeable system.

By using social capital, collective capacity, the right drivers, and implementation science, schools can effectively prepare, implement, scale up, and sustain the recommended changes. Successful change efforts, however, need to involve those most impacted by the changes—students and teachers. Effective change will also require collaboration among and between key groups such as teachers, students, schools, and communities. Working together for the betterment of all is not commonplace in the United States where we are accustomed to operating independently. Nonetheless, it is an important and necessary endeavor for educational change.

This book was intended to be for and about students, but we cannot empower students without empowering educators. For educators to become liberators of young people, rather than agents of oppression, they too must be empowered. Deinstitutionalizing our school systems will help to empower students and staff. It will also help schools to more closely resemble the democratic society we purport to be.

Powerful opportunities for transformation await, but the responsibility for change does not lie solely with teachers and schools. Policymakers and lawmakers, individual citizens, and society as a whole all have significant roles in determining whether our schools will evolve to meet the needs of students and the demands of the times. And it is not a matter of educators doing more with less, it is a matter of doing more with more—more support, more training, more opportunities to collaborate, more time and resources, and more respect as a profession. So as Charlie would advise new leadership classes, "It isn't just politicians or old people that can make change, you can too! You just have to start, start somewhere, do something, just start!"

Resources

STUDENT-CENTERED LEARNING

1. Students at the Center
   http://www.studentsatthecenter.org/
2. Putting Students at the Center Reference Guide
   http://www.studentsatthecenter.org/sites/scl.dl-dev.com/files/field_attach_file/NMEF_sclreframeweb.pdf
3. *Anytime, Anywhere: Student-Centered Learning for Schools and Teachers* (book), Rebecca E. Wolfe, Adria Steinberg, and Nancy Hoffman (Cambridge: Harvard Education Press, 2013).

WHOLE-CHILD EDUCATION

1. ASCD: The Whole Child Initiative (+ School Improvement Tool)
   http://www.ascd.org/whole-child.aspx
2. Whole Child Education
   http://www.wholechildeducation.org/

POSITIVE YOUTH DEVELOPMENT

1. Putting Positive Youth Development into Practice: A Resource Guide
   http://ncfy.acf.hhs.gov/sites/default/files/PosYthDevel.pdf
2. 2008 Positive Youth Development Toolkit
   http://www.nrcyd.ou.edu/publication-db/documents/2008-positive-youth-development-toolkit.pdf

YOUTH/STUDENT VOICE, DECISION MAKING, AND INVOLVEMENT IN SCHOOL CHANGE

1. Youth on Board (multiple resources)
   http://www.youthonboard.org
2. Meaningful Student Involvement: Guide to Students as Partners in School Change
   http://soundout.org/MSIGuide.pdf
3. SoundOut.org
   http://soundout.org/
4. Youth Engagement in Educational Change: Working Definition and Self-Assessment
   http://forumfyi.org/files/
   Youth%20Engagement%20in%20Educational%20Change.pdf
5. Youth Action for Educational Change
   http://forumfyi.org/files/Youth%20Action%20Ed%20Change.pdf
6. Education Change and Youth Engagement: Strategies for Success
   http://www.yli.org/media/docs/2648_
   Educationchangeandyouthengagement.pdf
7. Student and Youth Voice: Asking, Listening, and Taking Action
   http://www.whatkidscando.org/specialcollections/student_voice/
   index2.html
8. Spectrum of Student Voice–Oriented Activity (page 3)
   http://www.studentsatthecenter.org/sites/scl.dl-dev.com/files/field_
   attach_file/Exec_Toshalis%26Nakkula_032312.pdf
9. Conditions for Student Voice and Level of Student Involvement in School Improvement (tables, pages 134–36) http://www.edugains.ca/
   resourcesSV/StudentVoiceResearch/
   StudentsasRadicalPartnersofChange.pdf

YOUTH-ADULT PARTNERSHIPS

1. Being Y-AP Savvy: A Primer on Creating & Sustaining Youth-Adult Partnerships
   http://fyi.uwex.edu/youthadultpartnership/files/2011/02/YAP-
   Savvy12.pdf
2. Innovation Center for Community & Youth Development
   http://www.theinnovationcenter.org/catalog/toolkits/resources
3. Youth Adult Partnerships in Evaluation: A Resource Guide for Translating Research into Practice
   http://fyi.uwex.edu/youthadultpartnership/files/2012/10/YAP-
   Resource-Guide.pdf

INQUIRY-, PROJECT-, AND COMMUNITY-BASED LEARNING

1. Edutopia: What Works in Education
   http://www.edutopia.org/project-based-learning
   http://www.edutopia.org/video/five-keys-rigorous-project-based-learning
   http://www.edutopia.org/stw-maine-project-based-learning-six-steps-planning
2. Schools That Change Communities (video)
   http://www.docmakeronline.com/schoolsthatchangecommunities.html
3. Powerful Learning: What We Know About Teaching for Understanding (book)
   Linda Darling-Hammond et al. (San Francisco: Jossey-Bass, 2008).
4. Teaching for Meaningful Learning: A Review of Research on Inquiry-Based and Cooperative Learning
   http://www.edutopia.org/pdfs/edutopia-teaching-for-meaningful-learning.pdf
5. Buck Institute for Education—a nonprofit that creates, gathers, and shares high-quality project-based instructional practices, products, and services
   http://bie.org/
6. Expeditionary Learning
   http://elschools.org/
7. Project-Based Learning
   http://www.bigpicture.org/
8. Bob Pearlman
   http://www.bobpearlman.org/BestPractices/PBL.htm

STUDENT ENGAGEMENT IN LEARNING

1. Motivation, Engagement, and Student Voice Toolkit (Student Centered)
   http://www.studentsatthecenter.org/sites/scl.dl-dev.com/files/1_SATC_Motivation_Toolkit_051713.pdf
2. High School Survey of Student Engagement
   http://ceep.indiana.edu/hssse/index.shtml

SERVICE LEARNING

1. Engaging Students through Academic Service Learning

National Guide to Implementing Quality Academic Service-Learning
http://ncasl.org/wp-content/uploads/Engaging-Students-Through-Academic-Service-Learning-Implementation-Guide.pdf
2. National Youth Leadership Council
http://www.nylc.org/
3. Service Learning + Project-Based Learning
http://eastinitiative.org/

TWENTY-FIRST-CENTURY LEARNING

1. Partnership for 21st Century Skills
http://www.p21.org/
2. P21 Resources for Educators
http://www.p21.org/our-work/resources/for-educators
3. Learning Environments: A 21st Century Skills Implementation Guide
http://www.p21.org/storage/documents/p21-stateimp_learning_environments.pdf
4. *21st Century Skills: Learning for Life in Our Times* (book)
Bernie Trilling and Charles Fadel (San Francisco: Jossey-Bass, 2009)

GROWTH MINDSET

1. Growth Mindset Assessment
http://www.studentsatthecenter.org/resources/growth-mindset-assessment

PARTNERSHIPS (ORGANIZATIONAL)

1. Broader Partnerships Toolkit
http://www.readyby21.org/toolkits/broader-partnerships-toolkit
2. The Forum for Youth Investment
http://forumfyi.org/
3. Building Mutually-Beneficial Relationships Between Schools and Communities: The Role of a Community Connector.
http://www.abcdinstitute.org/docs/Building%20Mutually%20Beneficial%20School-Community%20Relationships.pdf.

IMPLEMENTATION SCIENCE

1. State Implementation and Scaling-Up of Evidence-Based Practices Center Fact Sheet
   http://sisep.fpg.unc.edu/
2. National Implementation Research Network
   http://nirn.fpg.unc.edu/
3. A Guide to Evidence and Innovation
   http://evidence-innovation.findyouthinfo.gov/investing-what-works-forum-issue-briefs

For additional resources, contact the author at http://www.mpowersolutions.org.

Bibliography

"About MetWest." MetWest. Accessed January 25, 2015.http://www.ousd.k12.ca.us/domain/ 1996.

"About the 21st Century Learning Exemplar Program." Partnership for 21st Century Skills. Accessed January 25, 2015.http://www.p21.org/storage/documents/exemplars/P21_ Patterns_of_Innovation_Final.pdf.

"Adolescence: An Age of Opportunity." Executive Summary. In *The State of the World's Children 2011*. New York: United Nations Children's Fund, 2011.

"Adolescent Development E-Learning Module." Office of Adolescent Health. U.S. Department of Health & Human Services. Accessed January 9, 2015.http://www.hhs.gov/ash/oah/ resources-and-publications/learning/ad_dev/.

Allbritten, Drew, Richard Mainzer, and Deborah Ziegler. "Will Students with Disabilities Be Scapegoats for School Failures?" *Educational Horizons* 82, no. 2 (2004).

Anderson, Doug PhD, LP, Trainer and Consultant, Solution-Focused Practices. Interview with Maure Ann Metzger. Personal Interview, April 8, 2014.

Anyon, Yolanda, and Sandra Naughton. *Youth Empowerment: The Contributions and Challenges of Youth-Led Research in a High-Poverty, Urban Community*. Issue Brief. John W. Gardner Center for Youth and Their Communities, 2003. Accessed January 2, 2015. http:// gardnercenter.stanford.edu/resources/publications/JGC_IB_ ContributionsChallengesYouthLedResearch2003.pdf.

Appleton, James J., Sandra L. Christenson, and Michael J. Furlong. "Student Engagement with School: Critical Conceptual and Methodological Issues of the Construct." *Psychology in the Schools* 45, no. 5 (2008): 369–86.

Arnold, Nicki G. "Learned Helplessness and Attribution for Success and Failure in LD Students." LDOnline, 1996. Accessed December 6, 2014.http://www.ldonline.org/article/6154/.

Astroth, Kirk A. "Beyond Ephebiphobia: Problem Adults or Problem Youth?" *Phi Delta Kappan* 75, no. 5 (1994): 411–13.

Balfanz, Robert, John M. Bridgeland, Joanna Hornig Fox, Jennifer L. DePaoli, Erin S. Ingram, and Mary Maushard. *Building a Grad Nation: Progress and Challenge in Ending the High School Dropout Epidemic*. Civic Enterprises, 2014. Accessed December 17, 2014.http:// gradnation.org/sites/default/files/17548_BGN_Report_FinalFULL_5.2.14.pdf.

Bandura, Albert. "Self-Efficacy." In *Encyclopedia of Human Behavior* 4. Edited by V. S. Ramachaudran. New York: Academic Press, 1994. Accessed December 6, 2014.http://www. uky.edu/~eushe2/Bandura/BanEncy.html.

Barron, Brigid, and Linda Darling-Hammond. *Teaching for Meaningful Learning: A Review of Research on Inquiry-Based and Cooperative Learning*. Edutopia, The George Lucas Foundation, 2008. Accessed January 16, 2015.http://www.edutopia.org/pdfs/edutopia-teaching-for-meaningful-learning.pdf.

Beane, James A. "Sorting Out the Self-Esteem Controversy." *Educational Leadership* 49, no. 1 (1991): 25–31. Accessed December 6, 2014.http://www.acsd.org/ACSD/pdf/journals/ed_lead/el_199109_beane.pdf.

Bell, John. "Understanding Adultism: A Major Obstacle to Developing Positive Youth-Adult Relationships." YouthBuild USA, 1995. Accessed October 28, 2014. https://www.scoe.net/actioncivics/pdf/Understanding-Adultism.pdf.

Blank, Martin, and Amy Berg. *All Together Now: Sharing Responsibility for the Whole Child.* Coalition for Community Schools at the Institute for Educational Leadership, Washington, DC, 2006. Accessed January 25, 2015. http://www.ascd.org/ASCD/pdf/sharingresponsibility.pdf.

Blank, Martin, Bela Shah, Sheri Johnson, William Blackwell, and Melissa Ganley. "Reforming Education: Developing 21st-Century Community Schools." In *Applied Developmental Science: An Advanced Textbook.* Edited by Richard M. Learner, Francine Jacobs, and Donald Wertlieb, 227–46. Thousand Oaks, CA: Sage Publications, 2005.

Bonwell, Charles C., and James A. Eison. *Active Learning: Creating Excitement in the Classroom.* ASHE-ERIC Higher Education Report No. 1. Washington, DC: The George Washington University, School of Education and Human Development, 1991.

Bostrom, Meg. "Teenhood: Understanding Attitudes toward Those Transitioning from Childhood to Adulthood." FrameWorks Institute, 2000. Accessed October 21, 2014.http://www.frameworksinstitute.org/assets/files/PDF/youth_understanding_attitudes.pdf.

Bridgeland, John M., Robert Balfanz, Laura A. Moore, and Rebecca S. Friant. *Raising Their Voices: Engaging Students, Teachers, and Parents to Help End the High School Dropout Epidemic.* A Report by Civic Enterprises in association with Peter D. Hart Research Associates, 2010. Accessed January 25, 2015.http://www.civicenterprises.net/MediaLibrary/Docs/raising_their_voices.pdf.

Bridgeland, John M., John J. Dilulio Jr., and Karen Burke Morison. *The Silent Epidemic: Perspectives of High School Dropouts.* A Report by Civic Enterprises in association with Peter D. Hart Research Associates for the Bill and Melinda Gates Foundation, 2006. Accessed January 16, 2015.http://files.eric.ed.gov/fulltext/ED513444.pdf.

Bridgeland, John M., John J. Dilulio Jr., and Stuart C. Wulsin. *Engaged for Success: Service Learning as a Tool for High School Dropout Prevention.* A Report by Civic Enterprises in association with Peter D. Hart Research Associates, 2008. Accessed January 16, 2015.http://civicenterprises.net/MediaLibrary/docs/engaged_for_success.pdf.

Brown, Christopher. *Patterns of Innovation: Showcasing the Nation's Best in 21st Century Learning.* Pearson Foundation, Partnership for 21st Century Skills, 2013. Accessed January 25, 2015.http://www.p21.org/storage/documents/exemplars/P21_Patterns_of_Innovation_Final.pdf

Burcum, Jill, and the *Star Tribune* Editorial Board. "Separate and Unequal." *Star Tribune*, December 10, 2014. Accessed February 7, 2015.http://www.startribune.com/opinion/285613631.html.

Caine, Geoffrey, and Renate Nummela Caine. *The Brain, Education, and the Competitive Edge.* Lanham, MD: Scarecrow Press, 2001.

———. *Education on the Edge of Possibility.* Alexandria, VA: ASCD/Association for Supervision and Curriculum Development, 1997.

Camino, Linda, and Shepherd Zeldin. "From Periphery to Center: Pathways for Youth Civic Engagement in the Day-to-Day Life of Communities." *Applied Developmental Science* 6, no. 4 (2002): 213–20.

Cervone, Barbara, and Kathleen Cushman. "Learning from the Leaders: Core Practices of Six Schools." In *Anytime, Anywhere: Student-Centered Learning for Schools and Teachers.* Edited by Rebecca E. Wolfe, Adria Steinberg, and Nancy Hoffman, 15–53. Cambridge, MA: Harvard Education Press, 2013.

———. "Moving Youth Participation into the Classroom: Students as Allies." In *New Directions for Youth Development 26.* Edited by Benjamin Kirshner, Jennifer L. O'Donoghue, and Milbrey McLaughlin, 27–46. San Francisco: Jossey-Bass, Winter 2002.

"Challenging Adultism." The Free Child Project. Accessed October 30, 2014.http://www. freechild.org/adultism.htm.

Checkoway, Barry. *Adults as Allies*. School of Social Work, University of Michigan, W. J. Kellogg Foundation, 2001. Accessed January 2, 2015. https://ppoe.at/scoutdocs/yi/Adults as Allies.pdf.

Cohen, Richard. "Adultism." *The School Mediator* 3. School Mediation Associates, 2004. Accessed October 28, 2014.http://www.schoolmediation.com/newsletters/2004/01_04.html.

Community Programs to Promote Youth Development. Institute of Medicine, National Research Council of the National Academies, 2004. Accessed January 2, 2015. http://www. iom.edu/~/media/Files/Report%20Files/2004/Community-Programs-to-Promote-Youth-Development/FINALCommunityPrograms8Pager.pdf.

"Convention on the Rights of the Child: FAQs and Resources." UNICEF. Accessed January 8, 2015. http://www.unicef.org/crc/index_30225.html.

Cook-Sather, Alison. "Authorizing Students' Perspectives: Toward Trust, Dialogue, and Change in Education." *Educational Researcher* 31, no. 4 (2002). Accessed January 2, 2015.http://edr.sagepub.com/content/31/4/3.full.pdf+html.

———. "What Would Happen If We Treated Students as Those with Opinions That Matter? The Benefits to Principals and Teachers of Supporting Youth Engagement in School." *NASSP Bulletin* 91, no. 4 (2007): 343–62.

Copeland, Larry. "Texting in Traffic: Adults Worse than Teens." *USA Today*, March 28, 2013. Accessed October 28, 2014.http://www.usatoday.com/story/news/nation/2013/03/28/adults-worse-than-teens-about-texting-behind-wheel/2026331/.

Costello, Joan, Mark Toles, Julie Spielberger, and Joan Wynn. "How History, Ideology, and Structure Shape the Organizations that Shape Youth." In *Trends in Youth Development: Visions, Realities and Challenges*. Edited by Peter L. Benson and Karen Johnson Pittman. Norwell, MA: Kluwer Academic Publishers, 2001.

Darling-Hammond, Linda. "From 'Separate But Equal' to 'No Child Left Behind': The Collision of New Standards and Old Inequalities." In *Many Children Left Behind: How the No Child Left Behind Act Is Damaging Our Children and Our Schools*. Edited by Deborah Meier and George Wood. Boston: Beacon Press, 2004.

———. "U.S. vs. Highest-Achieving Nations in Education." Guest post on Victoria Strauss, *Washington Post*, March 23, 2011. Accessed February 7, 2015.http://www.washingtonpost. com/blogs/answer-sheet/post/darling-hammond-us-vs-highest-achieving-nations-in-education/2011/03/22/ABkNeaCB_blog.html.

———. *What We Can Learn from Finland's Successful School Reform*. National Education Association, 2010. Accessed February 7, 2015.http://www.nea.org/home/40991.htm.

Deci, Edward L., and Richard Flaste. *Why We Do What We Do: Understanding Self-Motivation*. New York: Penguin Books, 1995.

Deci, Edward L., and Richard M. Ryan. *Handbook of Self-Determination Research*. Rochester, NY: The University of Rochester Press, 2002.

Dewey, John. *Experience and Education*. New York: Touchstone, 1997.

Diamond, Marian C., and Janet Hopson. "Learning Not by Chance: Enrichment in the Classroom." In *The Jossey-Bass Reader on the Brain and Learning*. San Francisco: John Wiley & Sons, 2008, 70–88.

DiBenedetto, A. "Youth Groups: A Model for Empowerment." *Networking Bulletin* 2, no. 3 (1992): 19–24.

Donahue, Nicholas C. Foreword to *Anytime, Anywhere: Student Centered Learning for Schools and Teachers*. Edited by Rebecca E. Wolfe, Adria Steinberg, and Nancy Hoffman. Cambridge, MA: Harvard Education Press, 2013.

Dweck, Carol. *Mindset, The New Psychology of Success: How We Can Learn to Fulfill Our Potential*. New York: Ballantine Books, 2006.

"EAST Initiative." EASTCore. Accessed January 25, 2015.http://core.eastinitiative.org/home/ EAST-Initiative.aspx.

Education Change and Youth Engagement: Strategies for Success. Youth Leadership Institute, 2009. Accessed January 2, 2015. http://www.yli.org/media/docs/2648_ Educationchangeandyouthengagement.pdf.

"Educational Expenditure Statistics 2013." European Commission. Accessed January 9, 2015.http://ec.europa.eu/eurostat/statistics-explained/index.php/Educational_expenditure_ statistics.

"Empowerment." Wikipedia. Accessed January 2, 2015.https://en.wikipedia.org/wiki/ Empowerment.

"Engaging Learning Strategies." What Works, The Whole Child. Accessed January 16, 2015.http://www.wholechildeducation.org/what-works.

Facilitator's Guide. ASPIRA Youth Leadership Development Curriculum. Accessed January 2, 2015.http://www.aspira.org/sites/default/files/Facilitator%27s Guide 2012-V3.pdf.

"FAQ." Partnership for 21st Century Skills. Accessed January 25, 2015.http://www.p21.org/ about-us/p21-framework.

Ferber, Thaddeus, Elizabeth Gaines, and Christi Goodman. "Positive Youth Development: State Strategies." *Strengthening Youth Policy—Research and Policy Report.* Prepared for the National Conference of State Legislators, October 2005. Accessed January 2, 2015.http:/ /www.ncsl.org/print/cyf/final_positive_youth_development.pdf.

Fielding, Michael. "Radical Collegiality: Affirming Teaching as an Inclusive Professional Practice." *Australian Educational Researcher* 26, no. 2 (1999): 1–34.

———. "Students as Radical Agents of Change." *Journal of Educational Change* 2, no. 2 (2001): 123–41. Accessed January 2, 2015. http://www.edugains.ca/resourcesSV/ StudentVoiceResearch/StudentsasRadicalPartnersofChange.pdf.

Fletcher, Adam. *Meaningful Student Involvement: Guide to Inclusive School Change.* Olympia, WA: SoundOut, 2003. Accessed January 2, 2015.http://www.soundout.org/ MSIInclusiveGuide.pdf.

———. "Overcoming Barriers to Student Voice." SoundOut, 2007. Accessed January 2, 2015. http://www.soundout.org/overcoming-barriers-to-student-voice.

———. "What Is Student Voice About?" SoundOut. Accessed January 2, 2015.http://www. soundout.org/article.107.html.

"Framework for 21st Century Learning." Partnership for 21st Century Skills. Accessed January 25, 2015.http://www.p21.org/about-us/p21-framework.

A Framework for Success for All Students. Schools for a New Society Initiative and Carnegie Corporation of New York, 2006. Accessed January 2, 2015.http://annenberginstitute.org/ pdf/SNS_cogs.pdf.

Fullan, Michael. *All Systems Go: The Change Imperative for Whole System Reform.* Thousand Oaks, CA: Corwin and Ontario Principals Council, 2010.

———. *Choosing the Wrong Drivers for Whole System Reform.* Seminar Series 204. Center for Strategic Education, 2011. Accessed January 25, 2015.http://edsource.org/wp-content/ uploads/Fullan-Wrong-Drivers1.pdf.

Furco, Andrew, and Susan Root. "Research Demonstrates the Value of Service Learning." *Phi Delta Kappan* 91, no. 5 (2010): 16–20. Accessed January 16, 2015.http:// nmcommunityservicelearning.wikispaces.com/file/view/research+demonstrates+value+of+ csl.pdf.

"Gallup Student Poll, Montgomery County Public Schools, MD." Gallup, Inc., 2012. Accessed December 24, 2014.http://www.montgomeryschoolsmd.org/uploadedFiles/info/gallup/ GallupStudentResults.pdf.

2013 Gallup Student Poll: Overall U.S. Results. Gallup Student Poll, 2014. Accessed January 16, 2015.http://www.gallupstudentpoll.com/174020/2013-gallup-student-poll-overall-report.aspx.

Garza, Ruben. "Latino and White High School Students' Perceptions of Caring Behaviors: Are We Culturally Responsive to Our Students?" *Urban Education* 44, no. 3 (2009): 297–321. Accessed January 9, 2015. http://www.education.txstate.edu/ci/people/faculty/Garza/ contentParagraph/03/document/Garza+2.pdf.

Garza, Ruben, Gail Ryser, and Kathryn Lee. "Illuminating Adolescent Voices: Identifying High School Students' Perceptions of Teacher Caring." *Academic Leadership Journal* 7, no. 4 (2009). Accessed January 9, 2015.http://contentcat.fhsu.edu/cdm/compoundobject/ collection/p15732coll4/id/420/rec/1.

Gilliam, Franklin D. Jr., and Susan Ball Nales. "Strategic Frame Analysis: Reframing America's Youth." Society for Research in Child Development, Social Policy Report 15, no. 3 (2001).

Ginwright, Shawn, and Taj James. "From Assets to Agents of Change: Social Justice, Organizing and Youth Development." *New Directions for Youth Development* 26. Edited by Benjamin Kirshner, Jennifer L. O'Donoghue, and Milbrey McLaughlin, 27–46. San Francisco: Jossey-Bass, Winter 2002.

Goodwin, Bryan. *Simply Better: Doing What Matters Most to Change the Odds for Student Success.* Alexandria, VA: ASCD, 2011.

Gordon, Robert, and Myrna Gordon. *The Turned-Off Child: Learned Helplessness and School Failure.* Salt Lake City, UT: Millennial Mind Publishing, 2006.

Goswami, Usha. "Neuroscience and Education." In *The Jossey-Bass Reader on the Brain and Learning.* San Francisco: John Wiley & Sons, 2008.

Gregoire, Carolyn. "American Teens Are Even More Stressed Than Adults." *Huffington Post,* February 11, 2014. Accessed January 9, 2015.http://www.huffingtonpost.com/2014/02/11/american-teens-are-even-m_n_4768204.html.

Hanson, Kathryn, and Deborah Stipek. "Schools v. Prisons: Education's the Way to Cut Prison Population." *San Jose Mercury News,* May 16, 2014. Accessed January 9, 2014.http://www.mercurynews.com/opinion/ci_25771303/schools-v-prisons-educations-way-cut-prison-population.

Hernandez, Donald J. *Double Jeopardy: How Third-Grade Reading Skills and Poverty Influence High School Graduation.* The Annie E. Casey Foundation, 2012. Accessed December 6, 2014.http://www.aecf.org/m/resourcedoc/AECF-DoubleJeopardy-2012-Full.pdf.

"High School Dropout Rates." Child Trends Data Bank, Appendix 1. Accessed December 9, 2014.http://www.childtrends.org/wp-content/uploads/2012/10/01_appendix1.pdf.

Hinton, Christina, Kurt W. Fischer, and Catherine Glennon. *Anytime, Anywhere: Student-Centered Learning for Schools and Teachers.* Edited by Rebecca E. Wolfe, Adria Steinberg, and Nancy Hoffman. Cambridge, MA: Harvard Education Press, 2013.

———. *Mind, Brain, and Education.* Students at the Center, 2012. Accessed January 25, 2015.http://www.studentsatthecenter.org/sites/scl.dl-dev.com/files/Mind Brain Education.pdf.

Immordino-Yang, Mary Helen, and Antonio Damasio. "We Feel, Therefore We Learn: The Relevance of Affective and Social Neuroscience to Education." In *The Jossey-Bass Reader on the Brain and Learning.* San Francisco: Jossey Bass, 2008.

"Innovation Tech High School." OCMBOCES. Accessed January 25, 2015.http://www.ocmboces.org/teacherpage.cfm?teacher=2445.

"Institutionalization." Changing Minds. Accessed October 20, 2014.http://changingminds.org/disciplines/sociology/articles/institutionalization.

Irvin, Judith L., Julie Meltzer, and Melinda S. Dukes. *Taking Action on Adolescent Literacy: An Implementation Guide for School Leaders.* Alexandria, VA: Association for Supervision & Curriculum Development, 2007.

Jensen, Eric. *Teaching with the Brain in Mind.* Alexandria, VA: ASCD/Association for Supervision and Curriculum Development, 1998.

———. *Teaching with Poverty in Mind: What Being Poor Does to Kids' Brains and What Schools Can Do About It.* Alexandria, VA: ACSD/Association for Supervision and Curriculum Development, 2009.

Joselowsky, Francine. "Students as Co-Constructors of the Learning Experience and Environment: Youth Engagement and High School Reform." *Voices in Urban Education* 8 (Summer 2005). Accessed January 2, 2015.http://vue.annenberginstitute.org/sites/default/files/issuePDF/VUE8.pdf.

———. "Youth Engagement, High School Reform, and Improved Learning Outcomes: Building Systemic Approaches for Youth Engagement." *NASSP Bulletin* 91, no. 3 (2007): 257–76. Accessed January 2, 2015.http://www.leadingnow.org/sites/default/files/pdf/Youth_Engagement_High_School_Reform.pdf.

Kerckhoff, Alan C. "The Transition from School to Work." In *The Changing Adolescent Experience: Societal Trends and the Transition to Adulthood.* Edited by Jeylan T. Mortimer and Reed W. Larson, 52–87. New York: Cambridge University Press, 2002.

2014 Kids Count Data Book: State Trends in Child Well-Being. The Annie E. Casey Foundation. Accessed December 6, 2014. http://www.aecf.org/m/resourcedoc/aecf-2014kidscountdatabook-2014.pdf.

King, Patricia, and Tak Cheung Chan. "Teachers' and Students' Perceptions on Teachers' Caring Behaviors." Paper presented at Annual Meeting of Gera, 2011. Accessed January 9, 2015.http://files.eric.ed.gov/fulltext/ED525290.pdf.

Kivel, Paul. "Adultism." Getting Together for Social Justice, 2009. Accessed October 28, 2014.http://www.paulkivel.com/component/jdownloads/finish/1/81/0?Itemid=31.

———. *Adultism.* 2006. Accessed October 28, 2014.http://www.paulkivel.com/component/jdownloads/finish/1/5/0?Itemid=31.

Kleinfeld, Judith. "Effective Teachers of Eskimo and Indian Students." *School Review* 83, no. 2 (1975): 301–44.

Klem, Adena M., and James P. Connell. "Relationships Matter: Linking Teacher Support to Student Engagement and Achievement." *Journal of School Health* 74, no. 7 (2004): 262–73. Accessed January 16, 2015.http://ceep.indiana.edu/hssse/Klem.pdf.

Knesting, Kimberly. "Students at Risk for School Dropout: Supporting Their Persistence." *Preventing School Failure* 52, no. 4 (2008): 3–10. Accessed December 19, 2014.http://cpedinitiative.org/files/Students%20at%20Risk%20for%20School%20Dropout.pdf.

Kohn, Alfie. "Choices for Children: Why and How to Let Students Decide." *Phi Delta Kappan* 75, no. 1 (1993): 8–21. Accessed January 2, 2015.http://www.alfiekohn.org/teaching/cfc.htm.

Kotulak, Ronald. "The Effect of Violence and Stress in Kids' Brains." In *The Jossey-Bass Reader on the Brain and Learning.* San Francisco: John Wiley & Sons, 2008.

Kronley, Robert A., and Claire Handley. *Sustaining Partnerships: Emerging Lessons from the Carnegie Corporation's Schools for a New Society Initiative.* Kronley & Associates, 2006. Accessed February 15, 2015.http://www.kronley.com/documents/SustainingPartnerships-Carnegie.pdf.

Laitsch, Dan, Theresa Lewallen, and Molly McCloskey. "A Framework for Education in the 21st Century." *Whole Child, InfoBrief* 40 (2005): 1–8.

The Learning Compact Redefined: A Call to Action, A Report of the Commission on the Whole Child, 2007. Association for Supervision and Curriculum Development. Accessed January 9, 2015.http://www.ascd.org/ASCD/pdf/Whole%20Child/WCC%20Learning%20Compact.pdf.

Learning Opportunities for Children and Youth: Expanding Commitments, Blurring the Lines. Forum for Youth Investment, 2002. Accessed January 25, 2015.http://forumfyi.org/files/Expanding%20Commitments%20Blurring%20Lines.pdf.

Lerner, Richard M. *Promoting Positive Youth Development: Theoretical and Empirical Bases.* Paper prepared for the Workshop on the Science of Adolescent Health and Development. National Research Council, National Research Council/Institute of Medicine, and the National Academy of Sciences, Washington, D.C. 2005. Accessed January 2, 2015.http://ase.tufts.edu/iaryd/documents/pubPromotingPositive.pdf.

Levin, Benjamin. "Putting Students at the Centre in Education Reform." *Journal of Educational Change* 1, no. 2 (2000): 155–72.

Lopez, Shane J. *Youth Readiness for the Future: A Report on Findings from a Representative Gallup Student Poll Sample.* Gallup Student Poll. Accessed on January 16, 2015.http://www.gallup.com/poll/141842/youth-readiness-future.aspx.

Mathis, William J. "NCLB and High Stakes Accountability: A Cure? Or a Symptom of the Disease?" *Educational Horizons* 82, no. 2 (2004).

McGuire, Kim. "Valley View Elementary Students Beat the Odds." *Star Tribune,* September 20, 2014. Accessed February 15, 2015.http://www.startribune.com/local/north/275902881.html.

McMillan, James, and Daisy Reed. *Defying the Odds: A Study of Resilient At-Risk Students*. Virginia Commonwealth University, 1993. Accessed January 16, 2015.http://files.eric.ed. gov/fulltext/ED389780.pdf.

McNeely, Clea, and Jayne Blanchard. *The Teen Years Explained: A Guide to Healthy Adolescent Development*. John Hopkins University, 2010. Accessed January 9, 2015.http://www. jhsph.edu/research/centers-and-institutes/center-for-adolescent-health/_includes/ interactive%20guide.pdf.

Measuring Innovation in Education: A New Perspective. Educational Research and Innovation, OECD Publishing, 2014. Accessed February 7, 2015. http://www.keepeek.com/Digital-Asset-Management/oecd/education/measuring-innovation-in-education_9789264215696-en -page1.

Medina, John. *Brain Rules: 12 Principles for Surviving and Thriving at Work, Home, and School*. Seattle, WA: Pear Press, 2008.

Melaville, Atelia, Amy C. Berg, and Martin J. Blank. *Community-Based Learning: Engaging Students for Success and Citizenship*. Coalition for Community Schools, 2006. Accessed December 6, 2014.http://www.communityschools.org/assets/1/AssetManager/CBLFinal. pdf.

Metcalf, Linda. *Teaching Towards Solutions: Improve Student Behavior, Grades, Parental Support and Staff Morale*. Norwalk, CT: Crown House Publishing, 2005.

Metzger, Maure Ann. "An Appreciative Inquiry of Youth Perspective on Effective Youth Leadership Programming." EdD dissertation, St. Mary's University, 2007.

Metzger, Maure Ann, and Richard S. Scott. *Solution-Focused Practices: Listening Groups Summary Report*. Carver-Scott Educational Cooperative, 2010.

Mitra, Dana. "Amplifying Student Voice." *Educational Leadership* 66, no. 3 (2008): 20–25. Accessed January 2, 2015.http://www.academia.edu/2005795/Amplifying_student_voice.

———. "Increasing Student Voice and Moving Toward Youth Leadership." *The Prevention Researcher* 13, no. 1 (2006): 7–10. Accessed January 2, 2015.https://eboardsecure.dcsdk12. org/attachments/080aee20-ba2b-4149-b28f-7d402eb4de1c.pdf.

———. "The Significance of Students: Can Increasing 'Student Voice' in Schools Lead to Gains in Youth Development?" *Teachers College Record* 106, no. 4 (2004): 651–88. Accessed January 2, 2015.http://www.new.promente.org/files/research/ESPdocs/12633733. pdf.

———. "Strengthening Student Voice Initiatives in High Schools: An Examination of the Supports Needed for School-Based Youth-Adult Partnerships." *Youth & Society* 40, no. 3 (2009): 311–35.

———. "Student Voice in School Reform: Reframing Student-Teacher Relationships." *McGill Journal of Education* 38, no. 2 (2003): 289–304. Accessed January 2, 2015.https://www. bcps.org/offices/oea/pdf/student-voice.pdf.

———. "Student Voice or Empowerment? Examining the Role of School-Based Youth-Adult Partnerships as an Avenue Toward Focusing on Social Justice." *International Electronic Journal for Leadership in Learning* 10, no. 22 (2006). Accessed January 2, 2015.http://iejll. synergiesprairies.ca/iejll/index.php/ijll/article/viewFile/622/284.

Mitra, Dana, Stephanie Serriere, and Donnan Stoicovy. "The Role of Leaders in Enabling Student Voice." *Management in Education* 26, no. 3 (2012): 104–12. Accessed January 2, 2015. http://www.academia.edu/2005772/The_role_of_leaders_in_enabling_student_voice.

National Coalition for Academic Service-Learning. *Engaging Students Through Academic Service-Learning: National Implementation Guide to Implementing Quality Academic Service-Learning*. Learn and Serve America National Service-Learning Clearinghouse, 2012. Accessed January 25, 2015.http://ncasl.org/wp-content/uploads/Engaging-Students-Through-Academic-Service-Learning-Implementation-Guide.pdf.

National Research Council Institute of Medicine. *Engaging Schools: Fostering High School Students' Motivation to Learn*. Washington, DC: The National Academies Press, 2004.

Nelsen, Jennifer. "At Risk Youth: Give Them the Knowledge to Shine." Presentation at the Minnesota Social Services Association Annual Training Conference and Expo. Minneapolis, Minnesota, March 2011.

Nelson, Alison. "Person Centered Services & Outcome Development." Presented at the Minnesota Social Services Association Annual Training Conference & Expo, Minneapolis, Minnesota, March 2011.

Nelson, Ruth. "Andy Hargreaves Discusses the Importance of Professional Capital in School Improvement Efforts." HOPE Foundation, November 19, 2012. Accessed February 15, 2015.http://www.hopefoundation.org/andy-hargreaves-discusses-the-importance-of-professional-capital-in-school-improvement-efforts/.

Neuman, Susan B. *Changing the Odds for Children at Risk: Seven Essential Principles of Educational Programs That Break the Cycle of Poverty.* Westport: CT: Praeger, 2009.

"A New Approach to Schools." The School without Walls High School. Accessed January 25, 2015.http://www.swwhs.org/.

"Our History." Partnership for 21st Century Skills. Accessed January 25, 2015.http://www.p21.org/about-us/our-history -SkillsMaps.

Page, Nanette, and Cheryl E. Czuba. "Empowerment: What Is It?" *Journal of Extension* 37, no. 5 (October 1999). Accessed January 2, 2015.http://www.joe.org/joe/1999october/comm1.php.

Palmer, Parker J. *The Courage to Teach: Exploring the Inner Landscape of a Teacher's Life.* San Francisco: John Wiley & Sons, 2007.

"Pathways for Youth: Draft Strategic Plan for Federal Collaboration." Interagency Working Group on Youth Programs, 2013. Accessed February 15, 2015.http://www.findyouthinfo.gov/docs/Pathways_for_Youth.pdf.

Perez, Samuel A. "An Ethic of Caring in Teaching Culturally Diverse Students." *Education* 121, no. 1 (2000): 102–5.

Pink, Daniel H. *A Whole New Mind: Why Right-Brainers Will Rule the Future.* New York: Riverhead Books, 2006.

Pittman, Karen J. "College and Career Readiness." *The School Administrator* 67, no. 6 (2010): 10–14. Accessed January 25, 2015. http://forumfyi.org/files/School%20Administrator%20Article%206-10.pdf.

Pittman, Karen, Merita Irby, and Thaddeus Ferber. "Unfinished Business: Further Reflections on a Decade of Promoting Youth Development." In *Trends in Youth Development: Visions, Realities, and Challenges.* Edited by Peter L. Benson and Karen Johnson Pittman, 3–50. Norwell, MA: Kluwer Academic Publishers, 2001.

Pittman, Karen J., and Marlene Wright. *Bridging the Gap: A Rationale for Enhancing the Role of Community Organizations in Promoting Youth Development.* The Task Force on Youth Development and Community Programs at the Carnegie Council on Adolescent Development, 1991. Accessed January 24, 2015.http://files.eric.ed.gov/fulltext/ED364804.pdf.

Positive Youth Development Toolkit: Engaging Youth in Program Development, Design, Implementation, and Service Delivery. National Resource Center for Youth Services, 2008. Accessed January 2, 2015. http://www.nrcyd.ou.edu/publication-db/documents/2008-positive-youth-development-toolkit.pdf.

Prann, Elizabeth. "States Spend Almost Four Times More Per Capita on Incarcerating Prisoners Than Educating Students." Fox News, March 14, 2011. Accessed on January 9, 2015.http://www.foxnews.com/politics/2011/03/14/states-spend-times-incarcerating-educating-studies-say-464156987/.

Princiotta, Daniel, and Ryan Reyna. *Achieving Graduation for All: A Governor's Guide to Dropout Prevention and Recovery.* National Governor's Association Center for Best Practices, 2009. Accessed January 16, 2015.http://www.nga.org/files/live/sites/NGA/files/pdf/0910ACHIEVINGGRADUATION.PDF.

"Principles of Student Voice in Schools." SoundOut. Accessed February 8, 2015.http://www.soundout.org/principles.html.

Profile of Teachers in the U.S. 2005. National Center for Education Information, 2005. Accessed February 7, 2015.http://www.ncei.com/POT05PRESSREL3.htm.

"Project-Based Learning." New Tech Network. Accessed January 25, 2015.http://www.newtechnetwork.org/about/project-based-learning.

The Promise of Urban Schools: In Search of Excellence. Senior Fellows in Urban Education. Annenberg Institute for School Reform, 2000. Accessed January 2, 2015. http://annenberginstitute.org/pdf/Promise.pdf.

Putting Positive Youth Development into Practice: A Resource Guide. National Clearinghouse on Families & Youth on behalf of the Family and Youth Services Bureau, 2007. Accessed January 2, 2015.http://ncfy.acf.hhs.gov/sites/default/files/PosYthDevel.pdf.

Reeve, Johnmarshall. "Self-Determination Theory Applied to Educational Settings." In *Handbook of Self-Determination Research.* Edited by Edward L. Deci and Richard M. Ryan. Rochester, NY: University of Rochester Press, 2002.

Reivich, Karen. "Self-Efficacy: Helping Children Believe They Can Succeed." *Communique Handout* 39, no. 3 (2010). Accessed December 6, 2014.http://www.nasponline.org/publications/cq/39/3/pdf/V39N3_FT_Self-Efficacy.pdf.

Research on the Use of Khan Academy in Schools. Research Brief, 2014. Accessed February 7, 2015.http://www.sri.com/sites/default/files/publications/2014-03-07_implementation_briefing.pdf.

Rose, David H., and Jenna W. Gravel. "Using Digital Media to Design Student-Centered Curricula." In *Anytime, Anywhere: Student Centered Learning for Schools and Teachers.* Edited by Rebecca E. Wolfe, Adria Steinberg, and Nancy Hoffman, 77–101. Cambridge, MA: Harvard Education Press, 2013.

Rourke, Matt. "PA Teacher Strikes Nerve with 'Lazy Whiners' Blog." *USATODAY.* February 16, 2011. Accessed October 21, 2014.http://usatoday30.usatoday.com/news/education/2011-02-16-teacher-blog-suspended_N.htm.

Ryan, Richard M., and Edward L. Deci. "Intrinsic and Extrinsic Motivations: Classic Definitions and New Directions." *Contemporary Educational Psychology* 25, no. 1 (2000): 54–67. Accessed January 16, 2015.http://www.selfdeterminationtheory.org/SDT/documents/2000_RyanDeci_IntExtDefs.pdf.

———. "Self-Determination Theory and the Facilitation of Intrinsic Motivation, Social Development, and Well-Being." *American Psychologist* 55, no. 1 (2000): 68–78.

Sahlberg, Pasi. *Finnish Lessons: What Can the World Learn from Educational Change in Finland?* New York: Teachers College Press, 2011.

———. "Five U.S. Innovations That Helped Finland's Schools Improve But That American Reformers Now Ignore." Guest post on Victoria Strauss. *Washington Post*, July 25, 2014. Accessed February 7, 2015.http://www.washingtonpost.com/blogs/answer-sheet/wp/2014/07/25/five-u-s-innovations-that-helped-finlands-schools-improve-but-that-american-reformers-now-ignore/.

———. "Global Education Reform Movement Is Here!" *The Pasi Sahlberg Blog.* Accessed February 7, 2015.http://pasisahlberg.com/global-educational-reform-movement-is-here/. http://carnegie.org/fileadmin/Media/Publications/PDF/SNS-BrochureForWeb.pdf.

———. "How GERM Is Infecting Schools Around the World." Guest post on Victoria Strauss. *Washington Post*, June 29, 2012. Accessed February 7, 2015.http://www.washingtonpost.com/blogs/answer-sheet/post/how-germ-is-infecting-schools-around-the-world/2012/06/29/gJQAVELZAW_blog.html.

———. Presentation for 2014 Education Minnesota Conference, October 16, 2014. Accessed February 7, 2015. http://pasisahlberg.com/wp-content/uploads/2013/07/Minnesota-Talk-2014.pdf.

———. "What Can the World Learn from Educational Change in Finland?" Presentation at NYSAIS Conference, Mohonk Mountain, New York, November 7, 2014. Accessed February 7, 2015.http://pasisahlberg.com/wp-content/uploads/2013/07/NYSAIS-Talk-2014.pdf.

———. "What If Finland's Great Teachers Taught in U.S. Schools?" Guest post on Victoria Strauss. *Washington Post*, May 15, 2013. Accessed February 7, 2015.http://www.washingtonpost.com/blogs/answer-sheet/wp/2013/05/15/what-if-finlands-great-teachers-taught-in-u-s-schools-not-what-you-think/.

———. "What the U.S. Can't Learn from Finland about Ed Reform." Guest post on Valerie Strauss. *Washington Post,* April 17, 2012. Accessed February 7, 2015.http://www.washingtonpost.com/blogs/answer-sheet/post/what-the-us-cant-learn-from-finland-about-ed-reform/2012/04/16/gIQAGIvVMT_blog.html.

Sazama, Jenny, and Karen S. Young. *Get the Word Out!* Somerville, MA: Youth On Board, 2001.

Schlosser, Linda Kramer. "Teacher Distance and Student Disengagement: School Lives on the Margin." *Journal of Teacher Education* 43, no. 2 (1992): 128–40.

"School Climate." National School Climate Center, 2015. Accessed January 16, 2015.http://www.schoolclimate.org/climate/.

Schools for a New Society Leads the Way. Schools for a New Society, Carnegie Corporation of New York, 2004. Accessed February 15, 2015.http://carnegie.org/fileadmin/Media/Publications/PDF/SNS-BrochureForWeb.pdf.

"Schools That Change Communities." DOCMAKERonline.com. Accessed January 25, 2015.http://www.docmakeronline.com/schoolsthatchangecommunities.html.

"Schools That Change Communities." The Video Project. Accessed January 25, 2015.http://www.videoproject.com/schoolschange.html.

Schussler, Deborah L., and Angelo Collins. "An Empirical Exploration of the Who, What, and How of School Care." *Teachers College Record* 108, no. 7 (2006): 1460–95.

Siegle, Del. "An Introduction to Self-Efficacy." Accessed December 6, 2014.http://www.gifted.uconn.edu/Siegle/SelfEfficacy/section1.html.

The State of America's Children 2014. Children's Defense Fund. Accessed January 9, 2014.http://www.childrensdefense.org/library/state-of-americas-children/2014-soac.pdf.

"Statistics on Native Students." National Indian Education Association. Accessed December 6, 2014.http://www.niea.org/Research/Statistics.aspx -Grad.

Steele, Claude M., and Joshua Aronson. "Stereotype Threat and the Intellectual Test Performance of African Americans." *Journal of Personality and Social Psychology* 69, no. 5 (1995): 797–811. Accessed December 6, 2014.http://mrnas.pbworks.com/f/claude+steele+stereotype+threat+1995.pdf.

Stetser, Marie C., and Robert Stillwell. *Public High School Four-Year On-Time Graduation Rates and Event Dropout Rates: School Years 2010–11 and 2011–12: First Look,* 2014. National Center for Education Statistics, U.S. Department of Education. Accessed December 6, 2014.http://nces.ed.gov/pubs2014/2014391.pdf.

A Summary of Research on Using Student Voice in School Improvement Planning. The Education Alliance, Business and Community for Public Schools, 2004. Accessed January 16, 2015.http://maaikerotteveel.pbworks.com/f/UsingStudentVoice+soort+literatuurstudie.pdf.

A Summary of the Rights under the Convention on the Rights of the Child. UNICEF. Accessed January 8, 2015.http://www.unicef.org/crc/files/Rights_overview.pdf.

Tapscott, Don. *Grown Up Digital: How the Net Generation Is Changing Your World.* New York: McGraw-Hill, 2008.

Tawil, Sobhi, and Marie Cougoureux. *Revisiting Learning: The Treasure Within; Assessing the Influence of the 1996 Delores Report,* 2013. Accessed February 7, 2015.http://unesdoc.unesco.org/images/0022/002200/220050E.pdf.

"The Teenage Brain, How Youth Learn: A Portfolio to Inform and Inspire Educators, Students, Parents & More." What Kids Can Do, Next Generation Press. Accessed January 9, 2015.http://howyouthlearn.org/research_teenagebrain.html.

Tolman, Joel, Patrice Ford, and Merita Irby. *What Works in Education Reform: Putting Young People at the Center,* 2003. International Youth Foundation. Accessed January 2, 2015.http://www.iyfnet.org/sites/default/files/WW_Education_Reform.pdf.

Toshalis, Eric, and Michael Nakkula. *Motivation, Engagement, and Student Voice.* Students at the Center, April 2012. Accessed January 2, 2015.http://www.studentsatthecenter.org/sites/scl.dl-dev.com/files/Motivation%20Engagement%20Student%20Voice_0.pdf.

Trilling, Bernie, and Charles Fadel. "21st Century Learning Balance." Table, *21st Century Skills: Learning for Life in Our Times.* San Francisco: Jossey-Bass, 2009.

———. *21st Century Skills: Learning for Life in Our Times.* San Francisco: Jossey-Bass, 2009.

Van der Klift, Emma, and Norman Kunc. "The Human Service System: Pyramid or Circle?" Broadreach Counseling & Mediation. Accessed October 20, 2014.http://www.broadreachtraining.com/advocacy/arsystem.htm.

Velázquez, Jorge, Jr. and Maria Garin-Jones. "Adultism and Cultural Competence." *Children's Voice* 12 Child Welfare League of America (2003): 20–21.

Weinberger, Daniel R., Brita Elvevag, and Jay N. Giedd. *The Adolescent Brain: A Work in Progress*. The National Campaign to Prevent Teen Pregnancy, 2005. Accessed January 9, 2015.http://web.calstatela.edu/faculty/dherz/Teenagebrain.workinprogress.pdf.

"What Is the Convention on the Rights of the Child?" UNICEF. Accessed February 24, 2015.http://www.unicef.org/rightsite/433_468.htm.

"When *Just Do It! Doesn't Do It*: Purposeful Implementation Increases Success Rates." *Early Developments* 14, no. 2 (2013): 6–8. Accessed February 7, 2015.http://fpg.unc.edu/sites/fpg.unc.edu/files/resources/early-developments/FPG_EarlyDevelopments_v14n2.pdf.

"The Whole Child Approach to Education." The Whole Child. Accessed February 7, 2015.http://www.wholechildeducation.org/about.

Willis, Judy. *Research-Based Strategies to Ignite Student Learning: Insights from a Neurologist and Classroom Teacher*. Alexandria, VA: ASCD, 2006.

Wolfe, Rebecca E., Adria Steinberg, and Nancy Hoffman. Introduction in *Anytime, Anywhere: Student Centered Learning for Schools and Teachers*. Edited by Rebecca E. Wolfe, Adria Steinberg, and Nancy Hoffman, 1–12. Cambridge, MA: Harvard Education Press, 2013.

Yassie-Mintz, Ethan. *Charting the Path from Engagement to Achievement: A Report on the 2009 High School Survey of Student Engagement*. Center for Evaluation & Education Policy, Indiana University, 2010. Accessed December 21, 2014.http://ceep.indiana.edu/hssse/images/HSSSE_2010_Report.pdf.

Yohalem, Nicole, and Karen Pittman. Foreword to *The Teen Years Explained: A Guide to Healthy Adolescent Development*. Edited by Clea McNeely and Jayne Blanchard. John Hopkins University, 2010. Accessed January 9, 2015.http://www.jhsph.edu/research/centers-and-institutes/center-for-adolescent-health/_includes/interactive guide.pdf.

Youniss, James, and Allison J. Ruth. "Approaching Policy for Adolescent Development in the 21st Century." In *The Changing Adolescent Experience: Societal Trends and the Transition to Adulthood*. Edited by Jeylan T. Mortimer and Reed W. Larson, 250–71. New York: Cambridge University Press, 2002.

———. "Positive Indicators of Youth Development." Unpublished manuscript. The Catholic University of America, Washington, DC, 2000.

"Youth Empowerment." Wikipedia. Accessed January 2, 2015.http://en.wikipedia.org/wiki/Youth_empowerment.

Youth Engagement in Educational Change. The Forum for Youth Investment, 2005. Accessed January 2, 2015. http://forumfyi.org/files/Youth%20Engagement%20in%20Educational%20Change.pdf.

"Youth Engagement: Positive Youth Development." National Resource Center for Youth Development (NRCYD). Accessed January 2, 2015.http://www.nrcyd.ou.edu/youth-engagement/positive-youth-development.

"Youth Voice Glossary." The FreeChild Project. Accessed January 2, 2015.http://www.freechild.org/glossary.htm.

Zeldin, Shepherd. "Sense of Community and Positive Adult Beliefs Toward Adolescents and Youth Policy in Urban Neighborhoods and Small Cities." *Journal of Youth and Adolescence* 31, no. 5 (2002): 331–42.

Zeldin, Shepherd, Brian D. Christens, and Jane L. Powers. "The Psychology and Practice of Youth-Adult Partnership: Bridging Generations for Youth Development and Community Change." *American Journal of Community Psychology* 51, nos. 3–4 (2012): 385–97. Accessed January 2, 2015.http://fyi.uwex.edu/youthadultpartnership/files/2012/10/Am-Journal-of-Community-Psych-paper.pdf.

Zeldin, Shepherd, Annette Kusgen McDaniel, Dimitri Topitzes, and Matt Calvert. *Youth In Decision-Making: A Study on the Impacts of Youth on Adults and Organizations*. The Innovation Center for Community and Youth Development and the National 4-H Council, 2000. Accessed January 2, 2015.http://www.theinnovationcenter.org/files/Youth_in_Decision_Making_Brochure.pdf.

Zeldin, Shepherd, and Julie Petrokubi. "Youth-Adult Partnership: Impacting Individuals and Communities." *The Prevention Researcher* 15, no. 2 (2008): 16–20. Accessed January 2, 2015,http://fyi.uwex.edu/youthadultpartnership/files/2011/07/Zeldin-Petrokubi-Prevention-Researcher-2008.pdf.

Zeldin, Shepherd, and Dimitri Topitzes. "Neighborhood Experiences, Community Connection, and Positive Beliefs about Adolescents among Urban Adults and Youth." *Journal of Community Psychology* 30, no. 6 (2002): 647–69.

Zull, James E. *From Brain to Mind: Using Neuroscience to Guide Change in Education.* Sterling, VA: Stylus Publishing, 2011.

Index

academic operating system: components of, 63; essentials of, 63

active learning, 143–144

adolescent development, 100; brain functioning during, 102; different rates of, 101; exposure to positive experiences in, 101; as individualized process, 101; -led organizations support of youth voice, 129; ongoing staff education in, 102; Pittman and Wright on basic needs and competencies of, 100; shaping identities in, 102–103; valuation decline of, 92–93. *See also* Positive Youth Development

Adrian: on decision making, 118, 121, 127; on negative perceptions of teens, 39

adultism: Andrew on, 38; Bell on, 35, 36–38; Ben on, 37–38; in community, 37; concept of, 36; consequences of, 35, 36; definition of, 35; holds power and blames youth for failures, 38–39; in institutions, 37; manifestations of, 35–36; oppressive nature of, 39; Richard on, 38; in schools, 36; in verbal interactions, 37

AFSF. *See* Architectural Foundation of San Francisco

Aimee, on being nonjudgmental, 98

alternative schools, xii, 6, 7; GLBT students in, 10; layers of devaluation in, 93; minority students in, 10

Alyson, on being nonjudgmental, 99

Ana, on youth voice, 117, 127

Anderson, Doug, 171

Andrew: on adultism, 38; on class size, 19; on design of schools, 29; on empowerment, 26; on future prep for workforce, 139; on identity in school, 10–11, 103; on ineffective teaching methods, 51–52; on not giving up, 100; on stress, 58–59

Anthony, on underlying causes, 98

Architectural Foundation of San Francisco (AFSF), 150

Association for Supervision and Curriculum Development (ASCD), 78

AT&T survey on texting, 39–40

Austin Voices for Education and Youth, 183

Barron, Brigid, 144

Bell, John, on adultism, 35, 36–38

Ben: on adultism, 37–38; on "coming out", 11; on leadership class, 75, 140, 167; on purpose of education, 73; on reform, 71; on traumatizing episode in school, 4–5, 11

BIE. *See* Bureau of Indian Education

Big Picture Learning schools, 151

Bonwell, Charles C., 148

brain: effects of stress on, 58, 59–60; functioning during adolescent development of, 102; poverty affects function of, 62–63; -research in whole child approach, 78

Brandi, on prediction of failure in school, 7–8

Briggs, Delonte, 149

Bug-O-Nay-Ge-Shig school, conditions at, 83

Build San Francisco Institute (Build SF), 150

Bureau of Indian Education (BIE), 82

Caine, Geoffrey, 17, 18, 28

Caine, Renate Nummela, 17, 18, 28

Carnegie Corporation of New York's Schools for a New Society, 183

Cassie, on valuation, 92

Charlie, 115; on class size and support, 19; on college, 152; on difference in learning, 21; on "doing school", 51; on funding education, 105; on limited value of paper and pencil learning, 141; on purpose of education, 73; on racially motivated fights in school, 9; on relevancy, 160

Chesterfield County Public Schools, Virginia, 159

Children's Home and Aid Society, 183–184

Child Trends, 49

class size: Andrew on, 19; Charlie on support and, 19; in engagement, 162–163; Katie on support and, 18; Lorenzo on learning and, 19; Nehls on, 18

Client's Rights document, 44

cognitive engagement, 158

college: Charlie on, 152; opportunity for partnerships with, 183; preparation focus of U.S. education, 74; Richard on, 152; students' on own to pursue work or, 151–152, 152–153

communities: adultism in, 37; as classroom in real life learning, 149–150; partnerships in, 182–183, 183–184

community-based youth programs, 118; resources for, 193; use PYD principles, 118–120

Community Schools, Chicago, 183–184

Conceptual Age, high order skills in, 140

Convention on the Rights of the Child (CRC): core principles of, 45; as international instrument of human rights, 120; key rights in, 121

cooperative small-group learning, 147; Kimberly on, 147–148; Marie on, 147

CRC. *See* Convention on the Rights of the Child

cult of efficiency, 34

Danielle: on autonomy-supportive teacher, 169; on leaders, 107; on youth voice, 128

Darling-Hammond, Linda, 144

Daunte, motivation story of, 56

Deci, Edward, 57

decision making: Adrian on, 118, 121, 127; as form of engagement, 165, 197; Marie on, 122; resources for, 192; teens in, 43, 117–118, 121, 122

Department of Education, U.S., 185

Department of Health and Human Services, U.S., 185

Department of Justice, U.S., 185

design-based learning, 146

devaluation: example of, 42–43; layers in alternative schools and special education of, 93; of teens, 46–47

Dewey, John: on mechanical uniformity, 22; on oppressive environments, 22; on student learning, 21; on traditional education, 14, 20

disengagement, 64–65; boredom as temporary form of, 159; cascading effect of, 158; dropout rates due to, 49–50; nonacademic factors in, 50; slow process of, 50–51

EAST. *See* Environmental and Spatial Technology, Inc.

EBD. *See* emotional-behavior disorders

education: Ben on purpose of, 73; Charlie on, 73, 105; college preparation focus of, 74; current funding priorities in, 105–106; Dewey on traditional, 14, 20; educators' predicting failure of students in, 8; entrenched traditions in, 17; factory (assembly-line) model of,

17–20, 75, 103, 141, 183, 197; Feliz on purpose of, 34, 73; in Finland, 74; four pillars of, 80; as frozen in time, 14; hierarchical structure of, 34; improve funding for, 106; institutionalization of, 13–17; Katie on purpose of, 73; knowledge and skills gap in, 141; Lorenzo on purpose of, 73; mantra of, 8; mechanistic approach of, 17–18; minority and gay students in, 8–9; mutual adaptation lack in, 20, 21; new and better model of, 197; Newtonian view of, 17; obstacles in, 197; outdated model of, 71; purpose of, 34; reexamine and redefine purpose of, 73–74; Richard on purpose of, 73; severe inequities in, 82–83; students blamed for failures in, 20–21; transformation of, 197

educational reform, 85–86; asking same questions in, 72; Ben on, 71; blending traditional practices with newer methods in, 75–76; common themes of new generation learners, 75; drivers of, 83–84, 198; in Finland, 81; implementation science in, 85, 198; involving students in, 79; other questions about value of youth in, 72–73; student-centered questions for, 72; students underrepresented in, xii; systemic approach in, 85; 21st century learning balance, 76; underlying belief systems change in, 83

Einstein, Albert, 71

Eison, James A., 148

emotional-behavior disorders (EBD), 18, 27

emotional engagement, 158

empowerment, xiii, 133, 197; adults need to foster, 127; Andrew on, 26; benefits of, 122–123; changing traditional structures as obstacle to, 124; conditions that create, 114; definition of, 114; diverse roles of youth in, 128; environments for, 129–131; influencing factors of, 115; involves youth, 115–116; key aspect of, 115; in leadership class, xii; limited opportunities in schools of, 115;

obstacles in, 123–125; school conditions for, 113–114, 115, 132; shift to relational power as obstacle to, 124; Stephanie on, 113; structural and cultural barriers in, 124–125; of students, 33–34; trust as obstacle to, 124; YAP as critical to, 125–127; youth needing assistance in, 114–115

engagement, xiii, 174; belonging as element of, 161–162; caring and committed teachers element in, 160–161; class and school size matter in, 162–163; as emotional experience, 165; importance of, 49; Katie on, 49; learning approaches that foster, 166; novelty and variation as form of, 164; personalized learning environment as, 160; relevancy of learning element in, 160; resources for, 193; risk taking and decision making as forms of, 165, 197; in school, 162–163, 163; as strong predictor of achievement, 157–158; of teachers, 159, 160–161, 173; three dimensions of, 158; use of fun as, 163–164; as vital strategy, 157; voice and choice as, 166–167; working and learning with peers as, 159

Environmental and Spatial Technology, Inc. (EAST), model of education, 147

environments, xii; Dewey on oppressive, 22; for empowerment, 129–131; factors in stress, 59; personalized learning, as engagement, 160; as powerful influence on self-esteem, 55

Envision Schools, 145

ephebiphobia, 40

Expeditionary Learning, 145

Experience and Education (Dewey), 22

factory (assembly-line) model of education, 17–20, 75, 103, 141, 183, 197

fear, as standard management tool, 23

Feliz: on PBL, 144–145; on purpose of education, 34, 73; on respect, 97; on struggles in school, 5–6

Finland: dual system of schooling and job training in, 150; educational reform in, 81; enhancing equity in, 82; focus on

school effectiveness, 180; purpose of
education in, 74; teacher training differs
from U.S., 80; U.S. education differs
from, 80

FIRST robotics, 146

Framework for 21st Century Learning
(P21), 140

Fullan, Michael, 185; on drivers of reform,
83

Gallup Student Poll (2013), 158

George Washington University, 149

GERM. *See* Global Educational Reform
Movement

Germany, dual system of schooling and job
training in, 150

giving up: Andrew on not, 100; Jacquelyn
on not, 99–100

Global Educational Reform Movement
(GERM), 81

Gonzalo Garza Independence High School,
183

Groves, Lynn, 28; on disillusionment, 14;
on SFP, 165; on stress, 60–61

growth mindset, 172–173, 174, 194

"hammering", 23–24

High School Survey of Student
Engagement (HSSSE) (2009), 56–57,
159, 161; three dimensions of
engagement by, 158

High Technology High School, 145, 184

HSSSE. *See* High School Survey of
Student Engagement

identities: adolescent development shaping
of, 102–103; Andrew on, 10–11, 103

implementation science: in educational
reform, 85, 198; resources for, 195

Industrial Age: approach of school, 76–77;
to Knowledge Age economy in real life
learning, 139–140

inquiry-based learning approaches, 144,
197; cooperative small-group learning
as, 147–148; design-based learning as,
146; implementation barriers in, 148;
problem-based learning as, 146–147;
project-based learning, 144–145;
resources for, 193; service learning as,

146–147; three methods of, 144

Institute of Medicine, 116

institutions: adultism in, 37; constraints
and standardization in, 14–15; masses
served by, 29; oppression as
consequence of, 20; schools as, 15, 74;
various systems in, 15

Interagency Working Group on Youth
Programs (IWGYP), 185

International Commission for Education in
the Twenty-First Century, four pillars
of education of, 80

International Youth Foundation,
"education for life" promoted by, 75

IWGYP. *See* Interagency Working Group
on Youth Programs

Jacquelyn: on being nonjudgmental, 93,
99; on not giving up, 99–100; on
solution-focused approach, 97; on
unconditional positive regard, 95; on
valuation, 92

Jake: on active learning, 143; on fun and
learning, 164; on YAP, 126

James, on painful experience in school,
3–4

Japan, U.S. education differs from, 80

Jennifer: on active learning, 143; on
optimal challenge, 168; on service
learning, 146–147; on youth voice, 128

Joseph, "4 E's for an Excellent Teacher"
presentation of, 173

Josh: on valuing youth, 91; on YAP, 126

Justin, on respect, 97

Kari, on youth voice, 121

Katie: on being engaged in learning, 49; on
class size and support, 18; on poverty,
61; on purpose of education, 73

Khan Academy, 74

Kimberly: on cooperative small-group
learning, 147–148; on Leadership class,
164

Kivel, Paul, 38–39

Korea, innovation measurement points of,
71

Kunc, Norman, 15–17

Kyle, on respect, 97

Leadership class, 42, 96, 103; active learning in, 143–144; Ben on value of, 75, 140, 167; empowerment in, xii; Kimberly on, 164; Marie on value of, 34; real life learning in, 142, 143; Shawn on, 157; valuation in, 107

Leadership Development, Youth Build, USA, 35

learned helplessness, 52, 64–65; attribution theory in, 53; deficits in, 52–53; educator's need to minimize, 61; motivational issues in, 53; of teachers, 28

Learning and Teaching Together project, 130, 183

learning strategies, xii

Listening Groups, 94, 97, 99

Lofquist, William, 118

Logan Square Neighborhood Association, 184

Lorenzo: on aspiration, 92; on being underrepresented, 131; on class size and learning, 19; on going against system, 21; on hurdle in school, 3, 7, 8, 9–10; on motivation, 55–56; on preparation for real life, 148–149; on purpose of education, 73; on racism, 9–10; on special education disability, 93; on stress, 57–58; on student voices, 33; on teachers, 8; on YAP, 125

lose-lose situation, 7

Mandela, Nelson, 108

Marana, 22; on restrictive student control, 22

Marie: on cooperative small-group learning, 147; on decision making, 122; on optimal challenge, 168; on value of leadership class, 34; on YAP, 126

Martin, on respect, 97

Maslow, Abraham, hierarchy of needs, 10

MetWest, 151

mindsets: fixed and growth, 172–173; motivation impacted by, 172–173; resources for, 194; of teachers, 173

Minnesota Comprehensive Assessments, 179

motivation: Daunte's story of, 56; external element in, 171, 172; impacted by

mind-sets, 172–173; internalization and integration in, 171–172; as intrinsic, 167; issues in learned helplessness of, 53; Lorenzo on, 55–56; optimal challenges in, 168; Richard on, 56; self-determination regarding, 167–171; underperforming students perceived as lacking, 55

Munroe, Mrs., 43

NCLB. *See* No Child Left Behind

Nehls, Jeanne, 18, 19; on class size, 18; on demands of teachers, 27–28

Nellie Mae Foundation, on student-centered education, 77

Neuman, Susan, 52

New Tech schools, 145

1960s student empowerment movement, 116

No Child Left Behind (NCLB), 13

nonjudgmental: Aimee on being, 98; Alyson on being, 99; Jacquelyn on being, 93, 99; support as first responsibility of teachers, 92–93, 98–99; as valuation, 98–99

OECD. *See* Organisation for Economic Co-Operation and Development

oppression, xi, 91; adultism nature of, 39; as consequence of institutions, 20; Dewey on, 22; long-term effects of, 25; in schools, 38; as silent weapon, 25; of teachers, 26–28

Organisation for Economic Co-Operation and Development (OECD), 71

paper and pencil learning, 141

Partnership for 21st Century Skills (P21), 140, 145, 184; resources for, 194; three skill sets of, 140

partnerships, 197; challenges in, 184; coalition building in, 184; collective capacity strategies in, 180, 198; in communities, 182–183, 183–184; engaged parental involvement in school as, 180–182; external change catalysts as, 183; formal contract or memorandum of understanding in, 184; key findings about, 184; policymakers and lawmakers in, 185, 198; previous school and community or organizational, as examples, 183–184; resources for, 194; school collaboration as, 180; social and human capital in, 179–180, 198; student-teacher as, 180; teacher collaboration (coteaching) as, 179; universities and colleges opportunity for, 183. *See also* Youth-adult partnerships

Patty, 26

PBL. *See* project-based learning

Pink, Daniel, 140

Pittman, Karen J., 100

policymaking: idealism of, 13–14; and lawmakers in partnerships, 185, 198; teens lack of representation in, 45

Positive Youth Development (PYD): community-based youth programs use of, 118–120; focus of, 118–119; implementation in school of, 120; key principal of, 119; resources for, 191

poverty, 64–65; affects brain function, 62–63; devastating consequences of, 62; Katie on, 61; lack of skills and prerequisites due to, 62; SES and cognitive ability regarding, 62–63; social and emotional challenges of children in, 63–64

prediction of failure, 5, 7–8, 24, 182

problem-based learning, 146–147

project-based learning (PBL), 144, 145, 166; Feliz on, 144–145; resources for, 193; schools using, 145

PYD. *See* Positive Youth Development

real life learning, 153–154, 197; active learning in, 143–144; boundaries between school and, 148–149; Conceptual Age in, 140; inquiry-based learning approaches in, 144–148; integration of school and life experience in, 142–143; Leadership class relation to, 142, 143; Lorenzo on, 148–149; paper and pencil limited value in, 141; shift from Industrial Age to Knowledge Age economy in, 139–140; theme-based programs in,

151; using city or community as classroom in, 149–150

relational power, 114, 124

resources: for community-based youth programs, 193; for decision making, 192; for engagement, 193; for implementation science, 195; for inquiry-based learning approaches, 193; for involvement in school change, 192; for mind-sets, 194; for P21, 194; for partnerships, 194; for PBL, 193; for PYD, 191; for service learning, 193–194; for student-centered education, 191; teens as assets and, 118–120; for whole child approach, 191; for YAP, 192; for youth voice, 192

respect: Feliz on, 97; Justin on, 97; Kyle on, 97; Martin on, 97; Richard on, 96–97; as valuation, 96–98

Richard, 13; on adultism, 38; on college, 152; on fights in school, 9; on motivation, 56; on perseverance, 61; on professionally addressing issues, 98; on purpose of education, 73; on respect, 96–97; on teacher caring, 93–94; on teen stereotypes, 41

Rocky Mountain Schools of Expeditionary Learning, 184

Ryan, Richard, 57

Sahlberg, Pasi, 81, 82, 185

school: adultism in, 36; Andrew on design of, 29; Andrew's identity in, 10–11; Ben's traumatizing episode in, 4–5, 11; boundaries between real life and, 148–149; Brandi's prediction of failure in, 7–8; Charlie on "doing", 51; Charlie racially motivated fights in, 9; children in poverty underserved in, 63–64; conditions for empowerment in, 113–114, 115, 132; critical elements and climate of engagement in, 162–163, 163; deficit-based view of students by, 119; deinstitutionalizing, 198; dual purpose of, 15; externally prescribed directives of, 26; Feliz's struggles in, 5–6; Industrial Age approach of, 76–77; as institutions, 15, 74; integration of real life learning in, 142–143; James's painful experience in, 3–4; knowledge and skills gap in, 141; Lorenzo's hurdle in, 3, 7, 8, 9–10; masses served by, 29; as microcosm of society, xiii; minority and gay students in, 8–9; movement and noise in, 22; oppression in, 38; participation rights lack of in, 45–46; partnerships in, 180, 180–182, 183–184; physical structure of, 29; pioneering efforts in, 197–198; as place of success, 197; as primary normative institution for youth, 74; PYD implementation in, 120; resources for change in, 192; Richard's fights in, 9; safety and survival in, 10, 11–12; Sergio's fighting incidents in, 6–7; threats and "hammering" as power-and-control response of, 23–24; using PBL, 145; valuation in, 34, 35, 46, 104–105, 107–108, 109; YAP difficulty in, 125–126, 126; youth voice in, 116–117, 127–128, 128–129

Schools for a New Society (SNS) initiative, 183, 184

Schools That Change Communities documentary, 149

schools-within-a-school (SWAS), 162

Schools without Walls High School (SWWHS), 149

SDT. *See* Self-Determination Theory

self-determination: autonomy as element of, 168–170; competence as element of, 167–168; motivation regarding, 167–171; relatedness as element of, 170–171

Self-Determination Theory (SDT), basic psychological needs of, 57

self-efficacy, 55, 64–65; definition of, 54; past successes and failures influence, 54; strong and weak, 54

self-esteem: environment as powerful influence on, 55; learning and school performance affects, 54–55; linked to self-efficacy, 55

Sense of Community and Positive Adult Beliefs Toward Adolescents and Youth Policy in Urban Neighborhoods and Small Cities study, 40

Sergio, on fighting incidents in school, 6–7

Service Learning, 6, 164; acquire twenty-first-century skills in, 146; benefits of, 166; as inquiry-based learning approach, 146–147; Jennifer on, 146–147; project on student rights, 44–45; resources for, 193–194; steps of, 146

SES. *See* socioeconomic status

SFP. *See* Solution-Focused Practices

Shawn, on Leadership class, 122, 157

Singapore, teacher training differs from U.S., 80

SNS. *See* Schools for a New Society

social engagement, 158

society, schools as microcosm of, xiii

socioeconomic status (SES), 62–63

Solution-Focused Practices (SFP), 131, 165; Groves on, 165; Jacquelyn on, 97; principles and elements of, 131

special education, xii; layers of devaluation in, 93; Lorenzo on, 93

Stephanie, on empowerment, 113

stereotypes: overcoming negative, 39–40; Richard on teen, 41; -threat phenomenon as stress, 59

stress, 64–65; Andrew on, 58–59; cumulative effects of, 58; educator's need to minimize, 61; effects of, on brain, 58, 59–60; effects of chronic or acute, on learning, 60; environmental factors in, 59; Groves on, 60–61; Lorenzo on, 57–58; psychological conditions impact on, 58–59; stereotype threat phenomenon as, 59; violence as cause of, 58

student: in alternative schools, 10; Andrew's identity as, 10–11; belief of incompetency about, 117–118; Ben's traumatizing episode as, 4–5, 11; blamed for failures in education, 20–21; Brandi's prediction of failure as, 7–8; Charlie racially motivated fights as, 9; control and coercion of, 24–25; current voice efforts regarding, 116; Dewey on learning, 21; in educational reform, 72, 79; educators' predicting failure of, 8; Feliz's struggles as, 5–6; high aspirations of, 56–57; James's painful experience as, 3–4; lack of valuation and validation of, 34; Lorenzo's hurdle as, 3, 7, 8, 9–10; Marana on restrictive control of, 22; marginalized or disenfranchised, benefit from valuation, 108–109; minority and gay, 8–9; on own to pursue college or work, 151–152, 152–153; perceptions of teacher caring, 95; Richard's fights as, 9; school deficit-based view of, 119; Sergio's fighting incidents as, 6–7; service learning project on rights of, 44–45; -teacher partnerships, 180; underperforming, perceived as lacking motivation, 55; underrepresented in school reform, xii; as unique personalities, 92; valuing and empowering of, 33–34; voices absence in education, xi, xii

student-centered education, xi; core elements in teaching practice of, 77–78; focus of, 15–17; four essential features of, 77; Nellie Mae Foundation on, 77; questions for educational reform, 72; resources for, 191; system-centered comparison to, 16; vision and mission statements showing, 104–105; whole child approach in, 78–79

student empowerment implementation: ensure participation of underrepresented in, 131; Learning and Teaching Together project on, 130; SFP as, 131; YELL initiative as, 129–130

succeedors, 51, 65, 197. *See also* Charlie

SWAS. *See* schools-within-a-school

SWWHS. *See* Schools without Walls High School

system-centered education, xi; focus of, 15–17; student-centered compared to, 16; vision and mission statements showing, 104–105

teachers: autonomy-supportive, 169–170; caring traits of, 94–95; collaboration as partnerships, 179; Danielle on autonomy-supportive, 169; educated, 173; energized, 173; engagement of, 159, 160–161, 173; experienced, 173; idealism of, 13–14; learned helplessness of, 28; Lorenzo on, 8;

mind-sets of, 173; Nehls on demands of, 27–28; nonjudgmental support as first responsibility of, 92–93, 98–99; oppression of, 26–28; other obstacles of, 26–27; pressured to teach "bubble" kids, 52; relationship building by, 96; Richard on caring of, 93–94; -student partnerships, 180; student perceptions of caring, 95; YAP model of, 126

"Teaching for Meaningful Learning" (Barron and Darling-Hammond), 144

teens (youth): Adrian on negative perceptions of, 39; adultism holds power and blames, for failures, 38–39; adults lack of trust in, 43, 127; as assets and resources, 118–120; continually prove worth of, 41–42; as decision makers, 43, 117–118, 121, 122; devaluation of, 42–43, 46–47; disturbing research regarding adult impressions of, 41; empowerment of, 114–115, 115–116, 128; Josh on valuing, 91; lack of representation in policymaking, 45; Lofquist on three views of, 118; mass media idea of, 40–41; negative and limited knowledge of, 42; negative responses to studies of, 40; other questions about value of, in educational reform, 72–73; overcoming negative stereotypes of, 39–40; Richard on stereotypes of, 41; service learning project on student rights, 44–45; valuation of, 46, 104; voice opportunities of, 121–122. *See also* youth voice

ThinkQuest competitions, 146

threats, 23–24, 59

"Time to Teach" program, 95

unconditional positive regard: contingent and noncontingent interactions in, 95; example of, 95–96; Jacquelyn on, 95; as valuation, 95–96

United Nations General Assembly, 120

United States (U.S.): bridges between school and work in, 151; college preparation focus of education in, 74; CRC failure to ratify by, 120; education innovation lowest in, 71–72; Finland